THE PAUL VIRILIO READER

European Perspectives

European Perspectives
A Series in Social Thought and Cultural Criticism

Lawrence D. Kritzman, Editor

European Perspectives presents outstanding books by leading European thinkers. With both classic and contemporary works, the series aims to shape the major intellectual controversies of our day and to facilitate the tasks of historical understanding.

For a complete list of books in the series, see pages 275–277.

The Paul Virilio Reader

EDITED BY STEVE REDHEAD

Columbia University Press   New York

For Laura and Ellie Redhead

Columbia University Press
Publishers since 1893
New York

First published in the United Kingdom by
Edinburgh University Press Ltd 2004

Selection and editorial material copyright © Steve Redhead 2004.
The texts are reprinted by permission (please see acknowledgements page).
All rights reserved

Library of Congress Cataloging-in-Publication Data
Virilio, Paul.
The Paul Virilio reader / edited by Steve Redhead.
p. cm. — (European perspectives)
Includes bibliographical references and index.
ISBN 0–231–13482–7 (cloth) — ISBN 0–231–13483–5 (pbk.)
1. Technology—Social aspects. 2. Civilization, Modern—1950– I. Redhead,
Steve, 1952– II. Title. III. Series.
HM846.V57 2005
303.48'3—dc22   2004050036

Columbia University Press books are printed on permanent and durable
acid-free paper.
Printed in Great Britain
c 10 9 8 7 6 5 4 3 2 1
p 10 9 8 7 6 5 4 3 2 1

Contents

'Time is the accident of accidents. We have reached the speed of light with e-mail, interactivity and telework. We are now creating a similar accident.'

Paul Virilio, in conversation with Philippe Petit,
Politics of the Very Worst

'History is a series of accidents; but if it has any discernible trend it is the growing power of human invention. What we commonly call the modern period is only a quickening of this process.'

John Gray, *Al Qaeda and What It Means to be Modern*

Acknowledgements

The extracts in this book are reprinted by permission as follows:

Paul Virilio, 'Bunker archaeology' and 'Cryptic architecture' in Paul Virilio and Claude Parent (1997), *Architecture Principe 1966 and 1996*, trans. George Collins, Besançon: Les Editions de l'Imprimeur, English edition, pp. xvii–xix.

Paul Virilio, 'Architecture principe' in Paul Virilio (1996), *The Function of the Oblique: The Architecture of Claude Parent and Paul Virilio 1963–1969*, trans. Pamela Johnston, London: The Architecture Association, pp. 11–13.

Paul Virilio, 'The end of the proletariat' in Paul Virilio (1986), *Speed and Politics*, trans. Mark Polizzotti, New York: Semiotext(e), pp. 96–118.

Paul Virilio, 'Pure power' in Paul Virilio (1990), *Popular Defense and Ecological Struggles*, trans. Mark Polizzotti, New York: Semiotext(e), pp. 18–36.

Paul Virilio (1991), *The Aesthetics of Disappearance*, trans. Philip Beitchman, New York: Semiotext(e), pp. 9–39.

Paul Virilio, 'The overexposed city' in Paul Virilio (1991), *The Lost Dimension*, trans. Daniel Moshenberg, New York: Semiotext(e), pp. 9–27.

Paul Virilio, 'The imposture of immediacy' in Paul Virilio (1989), *War and Cinema: The Logistics of Perception*, trans. Patrick Camiller, London: Verso, pp. 46–51.

Paul Virilio, 'The last vehicle' in Dietmar Kamper and Christoph Wulf (eds) (1989), *Looking Back on the End of the World*, trans. David Antal, New York: Semiotext(e), pp. 106–19.

Paul Virilio, 'Candid camera' in Paul Virilio (1994), *The Vision Machine*, trans. Julie Rose, London and Bloomington: British Film Institute, Indiana University Press, pp. 47–57.

Paul Virilio, 'Environment control' in Paul Virilio (2000), *Polar Inertia*, trans. Patrick Camiller, London: Sage, pp. 55–70.

Paul Virilio (2002), *Desert Screen*, trans. Michael Degener, London: Continuum, pp. 5–16.

Paul Virilio, 'The data coup d'état' in Paul Virilio (1995), *The Art of the Motor*, trans. Julie Rose, Minneapolis: University of Minnesota Press, pp. 23–34. English-language edition © 1995 by the University of Minnesota Press. Original French edition © 1993 by Editions Galilée, Paris.

Paul Virilio, 'From sexual perversion to sexual diversion' in Paul Virilio (1997), *Open Sky*, trans. Julie Rose, London: Verso, pp. 103–18.

Paul Virilio, 'Delirious New York' in Paul Virilio (2000), *A Landscape of Events*, trans. Julie Rose, Cambridge, MA: MIT Press, pp. 18–22.

Paul Virilio (2000), *The Information Bomb*, trans. Chris Turner, London: Verso, pp. 131–45.

Paul Virilio (2000), *Strategy of Deception*, trans. Chris Turner, London: Verso, pp. 61–82.

Paul Virilio, 'Silence on trial' in Paul Virilio (2003), *Art and Fear*, trans. Julie Rose, London: Continuum, pp. 69–82.

Paul Virilio (2002), *Ground Zero*, trans. Chris Turner, London: Verso, pp. 45–68.

Paul Virilio, 'The museum of accidents' in Paul Virilio (2003), *Unknown Quantity*, trans. Chris Turner, London: Thames and Hudson, pp. 59–65.

Editorial Introduction: Theory at the Speed of Light
by Steve Redhead

Not long ago Keith Patrick (Patrick 2003), the editor of hip British art magazine *Contemporary*, travelled to Paris to interview a 71-year-old French architecture professor, now retired and living on the coast in La Rochelle, about his part in the creation and curation of an exhibition on 'the accident' entitled (in French) *Ce Qui Arrive*. The exhibition, labelled *Unknown Quantity* in English translation, played well with the Paris public at the Fondation Cartier pour l'Art Contemporain – designed by the renowned French architect Jean Nouvel – until its closure in March 2003. The pensioner was Paul Virilio, a man whose time has indeed 'arrived', although that could have been said of him at any time in the last thirty-five years, ever since he initially became a professor at the Ecole Spéciale d'Architecture in Paris in the late 1960s in the wake of the events of May 1968. Speed in/of modernity in general, not just in relation to technology and war, has become associated with his name, almost anywhere in the world. A book of self-consciously intellectual, innovative, imaginative writing, created through rolling e-mail, was published early in the new century in Western Australia (Kinsella et al. 2002). The book, based on four dispersed writers e-mailing each other 300 words at a time, attempted to develop a kind of speed writing. Indeed, working from Virilio's now famous notation that every technology programmes its own accident, the writers tried to create 'the accident of writing'. The book explicitly took Paul Virilio as representing a series of jumping-off points, even reclaiming Virilio's notion of 'the vector': 'this book does not have a point at which it is authored, but a vector, these lines between,' it ventured, thereby at a stroke almost wiping out the Roland Barthes and Michel Foucault inspired post-structuralist strictures about the 'death of the author', and replacing them with the manifesto of another French theory hero. As the speeding-up of modernity – Virilio's special topic, in fact the entire intellectual 'territory' he has made his own – continued apace in these years of late late modernity, ever shortening the time between departure and arrival, Paul Virilio could be said to be always on the verge of his time 'coming' as a celebrity academic in the mould of his friend and fellow French theorist, Jean Baudrillard.

Perhaps just as Baudrillard's 'time' was the USA in the 1980s and 1990s, the 'noughties', the time of new heroes in the zeros, will be Virilio's. In the mid-1990s publishers and their coterie of referees, could say 'why Virilio?' to suggestions that he be featured in academic series about well-known thinkers. Today, that is unlikely to be the response. Indeed, Sage, as the publishers of the international journal *Theory, Culture and Society*, at the beginning of the twenty-first century, assembled a whole issue, edited by John Armitage, entirely comprising articles on Paul Virilio (Armitage 2000). Further, publishers commissioning a textbook profiling contemporary social theorists are also just as likely to make sure it features a section on Virilio alongside seasoned 'regulars' such as Michel Foucault or Pierre Bourdieu; Sage, again, brought out such a book in 2001 (Elliott and Turner 2001). Virilio's celebrity, however, will never be of the same order as Baudrillard. Unlike Baudrillard, Paul Virilio has not yet figured in the (slightly ironic) soccer shirts with snappy quotes produced by the London-based Philosophy Football organisation, despite probably having as many soccer-oriented quotations in his work for these outfitters of sporting distinction to choose from. ('Those absent from the stadium are always right,' a quirky Virilio statement to an interviewer in 1982, especially springs to mind.) Their fates, however, are often intertwined. As it happened, Baudrillard and Virilio were indeed the two French theorists chosen by New Left publishers Verso in 2002 for their mini series dedicated to the first anniversary of the events of 11 September 2001 in New York and

Washington. The other European theorist chosen for the series was Slavoj Zizek whose contribution *Welcome to the Desert of the Real!* was positively conventional by contrast with the two Frenchmen. Striking in design and production values, these three books were meant as 'analyses of the United States, the media and the events surrounding September 11 by Europe's most stimulating and provocative philosophers'. Baudrillard's *The Spirit of Terrorism* was certainly that; Paul Virilio's eighty-two page effort on the other hand defied any trade descriptions legislation. Published originally in France as *Ce Qui Arrive* – veritably a favoured phrase for Virilio in 2002 – and written only six weeks after 9/11, *Ground Zero* barely acknowledged the existence of the events of 11 September at all, except in passing. It was left to *Unknown Quantity*, the exhibition and the catalogue, to perform this function, in the context of Virilio's latter-day concentration on the confluence between the accident, disaster, catastrophe and the new world war terrain of small group terrorism.

The voyage of an art magazine like *Contemporary* to Paris to interview Paul Virilio is a significant event in itself. As the cultural theorist Scott Lash has correctly argued, Virilio and Jean Baudrillard have been taken up by the art world as much as by academia (Lash 1995). Writing in the mid-1990s Lash pointed to magazines such as *Traverses* (the magazine of the Pompidou Centre, which saw Virilio and Baudrillard working together from the mid-1970s until the early 1990s) in France and *Art in America* in the USA as a cultural milieu where two outriders of 'theory' might be found and, moreover, taken seriously. In the last few years magazines such as *Contemporary*, *Blueprint*, *Viewpoint*, *Frieze*, *Artforum*, *Wallpaper* and *Black and White* have become international currency for those interested in the cutting edge of creative industries such as fine art, architecture, design, fashion and digital technology. Virilio's ideas have often surfaced in these post-style culture texts, as indeed they did in an earlier era in style magazines like *i-D* and *The Face*, even when his name was not explicitly mentioned. In any case Virilio has immersed himself in what Lash calls the 'art world' for many years. He after all trained as a stained-glass painter, working with Matisse and Braque, before he studied academic subjects at the university of the Sorbonne in Paris. He has moreover been involved in a number of major art exhibitions and displays in his career. As well as the *Unknown Quantity* exhibition on the accident, he has worked, for instance, with the Fondation Cartier pour l'Art Contemporain on other topics such as *La Vitesse* (or in English translation *Speed*) in 1991 at Jouy-en-Josas in France. In the *Unknown Quantity* exhibition he not only wrote the long theoretical text for the catalogue but conceived the event itself. Although many people were involved in the exhibition, Virilio, and curator Leanne Sacramone, were the main protagonists. Virilio also featured in pictures at the exhibition via the thirty-minute film installation *Unknown Quantity* by Romanian theorist Andrei Ujica, which comprised the visual recording of Virilio interviewing Ukranian journalist Svetlana Aleksievich about Chernobyl, one of the media events most fascinating to Virilio, and a major example of the accident in his thinking. The text of the interview was also included in the exhibition catalogue.

'Architecture' on the one hand and 'philosophy' on the other are constantly in play in Virilio's discourse, and in his life. But his positioning is an uncomfortable fit into either 'architecture' or 'philosophy' pigeonholes. As architects assumed the role of modern soothsayers in the late twentieth century – a process which saw the likes of Daniel Libeskind and Rem Koolhaas rise to international superstardom not just for their buildings but for their social and cultural proclamations – interviews with architects proliferated and the interchange between 'architecture' and 'philosophy' was widespread. For example, in the late 1990s a project which involved a conference between architects and philosophers, entitled *Urban Passages*, took place in Virilio's home town of Paris. This comprised six encounters between architects and, as the organizers put it rather provocatively, 'writers'. One of them, a fascinating conversation between Jean Baudrillard and Jean Nouvel, both colleagues of Virilio in the intellectual milieu of Paris for over thirty years, was even subsequently published as a short book (Baudrillard and Nouvel 2002). The French edition was subtitled *Architecture et Philosophie*, seemingly contradicting Baudrillard's own frequent insistence that his work is 'pataphysical' not philosophical. Virilio figures in the discourse of the two conversants, occasionally and obliquely but, surprisingly perhaps, not for his architecture. He appears as a fellow 'theorist', either of the 'aesthetics of disappearance' for instance, or else of what architecture has borrowed from cinema, both of which ideas Baudrillard and Nouvel chew over in parts of their discussions on the dialogue between architecture and philosophy. In actuality Virilio did have a career, in the 1960s, as an architect, though he never qualified to become a practitioner. His collaboration with the architect Claude Parent in the 1960s is a little archived but important part of Virilio's life and work. In a sense, however, as far as architecture practice was concerned, Virilio was a kind of interloper. He was a painter of stained glass when he first met Claude Parent, already an established figure on the French architectural scene since the 1950s. In the initial collaboration with Parent in 1963 Virilio's role was merely as a 'discussion partner'. Parent's own notoriety meant he was often asked to participate in architectural debates and Virilio would tag along, formulating a joint Parent/Virilio response. Later, Virilio took to hanging out in his friend's architectural practice office in Paris. Eventually they worked on the written theoretical manifestos of the group Architecture Principe, which they collectively spawned. Furthermore they designed, and in some cases actually constructed, buildings created on their revolutionary architectural platform of the 'function of the oblique'. This 'oblique function' theory involved the radical questioning of 'verticality' and to some extent 'horizontality'. Eventually the younger Virilio fell out with the older Parent over participation in the events of May 1968 and by 1969 Architecture Principe was no more. Parent, however, did continue to encourage young architectural prospects, Jean Nouvel among them. Nouvel, like Virilio before him, worked in Claude Parent's office for quite a time at the end of the 1960s and in the early 1970s even built, with François Seigneur and Roland Baltera, a house based on the oblique function design of Parent and Virilio. Nouvel must have been trained well by Parent for he went on to become one of France's best-known architects internationally, designing buildings like the Fondation Cartier and the Arab World Institute in Paris and the Hotel Broadway in New York. Nouvel was awarded the Grand Prix d'Architecture of France, his nation's highest architectural award which his mentor Claude Parent had already won in 1979. Virilio himself wrote a pamphlet on Nouvel published by the Institut Française d'Architecture in Paris in 1987, the year Virilio was recognized by his country as Laureate of the Grand Prix National de la Critique Architecturale.

The contemporary military and political relevance of Paul Virilio and his work is never less than uncanny. In mid-2003 *The Guardian* newspaper in Britain reported that the Pentagon was planning a new generation of weapons, including huge hypersonic drones and bombs dropped from space. The scenario painted, originally by a US defence website, was almost pure Virilio. The idea was to allow the USA to strike its potential enemies at lightning speed from its own territory, thereby alleviating the need to create alliances with other countries displayed by the second Gulf War invasion of Iraq in March–April 2003, and alternating the problems raised by the continued US military presence in Middle Eastern nations acting as forward bases or even simulated land-locked aircraft carriers for the USA. This new generation of weapons technology was imagined quite seriously as producing global reach for the USA by 2025. The aim of the technological changes would be a reusable hypersonic cruise vehicle which was able to take off from a conventional military runway in America and strike targets 9,000 nautical miles away in less than two hours. The hypersonic cruise vehicle would be unmanned and carry a maximum payload of 5,450 kg. A top speed of ten times the speed of sound would be envisaged by 2025. In the meantime small launch vehicles would fill in for the more expensive, longer-term system. They would take a warhead into space and drop it over its target, effectively creating an unpowered bomb that would be guided to its objective as it plummeted to earth at high and accelerating velocity. Although such small launch vehicles would be able to carry 450 kg of explosives, they would probably not be needed because, at the speeds predicted, a simple titanium rod would be able to penetrate deeply buried bunkers or rocky mountains.

Paul Virilio has, over the years, been interviewed by a number of people, both academics and journalists. There is now even a book of collected, selected Virilio interviews in the bookstores (Armitage 2001). But the best guide to Virilio 'in conversation' is to read the whole of the various interviews with him conducted by Sylvère Lotringer. Now in his sixties, Lotringer is of the same generation as Virilio, although he is six years younger than Virilio. For many years Professor of French and Comparative Literature at Columbia University, New York, he has been a friend of Virilio's for over twenty years. The book-length official interviews he has conducted with Virilio have always been originally in French, taking place in either Paris or New York, and have spanned the period of their friendship, beginning in January 1982. No one else, apart from perhaps the French journalist Philippe Petit, has come closer to nailing the enigmatic Virilio style of theory than Lotringer, and the most reliable testimony that we have of the origins of Virilio's thought and writing is buried in the texts of the interviews by him. It is fitting that Lotringer in conversation with Virilio has always been such a fascinating encounter. Lotringer has himself authored a little-noticed book on sexuality called *Overexposed*, a study of the treatment of sexual perversion in America through satiation therapy whereby sex offenders have their desire bored to death. However, he is best known as the general editor of the journal *Semiotext(e)* and co-editor, with Jim Fleming, of the Foreign Agents and Native Agents series of the Semiotext(e) publishing venture. This famous 'little black book' series is itself a monument to small-scale independent intellectual thought which has published the likes of Virilio and Baudrillard, and many other writers, for three decades. The British author Don Watson has testified that 'post-punk' writer Kathy Acker (herself published, subsequently, by Semiotext(e)) relied in the 1980s on the New York/Columbia University Philosophy Hall-produced Semiotext(e) series for political and theoretical sustenance, and philosophical inspiration. Many others of her generation did precisely the same.

The principle, that in trying to understand and evaluate what Paul Virilio has said, there is no substitute for reading the conversations of Virilio with Lotringer, is also applicable more widely to what Virilio has written. There is no substitute for reading the texts of Virilio, from the 1950s to the present day. This book is an up-to-date, timely volume published alongside *Paul Virilio: Theorist for an Accelerated Culture*, the first single-authored book to be published about the life and work of Virilio, and a text devoted to explaining and analyzing what Virilio has actually written and said over the years and exactly when he published or spoke it. *The Paul Virilio Reader,* revealing what can be called 'Theory at the Speed of Light', is designed to bring together extracts of Virilio's writing in his many books and chapters in other books. This present book collects together extracts from *Ground Zero* and *Unknown Quantity,* from *Speed and Politics* and *War and Cinema*, as well as other representative pieces from the whole of his long publishing and writing career, and puts them in context. The aim is to showcase for the first time the writing of Virilio as it developed historically. It will be suitable for intermediate, advanced/graduate students and academic audiences in general, but is also designed to be an introduction for the general reader curious about Virilio. The reader cuts across many disciplines taught in today's international academy, including Cultural Studies, Literary Studies, Philosophy, Urban Studies, Sociology, Art and Architecture, and the humanities and social sciences in general. The book consists of selected extracts from English translations of Virilio's writings from the mid-1960s to the twenty-first century. Each specially selected extract is prefaced by a brief bibliographical and contextual commentary. The book is completed by a Directory on Paul Virilio, a guide to exploring his multiple writings, conversations and exhibitions. The Directory is meant as a map to guide the reading of Virilio's work in a way which can make sense of his often distinctive intellectual contribution to contemporary thinking and the gaps and absences which his work and thought set up. The selected extracts of Virilio's writing in the reader are carefully chosen to reflect the entirety of his diverse intellectual career and the range of subjects on which he has written: from war studies to art history. They are presented in the order in which they were written and originally published in French to show the development, and interconnectedness, of Virilio's work. Paul Virilio's oeuvre has always been difficult to obtain. Even if it has been possible to purchase 'a Virilio', the cost was often prohibitive, especially given Virilio's tendency to produce shorter and shorter books. I myself have spent many hours over the years in bookshops throughout the world hoping to discover a rare copy, in English or in French. This book provides extracts from Virilio's writing at different stages of his life, beginning with a piece written in 1958 but not published until the mid-1960s, and ending with an extract from his introduction to the art catalogue for the exhibition *Unknown Quantity*. If nothing else, its publication will surely help, for a time at least, to get this editor out of some of the wonderfully obscure bookshops of the world and into more productive employment.

References

Armitage, John (ed.) (2000), *Paul Virilio: From Modernism to Hypermodernism and Beyond,* London: Sage (originally published as special double issue of *Theory, Culture and Society*, vol. 16, nos 5–6).

Armitage, John (ed.) (2001), *Virilio Live: Selected Interviews*, London: Sage.

Baudrillard, Jean and Jean Nouvel (2002), *The Singular Objects of Architecture*, Minneapolis: University of Minnesota Press.

Elliott, Anthony and Bryan Turner (2001), *Profiles in Contemporary Social Theory*, London: Sage.

Kinsella, John, Bernard Cohen, Terri-ann White, McKenzie Wark (2002), *Speedfactory,* Fremantle: Fremantle Arts Centre Press.

Lash, Scott (1995), 'Dead symbols: an introduction', *Theory, Culture and Society*, vol. 12, no. 4.

Patrick, Keith (2003), 'The century of fear', *Contemporary*, nos 47–8.

CHAPTER ONE

Bunker Archaeology

Paul Virilio was born in Paris, France in 1932, son of an Italian communist from Genoa and a French Catholic mother. Religion played a major part in his life from the age of eighteen. War influenced him even earlier. He experienced the trauma of the Second World War first-hand as a child in Nantes. In the 1950s Virilio began photographing the German bunkers, or blockhouses, of the Atlantic Wall built during the Nazi occupation of his homeland. These were originally designed to keep out the Allies and they held an architectural fascination for the young Virilio during the war and long after the conflict was over. Once the nearby Saint-Nazaire submarine base fell to the Allies, he swam out to see the bunkers for himself. He has acknowledged that the 'research' of the bunkers was a highly personal, archaeological study over a number of years. 'Bunker Archéologie' was a very short piece written in 1958 but did it not see the light of day until 1966. By then Virilio, with the collaboration of his architect friend Claude Parent, and also the painter Michael Carrade and the sculptor Morice Lipsi, had formed the Architecture Principe group. Parent had previously been part of several other architectural groups, including Groupe Espace with Andre Bloc, which also included painters and sculptors. In 1963 when Virilio and Parent finally met and set up Architecture Principe, Virilio was a stained-glass painter who had trained with Braque and Matisse. Although he worked with Parent on the design and construction of buildings for years in the 1960s, Virilio never formally qualified as an architect. He has said, 'I don't like that culture. I love painting.' He has also described himself as 'a man of the theatre', reminiscing that 'as a kid I designed theatrical sets'. This piece, 'Bunker Archaeology' in English, reproduced in its entirety here, formed part of the *Architecture Principe* magazine issue no. 7 for September/October which was produced and distributed in Paris in 1966.

'Bunker Archaeology', from *Architecture Principe 1966 and 1996*, trans. George Collins, Besançon: Les Editions de l'Imprimeur, 1997.

Phenomena of a dramatic moment in contemporary history, 10,000 monuments disappear. Stripped of their functions, removed from topical contexts, these works bespeak of an unknown meaning.

With an archaeological approach, I sought in this underground universe one of the secret figures of our time.

The blueprint of the blockhouse is strangely reminiscent of Aztec temples, and its dissimulation recalls the Mastaba, the Etruscan necropolises, but what in the pyramidic or circular form of ancient monuments evoked the sacred symbol, as cosmic image, here is implicit as involuntary.

The geometry is no longer affirmative, but eroded, worn. The angle is no longer right, but depressed, resisting apprehension; the mass is no longer anchored in the ground, but centred on itself, independent, capable of movement and articulation. This architecture floats on the surface of an earth which has lost its materiality. Approaching one of these beach monoliths, it suddenly appeared to me almost animal in nature, an empty carcass, abandoned, toppled over into the sand, like the skin of a defunct species. On entering, a particular heaviness oppresses me, the thickness of the walls is tangible, a second physiological envelope, amplifying certain senses and protecting movements. Here there are no windows to light the interior, the embrasure only lights the exterior, but with the precision of a lighthouse.

In this survival apparatus, life is not neutral. It takes an effort to become more subtle, more essential.

Banal remnants, these works have taken on the basic consistence of slopes that are protected only because they are so difficult to demolish. Astounding examples of the blindness of an epoch to itself, these primitive works announce a new architecture founded no longer on the physical proportions of man but on his psychic faculties, an urbanism in which, the elementary analysis of social reality finally overcome, habitat can finally unite with the secret possibilities of individuals.

CHAPTER TWO

Cryptic Architecture

This piece was originally written in September 1965 and published a year later in *Architecture Principe* no. 7. It appears here in full in English translation. The texts 'Bunker Archéologie' and 'Architecture Cryptique' were separated in the original French issue of the journal by fifteen photographs of Second World War German bunkers on the French coast, all of which had been taken by Paul Virilio himself between 1958 and 1965. Another Virilio photograph of a bunker adorned the cover of issue no. 7 of the magazine, which cost buyers four francs. This September/October 1966 issue touted a book to be entitled 'Cryptic Architecture' as 'to be' finished in 1965, having been apparently started in 1960. A photograph of a casually dressed thirtysomething Paul Virilio, with binoculars around his neck, taken at the coast, advertised the so-called forthcoming book. The issue also noted that he had undertaken several trips to Germany initially to study archives there and then, later, to research the 'anti-aircraft shelters of the major German cities, and the Maginot and Siegfried lines of defence'. Significantly, issue no. 7 also pointed to the origin of 'cryptic architecture' as a term in Virilio's writing and thought. According to the text, he had escaped from the Gestapo in Nantes with his family in 1941, as a nine-year-old child, because of the 'cryptic architecture' of the family home. The photographic archaeology of the Atlantic Wall and other German military architecture, undertaken by Virilio in the 1950s and 1960s, only eventually became known to an international English-speaking audience when a translation of *Bunker Archéologie* – a book authored and illustrated photographically by Paul Virilio and first published in France in 1975 – was issued by Princeton Architectural Press in the USA in 1994. That American volume was a translation from the second, revised edition of *Bunker Archéologie* brought out in France in 1991.

'Cryptic Architecture', from *Architecture Principe 1966 and 1996*, trans. George Collins, Besançon: Les Editions de l'Imprimeur, 1997.

Cryptic architectural design is obligatorily developed and understood in terms of the integrity of the autonomous bodies it contains and to whose process it is linked.

These bodies, considered themselves as primary architecture, are placed through their orifices of communciation in contact with the place – through the median zones of clothing, second 'portable' architecture, and objects, innumerable cryptic functions – down to the notion of territory, that is, of movement, in a possible space and through it up to the notion of time.

'Cryptic power' derives from access to these two principles, a power residing essentially in the potential to produce a 'continuum' by making the conditions of architectural appearance indissociable from those of disappearance.

The architecture results from the variations of a self-same energy, cryptic energy, itself indissociable from the survival of all living species. It is the energy of everything that hides itself. Considered by primitive societies as a primary dynamism, tending from the Neolithic age toward the perfection of 'everything that contains', cryptic architecture then progressively removed itself from the movements of social life starting with the Greek classical age which, substituting the evident thing for the containing thing, separated, for a time, action and invention.

To sum up, (a) associated first of all with the phenomena of vigilance and attention springing from a physical point of view, cryptic architecture tends (b), in terms of compensation for our phobias, (c), by the penetration of an element emptied of ordinary objective accidents, (d), to stimulate our faculties of genesis and thus (e), their ambitious aim on pre-existing reality and its meaning.

Passing historically through the gradations and degradations from (a) to (e), presenting itself in the form of inheritance or rapine, cryptic art nevertheless forms from its origin a continuous totality, whatever transformations it undergoes: religious,

racial, military, scientific, political, funerary, literary, philosophical or simply mineral.

Its explicit forms are directly relative as much to the desire for
power of a community as to the determined energy chosen by
such a community in its struggle.

Cryptic architecture is thus an infra-architecture. If physically
speaking it is the support and foundation of apparent architecture, it is more profoundly its central inspiring organ, thanks to
the historically necessary renewal of the invention by individuals and societies of their means of survival.

The isolation of cryptic energy, the observation of objects
which are charged with it, result in a calling into question of some
of today's widespread certainties concerning art and architecture.

In fact, whilst we erect an architecture of façade, flat surfaces,
imitation, speculation, décor or leisure, readily disposable finished objects (during each crisis, at each new cataclysm), an
intact architectural life goes on a few metres from ours, but unnoticed.

Art, that we no longer wish to conceive in anything else but in
gratuitous forms, amorphous and spoiled structures of physical
power, continues its initial task of resisting the ineluctable in
secret universes of compensation. Blinded by the discontinuous
proximity of objective givens, the diffusionists wonder about the
identity of worlds distant in millions of kilometres and several
millenniums.

Cities are episodic and cerebral, they are a permanent and
genetic crypt.

The accidental shape of cities can be objectively studied but
our systems of reference must be changed if the unit of inversion
of the other is to become intelligible. Mayan palaces devoid of
windows and chimneys, the impenetrable forests of Egyptian
columns, catacombs, the oval-shaped underground networks of
the Cathares, the Viet-Cong sanctuaries, Faust's hermetic home,
the copper mines of the Swiss mountains or the bunker. Our
version of art has only lived to a mediocre degree what cryptic
power has designed to reveal of itself, 2000 or 3000 years too late,
thanks to history or to archaeology. Our world is filled with anti-
objects, repulsive architecture in which the activities of the void

are opposed to those of the multiple, the invisible to the visible, the consistent to the complex, the continuous to the discontinuous, the anthropomorphic to the anonymous, a world of the limit-situation, of fear and reflex, born in the indistinct mixing of races, specialities, techniques, all ordained to the genetic powers of reality. After twenty years of relinquishment, the army has requisitioned the bunkers little by little, just as the Todt organization had refurbished the Vauban fortresses, Vauban the gallo-Roman sites which themselves had surged up out of tumuli. Thus the history of the content of places continues, beyond the episodic history of styles. If this postulate proves to be exact, the discontinuous notions of time and space becoming accessory, 'archaeology' might well be practised in the nearest of current affairs and cryptic civilization 'invented' in the immediate.

As I wished to suggest, without our being directly conscious of the fact, cryptic architecture is affecting us. It has spread out before our eyes its dwellings, its temples, the permanence without memory of its mentality.

CHAPTER THREE

Architecture Principe

'Archi-Principe', as Paul Virilio called it, did not outlast the 1960s. 'Five years, a flash', according to speed theorist Virilio at the end of the century. In 1963 the group Architecture Principe came together in Paris; by 1969 it was over. The magazine which was its permanent manifesto came out in 1966, more or less monthly, and there were nine issues in total in 1966. A tenth, thirty-year anniversary issue, entitled *Disorientation or Dislocation,* was published in 1996 and included pieces from Paul Virilio, Claude Parent and distinguished architectural guests such as Jean Nouvel, François Seigneur, Bernard Tschumi and Daniel Libeskind. As Virilio makes clear in the following extract from an Architectural Association publication on the architecture of Virilio and Parent in retrospect, Architecture Principe was literally about architectural 'principle', but, as his long-time interlocutor Sylvère Lotringer has said, what the architectural duo were doing in the mid-1960s in France was making architecture begin again (Lotringer stresses '*principium*' as the linguistic root). The theoretical basis for this creative beginning again was their idea of the 'oblique function'. This involved the theoretical and practical issues of building on an inclined plane, essentially questioning 'verticality' and, to a lesser extent, 'horizontality'. As Jean Baudrillard put it much more extremely, much later: 'All things are curves'. Parent and Virilio actually built buildings – especially churches though not dwelling houses – on the architectural principle of the 'function of the oblique'. 'What is negated is the vertical,' Virilio has stated, looking back on the origin of the idea. Inspired by cryptic architecture and bunker archaeology, Virilio was motivated by the concept of the body in motion, 'the idea of living on inclined planes and of having furniture coming out of the floor'. The architectural plan of Virilio and Parent, in the middle of the fanciful, radical 1960s, was nothing less than a new urban order of inclined cities.

'Architecture Principe', from *The Function of the Oblique*, trans. Pamela Johnston, London: Architectural Association, 1996.

I formed the Architecture Principe group in 1963, along with the architect Claude Parent, the painter Michel Carrade and the sculptor Morice Lipsi. Such multidisciplinary groups were in vogue at the beginning of the 1960s, and Claude Parent himself collaborated in several, including the Espace group founded by André Bloc.

My own research at the time was devoted to the architecture of Second World War bunkers. Since 1958 I had been studying not only the blockhouses of the Atlantic Wall and the Seigfried and Maginot lines, but also the military spaces of what was known as 'Fortress Europe', with its rocket-launching sites, air-defence systems, autobahns and radar stations.[1] This was an archaeological study, and a personal one, motivated by the desire to uncover the geostrategic and geopolitical foundations of the total war I had lived through as a young boy in Nantes, not far from the submarine base of Saint-Nazaire.[2] For me, the architecture of war made palpable the power of technology – and the now infinite power of destruction.

In my efforts to understand the spaces of conflict, I drew on *Gestalt* theory – the psychology of form and the phenomenology of perception. This approach revealed the extreme importance of the LOGISTICS (and fluxes) of circulation during the Blitzkrieg, and enabled me to realize the effect of the BALLISTICS of different projectiles on the configuration of contemporary military architecture.[3]

Already during that time, I was exploring in a number of experimental designs the possibility of a TOPOLOGICAL or at least non-orthogonal architecture. I was also working as a painter. I had made some stained-glass windows for churches, helping to execute Matisse's designs for Saint-Paul de Vence and those of Braque for Varengeville. It was through these connections in the domain of sacred art that I obtained the commission for the church of Sainte-Bernadette du Banlay in Nevers, which was built between 1964 and 1966 by Claude Parent and myself.

The Nevers church was followed by projects for the cultural centre in Charleville and the Mariotti house in Saint-Germain-en-Laye, which unfortunately were never built. The Thomson-Houston Aerospace Centre in Vélizy-Villacoublay, however, was successfully completed at the very end of our collaboration, in 1968–9, thanks to the good working relationship that I had with the engineer, Rami-Méziane.

In addition to these projects, it is important to mention the full-scale experimental model of an elevated oblique structure, 'The Pendular Destabilizer no. 1', that we set up at the University of Nanterre. It was our intention to live for several weeks within this structure, in an attempt to test the equilibrium and habitability of inclined slopes and to determine the best choice of angles for the different living spaces. But the 'events' of May 1968 – which began, as everyone knows, on the campus of Nanterre – effectively put a stop to our *psycho-physiological* experiment.

However, the most important work of the group is to be found elsewhere, in the development of the theory known as THE FUNCTION OF THE OBLIQUE . . . To elaborate the theory, it was absolutely essential to have a publication, a 'manifesto' – hence *Architecture Principe*, nine issues in total, edited jointly by me and Claude Parent, from 1966 on. That was thirty years ago.[4]

'The function of the oblique' had its origins in the concepts of disequilibrium and motive instability. The idea of using the earth's gravity as a motor for movement inspired a very Galilean utilization of the INCLINED PLANE – a building form in which the horizontal was used only as a means of establishing a 'threshold' between two slopes.

After the HORIZONTAL order of the rural habitat in the agricultural era, and the VERTICAL order of the urban habitat in the industrial era, the next logical (or, rather, topological) step was for us the OBLIQUE order of the post-industrial era.

To achieve this, it was necessary to discard the notion of the *vertical enclosure*, whose walls are made inaccessible by gravity, and to *define habitable space by means of wholly accessible inclined planes*, thereby increasing the usable surface areas. This was, in essence, the principle of HABITABLE CIRCULATION.

In contrast to partitions or vertical walls, which provoke an opposition between *in front* and *behind*, a combination of oblique and horizontal planes would result only in *above* and *below*; surface and soffit. Thus the artificial ground of the dwelling would become a LIVING GROUND enclosing all the various articles that are required for domestic life.

By setting the structure on an incline, and by making every part of the built surface (except for the underside) habitable and accessible, *the range of truly habitable spaces would be considerably increased*, at the scale of both the individual dwelling and the building as a whole, since the vertical façade would also cease to exist.

The objective of our research was to challenge outright the *anthropometric precepts of the classical era* – the idea of the body as an essentially static entity with an essentially static proprioception – in order to bring the human habitat into a dynamic age of the body in movement. In our work, the *traditional stability* (habitable stasis) of both the rural horizontal order and the urban vertical order gave way to the METASTABILITY (habitable circulation) of the human body in motion, in tune with the rhythms of life. The space of the body became MOBILE. The limbs of the individual became MOTIVE. And the inhabitant effectively became LOCOMOTIVE, propelled by the (relative) disequilibrium created by the gravity of planet earth, the habitat of our species.

Oblique architecture thus became a *generator of activity* which used physiological principles to make buildings more habitable. 'It is not the eye which sees,' according to the philosopher Maurice Merleau-Ponty, but '*the body as a receptive totality*'.

The typology of the inclined plane, by increasing usable surface space, also preserved that rare and extremely precious commodity: real space, as distinct from the space of the atmosphere or the liquid element of the hydrosphere.

In the work of the group, the 'making of the architectural

OBJECT' was superseded by the 'making of the JOURNEY'; the classical building finally gave way to the *bridging structure*, which, through the non-Euclidean geometry of its large inclined arches, allowed the full expanse of the landscape to unfold.

In this regard, I should indicate that the illustrations in the *Architecture Principe* magazine were obviously not of architectural or even urbanistic projects, but were simply statements of PRINCIPLE – concepts intended to outline the theory of 'habitable circulation' (with theory, in this instance, remaining true to its origins in the Greek *theoria*, which means both 'procession' (parade) and 'process').

In conclusion, I would like to mention that my interest in the oblique extended beyond the limits of my collaboration with Claude Parent. After I became co-director (with Anatole Kopp) of the Ecole Spéciale d'Architecture in Paris in 1972, my teaching concentrated on the development of technical research into the organization and the precise morphology of oblique volumes. Several student theses were devoted to this theme, but after a few years the overwhelming difficulties of building an oblique habitat led us to abandon this work, which seemed to offer no practical benefit to young architects starting out in the working world.

Since being forced to abandon the SPACE of the oblique, I have devoted myself to TIME – or more precisely to the diverse phenomena of acceleration in this era of the 'global village'. The focus of my research has shifted from TOPOLOGY to DROMOLOGY, i.e. the study and analysis of the impact of the increasing speed of transport and communications on the development of land-use. But that, as they say, is another story.

Notes

1. See *Bunker Archéologie*, Centre de Création Industrielle, 1975; second revised and expanded edition Demi-Cercle, 1991. This second edition has been published in English as *Bunker Archaeology*, Princeton Architectural Press, 1994.
2. See *L'Insécurité du Territoire*, Stock, 1976; revised edition Galilée, 1992.

3. See *Vitesse et Politique*, Galilée, 1977, p. 16. Published in English as *Speed and Politics*, Semiotext(e), 1986.

4. See *Architecture Principe*, L'Imprimeur, 1996, a new compilation of the nine issues of the manifesto magazine.

CHAPTER FOUR

The End of the Proletariat

By the mid-1970s Virilio had been a professor of architecture in Paris for six years. Effectively he went from the fall-out of the events of May 1968 to an academic position at the Ecole Spéciale d'Architecture, a post which he continued to hold for the next thirty years. The two books, he had published by this time were the long-awaited illustrated manuscript of *Bunker Archéologie* and the first full-length treatise wholly written while he was an academic, *L'Insécurité du Territoire*. These first editions were published in France in 1975 and 1976 respectively. Second editions of both books were published in French in the 1990s. In 1977 Editions Galilée published Virilio's third book, *Vitesse et Politique*. Semiotext(e) in the USA published an English translation, *Speed and Politics*, in its Foreign Agent Series in 1986. It is probably Virilio's best known and most frequently cited text, the one which defines for most readers, casual and otherwise, who he is, and where he stands. That is not to say that even this short book has been read from cover to cover by those who boldly quote Virilio. Mark Polizzotti's Semiotext(e) translation is extracted here in a late section of the book. *Speed and Politics* features Virilio's essay on what he calls 'dromology'. Dromos, in Greek, means race, and from this basic linguistic root Virilio, in the mid-1970s, was busy erecting a fragile theoretical edifice around the idea of a society of speed. The wide sweeps of historical and political referencing, not always obviously and immediately connected, which were to become a Virilio trademark in the years to come, are prominent in *Speed and Politics* as Virilio teases out the meaning of new concepts such as 'dromological' and 'dromocratic'. The author in fact becomes a self-styled 'dromologist' during the writing of the book. By September 1977, when the book was finished, the 1960s and their effects were well and truly over, and what Virilio labelled 'the new economy of survival' was taking over in France and elsewhere in Europe.

'The End of the Proletariat', from *Speed and Politics*, trans. Mark Polizzotti, New York: Semiotext(e), 1986.

You can have a proletarian insurrection on the condition that the others hold their fire. If they dump two tank battalions on you, the proletarian revolution is as good as nothing. (Andre Malraux, Interviews)

Evidently, dromological progress and what we conventionally call human and social progress coincided but did not converge. The development can be summarized as follows:

1. A society without technological vehicles, in which the woman plays the role of the logistical spouse, mother of war and of the truck.
2. The indiscriminate boarding of soulless bodies as metabolic vehicles.
3. The empire of speed and technological vehicles.
4. The metabolic vehicle competing with, then defeated by, the earthly technological vehicle.

We could logically conclude with a last paragraph:

5. The end of the dictatorship of the proletariat and of History in the war of Time.

If we come back to Goebbels' definition, or Engels', the invention of the militant – revolutionary-worker or otherwise – already makes for no more than a 'poor man's' version of the proletarian soldier. The proletarianization of the working classes is only one form of militarization – a temporary form.

From 1914 onward, the proletariat's motor – and thus political – power was no match for the European battlefields. This power, however, was still indispensable to the worksites of continental warfare. The military class, making sure to keep the proletariat under control, will thus allow it the illusion of being able to dominate, to submerge the bourgeois fortress. The latter is already ruined, pierced at all points by the expressway media (radio, telephone, television), condemned by its former defenders to instant destruction through the anti-city strategy of total war. Nonetheless, we will soon become familiar with the limits of this *military leave*, in Prague, Warsaw, Beirut . . . and in Paris, too, in May '68, when, after the taking of the Odeon theatre, the government predicts at any moment the intervention of armoured cars against the popular uprising. It is understandable that in the 1920s, while the 'Bolshevik threat' spread from Munich to the gates of India, the French government unleashed a new politics of social aid. All this was made necessary by the logistical redeployment of military-industrial nations in Europe and in the world. And yet everyone is surprised to discover that in Part XIII of the Preamble to the Treaty of Versailles it says that 'the living conditions of the working classes' – of 'the balance of military forces in the world' would be more appropriate! – 'are incompatible with world peace.'

This is the new mix that Junger partially reveals a little later, in 1932, in his essay *Der Arbeiter* (the figure of the worker encompasses the soldier and the industrialist), a work that was to win a large audience and rapidly become for the Germans a veritable political platform . . .

In the same way, the French Union of the Left is a trap insofar as it has insisted, in General Cluseret's words, on having 'the army constitute an unknown quantity in the social equation.' In short, its only strength has been its silence on the military question. It is inevitable that its undoing will be the problem of national Defence, and that the Communists, who have always accepted the Marxist model of military proletarianization, will find themselves confronting radicals and socialists who, since May 1968, have invested in a socialism 'with a human face', liable to assemble a new, somewhat depoliticized electorate. It was under the auspices of the Portuguese generals of the Armed Forces Movement that 'the end of the dictatorship of the proletariat' was decreed in Southern Europe. We should not see in this, as Georges Marchais will later claim, a cause for rejoicing, a softening of ideological will, 'the word "dictatorship" having an unpleasant sound since the fascist experience'. Indeed, we cannot accuse the Portuguese military leaders – returning to their country after a long and bloody campaign of colonial repression – of excessive humanism. In fact, with the Marxist generals courted by Cunhal, the dictatorship of the proletariat regains its original military significance; and as good technicians of war, they acknowledge that the time when the proletariat's kinetic energy dominated political life, after having dominated the battlefield, is reaching an end – the time when, as Lenin says, the working class suddenly found itself courted and solicited even by the capitalists.

From now on, the animal body of the worker is devalued as the bodies of other domestic species were before him. The end of the dictatorship of the proletariat is only the Communist version of facts already noted – by the French army, for example, when they did away with the review board (law of 9 July 1970), or in 1975, on the liberal side, by the 'Trilateral Commission' on the crisis of democracy: 'We have come to recognize that if there are potentially desirable limits to economic growth, there are also potentially desirable limits to the infinite expansion of democracy.' The crisis of these liberal democracies is the end of a form of mobilization of the citizenry. The central historical pseudo-figure of the dominating producer is simultaneously removed by the two great ideological blocs, the proletarian worker declared unusable along with the consumer-producer of the capitalist world. The revolutionary experiment of the Armed Forces Movement was in this context exemplary because it claimed to raise the Portuguese leftist forces to another level, that of an 'army civilization'. Thus in 1975, ship's captain Correia Jesuino, who had become 'Minister of Social Communication' (we are reminded here of the naval proletarianization under Louis XIV by M. de Valbelle, the former captain of the galleys), depicts the 'left-wing' officers as 'ethnologists studying a primitive people'. For, in his view, the Portuguese people is under-developed. Jean-François Revel, reporting these statements in *L'Express* (14 April 1975), indicated that the average salary of a Portuguese was comparable to that of a Breton or a Welshman, and didn't quite see where the 'under-development' was.

All of this, indeed, is inexplicable in economic terms; instead we must emphasize a dromological military philosophy that challenges everyone's participation in a state totality, making this participation problematic. In the same way, if the nuclear problem in 1977 caused the French Union of the Left to break apart, it was less a matter of megatons than of *the political vectors of the new nuclear power*. Without our realizing it, *the nuclear weapon logically modified the political constitution of the States in the world*. As one lawyer put it, 'We must recognize that the nuclear weapon has shown itself to be a source of constitutional right by modifying our actual constitution.'

Here again, it is not so much the final explosion that counts in deterrence; rather more it is questions such as those posed by Articles 5 and 15 of the French Constitution of 1958 to the solitary decision-maker that the Head of State and Supreme Commander of the Armies, the President of the Republic, guarantor of the national territory's integrity, has become. The speed of the political decision depends on the sophistication of the vectors: how to transport the bomb? how fast? The bomb is political, we like to repeat – political not because of an explosion that should never happen, but because it is the ultimate form of military surveillance.

The political bourgeoisie, like the 'revolutionary' parties, anaesthetized by a long period of coexistence and full employment, by the euphoria of continued growth, are proving in Europe that 'one can do anything with a bayonet except sit on it'. The proletarian revolution now *necessarily* goes through the revolutions of the military institutions in the heart of the State's constitutional apparatus and, in fact, the principal actors who have taken the initiative these last years are no longer the great political parties, but the army, the unions, and even the unions in the army.

It is useful to notice here the anational nature of these events. For if one of the French national labour unions (the C.F.D.T.) wholeheartedly supports military unionism, requesting a 'body politic of the soldier', at the same time the famous A.F.L.-C.I.O. has declared itself ready to take the American soldiers' unions under *its* wing. Here something fundamental is happening, which no one has clearly pointed out: a non-partisan dialogue is being created between the world's labour forces and the military class and, in the short term, a 'latinization' of Europe comparable to that of the South-American continent. If General Vargas Prieto, 'considered one of the most capable and progressive leaders in the Peruvian army' (*Le Monde*, 4 November 1975), declares in an interview that 'the true forerunners of the Peruvian revolution are its armed forces, the root and *institutional essence of the people because they are born from them*', we must understand that this really means a return to a situation that long precedes political Marxism, to a negation of the State-polis by the proletarian revolutionary forces.

Le Monde reported in August 1977 that General Pinochet had done away with the DINA, his political police, in favour of a military police force. Things are getting simpler . . . This is truly the end of the reasonable democratic State that engages in a non-partisan process in which the unions and the most disparate, the least 'socialized' groups, are called to play the primary role. We are heading toward an explosion of national production systems, toward union individuation as it exists in the United States, for example – human labour depending less on productivity than on the game of interests in the manpower market. This, along with the breakdown of the unity of political action, allows for every imaginable manoeuvre, even the wildest and most fragmented, on the level of the very survival of the old political States. The end of democracy in Chile was thus foreseen and orchestrated by the CIA, and pressure was exerted on the highway systems by the truckers' unions, telecommunications, etc.

But what should we think of the crisis situation in the old urban fortresses, in New York or Montreal? The union functions, relayed by mob associations, are entirely supplanting the administration and services of the old bourgeois employer. Order reigns in the Bronx thanks to the Mafia, which is itself becoming international, aiming now at a direct collaboration with the military class, as was revealed by a recent scandal that called into question the relations between the Israeli generals and members of international crime. Far from being a military-political function that is becoming deterritorialized, losing interest in any form of sedentary fixation, whether national or otherwise, both the petty criminals and the large gangs are seeing their local cottage industry undergo serious revaluation.

The military class, increasingly distanced from its bourgeois partner, abandons the street, the highway, those outmoded vectors, to the small and middle-sized business of the protection rackets. The city unions in New York are starting to replace their members' productive activity with simple crisis management, by becoming administrators and bankers.

In Italy, assassinations, abductions, crimes and incidents are on the rise. Financial interests are becoming inseparable from those of a multitude of little, so-called 'revolutionary' groups. Justice is in a quandary. They talk about 'liberating the people' and extort millions from them. Public opinion is in an uproar about the mix, but this criminal power rising from the masses is really only *a political demand* returning to an uncontrolled condition because the old national ethology – social ideals – has become secondary and no longer mobilizes.

We can thus interpret the unexpected visits of political leaders such as Messrs Marchais and Chevenement to the workers in their offices and factories not as a challenge to the bosses or the government, but as unavowed attempts by the representatives of the devalued revolutionary ideologies to take the grass roots back in hand. While the Communist Party in Portugal completely failed in its opportunistic attempts with the military masters, the French Communist Party, once hesitant, seemed to approach the courageous Italian solution of Mr Berlinguer, whose famous 'historical compromise' really only means a final, desperate union of the traditional parties before the threat of pure and simple disappearance that weighs on them from both within and without.

While in France they try to keep the masses tied to outmoded strategic and social convictions, the army is already deploying its personnel in key points of civilian activity and shadows the police in its surveillance tasks. The military proletariat's job is henceforth to police highways and airports, to collect garbage on public roads (where men like Democrat Abraham Beame, New York's 'little mayor', was ridiculed), as well as to provide telecommunications and assistance; to effect certain prestige operations such as the battle against pollution, campaigns for the defence of archaeological sites or cancer research, the organization of numerous athletic and cultural displays (Celebration in the Tuileries, the army at the Children's Fair); and to accomplish important international enterprises, such as saving children in Biafra, setting up surgical units in areas devastated by natural cataclysms . . . even 'rescuing' a group of hostages in Entebbe. In a threatening social universe, in which human societies are shown to be rife with criminal elements, the army seems to be a protective force, a refuge from the parade of subversive enterprises. The army continues to be greatly amused by the 'anti-militarists'' lack of information about, and static analysis of, its dynamic power.

The army's answer to the ecological celebration in Larzac, the Malville tragedy, was *Operation Demeter*, 'named for the Greek goddess who personified the Earth'. Why did they have to call it 'Demeter'? Why did they present themselves as occupiers and dominators of the planet Earth? Why did they violate and damage the fields? – unless the Larzac celebration had claimed, albeit inadvertently, to frustrate them in their primary function, the power to invade? Why was it that at that very moment the 'friends of the earth' lost contact with their planet, and haven't even demonstrated any resistance? In any case, the terminology used by Jacques Isnard in the 9 September 1977 issue of *Le Monde* gives us pause: 'Between the end of the harvest and the opening of the hunting season, the *land* army organized, in the Beauce and Perche regions, its first true manoeuvre in *open ground*, in other words, *away from the highways and roads*, in a region of 2,000 square kilometres of farm land and prairies.' They put on a 'show manoeuvre' in order to maintain *neighbourly relations between the army and the civilian populations*. The farmers, who remembered the army's help during the previous year's drought, accepted the Demeter exercise without, it seems, too much grumbling . . . 'Goddess Demeter is with us,' recognizes Colonel de Rochegonde, who commands the 2nd Motor Brigade. While another colonel states, 'We are but the *managers* of national Security and, as such, we too are held accountable.' 'The army takes advantage of these manoeuvres in open ground to lead, for example, offensive reconnaisssance missions fifty kilometres from its base, along with *public relations* operations in the Eure-et-Loire department.' You do not enclose dromocrats in gulags or camps, not even in Larzac.

The Institute of Advanced Studies in National Defense spent six months in collaboration with advertising experts setting up a three-year campaign (at a cost of sixty million francs) aimed at sensitizing the public to the notion of defence and protection, using every means of information at their disposal to change the army's image (*Le Monde*, 9 May 1975).

Joel le Theule, Gaullist deputy and chairman of the Finance Committee, thus has reason to worry, in his notes on 'the military budget for 1977–82', about 'the absence of numerical information on the use of funds'; for this *fuzziness* allows no appreciation of the shifts in our defence policies. The army insists on regaining its autonomy of action, on redefining itself as *a public service able to assume in a safe and orderly fashion* the greatest number – even the totality – of civil and military defence tasks, again increasing the communal and industrial undertakings of its parallel initiatives. We can thus see just how far military unionism, advocated by the Communist League, the Unified Socialist Party or the C.F.D.T. in the name of petty demands, finally enters into the army's social scheme. It is, moreover, revealing to see the creation of the first union branch in the 19th Army Engineering Corps, thus demonstrating that this body still remains at the forefront of military revolutionary thought!

Balzac, visiting the Wagram battlefield after 1830 in hopes of *expanding his social analysis*, already asked himself the *question of the veritable territory of historiality*, the strategic theatre that, thanks to the advance of the media (the use of the telegraph, for example), had suddenly become global – external and internal events henceforth able to interact almost immediately. This temporal limitation come from the battlefield had been answered by the new 'secret police', which Balzac considers the most important social revolution of his time – the moment when, after the long period of ostensible and bloody repression exerted against the civilian population by the Revolution's 'army of the interior', military violence stops being necessarily visible only from afar, by the soldier's uniform, and comes to rest on refined systems of surveillance and denunciation.

These first attempts at penetration, clandestine 'invasion' of the social corpus, had, as we saw, a specific aim: exploitation by the armed forces of the nation's raw potential (its industrial, economic, demographic, cultural, scientific, political and moral capabilities). Since then, social penetration has been linked to the dizzying evolution of military penetration techniques; each vehicular advance erases a distinction between the army and civilization.

Fascism, defining itself in Germany as *Ostkolonisation*, in other words the institution of a colonial situation on the European continent that claims to subvert existing socio-political groups, in fact reveals to us the great two-way movement of dromocratic totalitarianism between metropoles and colonies. Mapped out during the unprecedented logistical effort of the First World War, this movement will bring about the singular unity of Western civilization in the 1920s, 'the incorporation of colonial action in national life as a solution to the serious problems that human evolution will later impose on the world', as Albert Sarraut, French colonial minister, declared in 1921.

To understand dromocratic society and its establishment, it is no doubt more useful to read *the Black Code* of the Colonial Pact than any other so-called sociological work. 'We must not,' wrote Colbert, 'constitute in the colonies a *constant* civilization.' The ancient legislation that will subsist in our colonies until 1848 considers the negro to be *furniture*;[1] the black slave is first of all a *movable commodity*. His legal existence is solely a function of his movable/furniture quality, of the transportation he is subjected to. The vogue of Black-American jazz after 1914, the frenzied gesticulation revealed by the first American sound film that coloured the face of a white actor and bent his rhythm of the movable slave, reminds us of that country's dominant culture today, and of James Baldwin's profound reflection: 'Tomorrow you will all be negroes!'

In fact, from the beginning, the American system has not had a measure of comparison between the value of the messages delivered and the effort necessary for their transmission. More so than with the content of the message, the means of its mediatization appear instruments of primary necessity in the United States, first of all in their naval relation to metropolitan Europe, to the Africa that supplies its manpower, then for the constitution of a certain State centralism over a vast territory in which, in order to govern, one must first penetrate and then communicate.

The media are the privileged instruments of the Union. They alone are able to control the social chaos of American panhumanity; they are the guarantors of a certain civic cohesion, and thus of civil security itself. Inversely, as in the ancient colonial model, American democracy will make no real efforts to integrate its ethnic minorities, its factions, into a constant civilization, into a truly community-oriented way of life. For segregation is what sanctions the system's hegemony of the media, on which rests the nature of the American State's authority.

This is one reason for the survival of old racism among the *good citizens* of the 'land of the free'; and we will note as well that the great internal and external upheavals in the United States will be linked directly to dromological events, to the very techniques of penetration and transmission – from the delayed radio message of Pearl Harbor to the affair of the Watergate microphones or the Kennedy assassination: we could draw up a list. *Citizen Kane*, the most accomplished product of American civic culture (later baptised 'pop-culture'!), is less William Randolph Hearst, the newspaper magnate who served as Orson Welles' model, than Howard Hughes, the invisible citizen. Hearst still delivered information; Hughes was content to speculate indifferently on whatever delivered it. He singlehandedly constituted the most radical critique of Fuller's and McLuhan's global theories. This completely desocialized man, who vanished from the earth, who avoided human contact for fear of germs, who was terrified by the very breath of his rare visitors, nonetheless thought only of the media, from the aerospace industry to the cinema, from gasoline to airfields, from casinos to the star system, from the design of Jane Russell's bra to that of a bomber. His existence could be considered exemplary. Hughes cared only about that which passes in transit. His life rebounded from one vector to another, as has, for 200 years, the power of the American nation he adored. Nothing else interested him. He died in the open sky, in an aeroplane.

In the same way, American commercial methods triumphed in Europe in 1914 thanks to the unforeseen logistical dimensions taken by the conflict. The United States was to win on the continent one of the first gasoline wars, putting the French market in the hands of Standard Oil, driving back our army which had gone to the front with 400 tanker trucks while the Americans owned more than 20,000. Once more, the market was created not by the object of consumption but by its vector of delivery!

Once peace was restored, it is interesting to see America retreat from the European market, notably from France, where the company representatives were unable to effectively implant their products, 'having committed gross psychological errors in their advertising campaigns.' To speak plainly, European culture still victoriously resists American cultural overthrow. We will see totalitarian governments try to install comparable vectors. But, being all-too-often tangled up in elitist culture and used to giving more importance to the message than to the vehicle, they will have difficulty, using ideological propaganda, in attaining the perfect logistical efficiency of the American patriotic 'short-cut'.

Later, after total war – in other words after the extensive destruction of the European nations' identity (total war, like colonial war, aiming at the annihilation of constant civilizations) – we see the evacuation of American stocks toward Europe. But here again, we haven't sufficiently analyzed this flow of instruments and objects brought over by the *liberty ships*. We must still apply aesthetic, functional and other meanings to this world of giant cars; to the plethora of household objects in gleaming kitchens in which, significantly, nothing is cooked but sandwiches and canned foods; to the whole spectacle of a 'thoughtless objectivity that makes the very concept of consciousness meaningless'; to the clandestine interference in the ordinary vectors of exchange and communication by the technological codes that result from production systems.

Technologies of body and soul are thus strangely complexified in American pop-culture. The body without soul is, as we saw, a body assisted by technical prostheses. And since we're talking about America, we would do well to remember that the word 'comfort' comes from the old French *assistance*: a reference to the old social bestiary of bodies seized in motion, left along the road. Unleashed in the 1920s, the de-neutralization of the media paves the way for what has been called 'the war of the domestic market', a massive ideological campaign addressed directly to the family puzzle that it claims to put together, even to reinvent, as an 'infinite receptacle for consumer goods'.[2] This campaign will very quickly become a veritable animal domestication of the American citizen.

Significantly, the American government will not deem it necessary to establish a veritable welfare system on its own territory. It is convinced at the time that the promotion of a paternalistic and humanitarian *comfort* civilization will perfectly replace social aid through the *technical assistance of bodies*, from the household robot to the company psychiatrist or the latest model of car. Not unlike the way this country today nurtures a romantic taste for the revived bionic bodies of fascistic futurism, human bodies in which certain organs have been replaced by technological grafts, enabling these new heroes of surgical science to accomplish superhuman physical exploits.

But the politics of comfort was superseded by that of *social standing*. Everyone suddenly found himself exposed to the scrutiny of his neighbours, compared with the Identikit portrait of the ideal American consumer: a model of civic-mindedness whose gestures, quirks and attitudes toward life were henceforth broadcast without reprieve by the radio, the press, television and the cinema, and buried under commercial messages. Its political counterpart is the McCarthy period, a time of blacklisting, of anti-American witch hunts, of artists and intellectuals on trial – the same artists and intellectuals who were again designated in 1975 by the Trilateral Commission as a threat to democracy by their ability to constitute demobilizing and irredeemable margins.

In fact, American-style (social) security implies the population's cultural underdevelopment. It is remarkable to see modern democratic States bragging about their *silent majorities*. In this way, the silence of the American people has become just as oppressive as that of the Russian people; social standing has become a step toward the invention of the proletarian policeman.

The hierarchy of high speeds of penetration and assault made and unmade the spectre of the proletarian as if in a lap-dissolve – that mutation that begins with the all-too-clear social distribution commanded by the Convention, then continues with the cloudier look of Marx and Engels, who are unable to see the mythic figure of the Worker, even in the rich deposit of industrial proletarianization that is England in the nineteenth century. Engels cannot find *his specimen*, his neanderthal of historical evolution[3] . . . Only in June 1848 will the image finally take shape, in the streets of Paris, on a theatre of civil war 'as populated as that of the Battle of Leipzig', where 30,000–40,000 men are thrown into combat.

Just as the revolutionary process of the proletarianization of labour comes from the war of mass and movement, the myth of 'the worker of metaphysics' (Biblical image of man's first pain: cursed by God and cursing and killing in turn to replace Him in His creative works) also *takes shape* on the great battlefields of industrial war. Teilhard de Chardin, for example, believes along with most of his contemporaries that war is one of the principal ferments of technological progress; but the idea of 'unfinished man' suddenly strikes him during his 'unforgettable experience at the front', as he writes in 1917. In 1945, at the end of the total war, he notes, 'War is an *organic phenomenon of anthropogenesis* that Christianity cannot suppress any more than it can do away with death.' He adopts the voice of Tacitus to deplore the international Peace that will cover the world with 'the crust of banality, the veil of monotony' (*La nostalgie du front*, 1917). 'Something like a light will go out over the earth.' *Demobilization* will be, for the member of the 'Yellow Crusade' (that epic of automotive assault), *immobilization* in anti-revolution-evolution.

While preparation for war requires months, even years, the decisive assault lasts only an hour, perhaps only a few minutes. Something of the evolutionary-revolutionary gaze on bodies engaged in historical kineticism is held over from the fatal homosexuality of ancient generals, enlightened despots and sultans, who would force the 'militias that are very pleasant to watch, if you are not the one to receive the blows' to repeat their manoeuvres endlessly.[4] Each is seized by an immoderate desire for the subjected flesh of the proletarian soldier, the powerful mass of 'mobile machines . . . blindly obeying the impulses of their drivers' (Babeuf). The military workforces are obliged not so much to sell themselves as to *give* themselves to the war-entrepreneur. For him they are what the woman, then the mount, was for the knight in battle: they help him move forward, die under him or cause death. Alexander is nothing without the humours of Bucephalus; Richard the Third at Bosworth loses his life – and his kingdom – along with his horse. The military, than labouring, proletarian – kinetic, infinite, prolifically self-regenerating – carries into time and space the historical guide who straddles him, directs and inspires his movements, and who is also a chief of war: Lenin, Trotsky, Stalin, Mao.

In short, the revolutionary figure of the worker, sketched less by the industrial system than by the military one, fills the kinetic disparity between slow war and rapid war. The 'full steam ahead through the mud' of the nihilist Nechaiev, apostle of systematized terrorist warfare, is not a rhetorical figure but a serious technological proposition: compensate for the distortion born of the destructive assault's necessary brevity by accelerating the rhythm of attacks. Historical evolution is then kept moving literally *by a combustion engine*!

German fascism will have the same concerns. With Heidegger it becomes *'die Totale Mobil-Machung,'* 'the final stage of the will to power and the realization of the essence of technology: nihilism.' The proletarian soldier can in non-war pursue his revolutionary task, assault, which has become an aggression against nature. This is the pan-destruction of the world (Bakunin), the great geo-political sites that devote the earth to war, keeping its *visible surface* for the 'worker of metaphysics', or giving it to him by educating him. In practice, this begins as a kind of humanitarian aid to the German unemployed, then as a voluntary service to which Heidegger calls the intellectuals, 'a service of work, knowledge and arms'. This will become the exemplary development of the history of the camps that, in 1926, receive their first volunteers, mixing, in the most moving manner possible, workers, peasants and students.

The whole thing could have seemed extremely liberal at a time when, everywhere in the Western world, a crushing need for manpower was being felt. The insatiable requirements of industrial warfare, already forgotten after so few years, simultaneously put the populations to work and domesticated them with para-military State bureaucracies in Europe, across the Atlantic and overseas (between the two wars, moreover, the International Labor Office in Geneva handled all of the world's manpower problems).

In the colonies, American 'forcing' is answered by the *smotig*, the organization of penal labour; while in Bulgaria, for example, civilian labour is made obligatory from 1920 onward, for both sexes, under a general office attached to the Ministry of Public Works. But the beneficiaries usually work on construction projects headed by the Ministry of War: strategic roads, railways, airports, factories.

The fascist project as well, in the final account, is no more than a compromise in the conflict that has long opposed, in the heart of the State, the aristocracy, the military class and the bourgeoisie, each one fighting over its proletariat. In Germany, labour service will be made mandatory in 1928; those who try to avoid it become objects of scorn, social exclusion or denunciation, as the deserter or shirker was in time of war. In 1934, the completely standardized work camps become detention camps; and they will be transformed into concentration camps, into death camps, in the face of public apathy, without anyone even bothering to remove their original motto: '*Arbeit macht frei*'.

The slip from one to the other is in fact quite natural; the proletarian worker's flesh is no different from that of the proletarian soldier. As Clausewitz writes: 'Tools (soldiers) are there to be used, and use will naturally wear them out . . .'

For their part, the Communist countries ostensibly fulfilled Teilhard de Chardin's wish at the very moment he formulated it: *die Totale Mobil-Machung*. More than the suppression of the bourgeois class, this is the disappearance of its productive proletariat. In China, from 1964 onward, the revolutionary slogan was 'Take the army as your model'; and the entire population was forced to wear a similar uniform, a kind of ambiguous, asexual outfit. In France, on the other hand, the soldier was called upon more and more frequently to wear the combat uniform, the outfit of the labourer, even during official parades.

All greatness is in assault! – an inaccurate translation of Plato or a paraphrasing of American forcing?[5] Fascism was totalitarian only insofar as it intended to be totally dromocratic. The 'vital space' is only the disappearance of European geography, become

an area, a desert without qualities, expanded by a 'social' organization made entirely functional by the hierarchy of speed – the
same hierarchy that had produced National Socialism on the
streets of Berlin, before returning with total war to its elitist cultural origins. From the beginning, the superb body of the Man of
Assault, of the blond and naturistic Aryan, is willingly exhibited
by Nazi propaganda. What the Berlin stadium's celebration of the
Olympic liturgy shows is a hierarchy of bodies according to
speeds of penetration. The athletic body is prytanic – projectile
or projector. The excitement of the speed or distance record is
that of assault. This *countdown in time and space*, the very principle of athletic performance, is but the theatricalization of the race
toward its 'absolute greatness', of that military charge that begins
as a slow and geometric march, and continues as an increasingly
powerful acceleration of the body meant to give the final surge.

With total war, the '*Totale Mobil-Machung*' takes on its full
meaning. There is no longer any social comparison between the
triumphant body of the proletarian soldier – the superior being
who, according to the old expression, possesses the 'magnificence
of displacement'; the German soldier who rushes headlong into
the limitless expanse of the steppe or the desert – and the body
of the proletarian worker who is there only to support the logistical effort. A mass of the physically unfit, of forced residents, of
prisoners interned in camps, unable bodies, petty criminals . . .

For the Italian fascist passing directly from the athletic record
to absolute war, the intoxication of the speedbody is total; it's
Mussolini's 'Poetry of the bomber'. For Marinetti, after
d'Annunzio, the 'warrior-dandy' is the 'only able subject, *sur-
viving* and savouring in battle the power of the human body's
metallic dream'; coupling with technological equipment scarcely
more cumbersome than a horse, the old metabolic vehicle of the
warring elites: rapid launches or 'torpedos' straddled under the
sea by aristocratic frogmen in search of the British fleet. The
Japanese kamikaze will realize in space the military elite's syner-
gistic dream by voluntarily disintegrating with his vehicle-
weapon in a pyrotechnical apotheosis; for the ultimate metaphor
of the speedbody is its final disappearance in the flames of explosion. *The possible rebirth of fascism* is a fear shown by many after

the revelation of the Nazis' crimes against *humanity*. Whatever the case: since fascism never died, it doesn't need to be reborn. I'm not talking about little sadico-museographic or commericial trifles, but quite simply the fact that it represented one of the most accomplished cultural, political and social revolutions of the dromocratic West, like the naval empires or the colonial establishments. And it certainly has less to fear from 'the future' than does a Communism that no longer has anything Marxist about it but its name, and for which the end of the dictatorship of the proletariat was the admission of its historical failure.

Fascism is alive because total war, then total peace, have engaged the headquarters of the great national bodies (the armies, the forces of production) in a new spatial and temporal process, and the historical universe in a Kantian world. The problem is no longer one of a historiality in (chronological) time or (geographic) space, but in *what* space-time?

In a recent article, I stressed the necessity of reviewing our *physical concept of history*, of finally recognizing it for what it has become:

> Which in short would make of war's conductibility (the coherent plan devised in time and space that can, through repetition, be imposed upon the enemy) not the instrument but the origin of a totalitarian langauge of History. This language is the mutual effort of the European States, then of the world, toward the absolute essence of foreign or civil war (speed), thus giving it the stature of an absolute takeover of world history by Western military intelligence. Pure history, then, is only the translation of a pure strategic advance over terrain. Its power is to precede and be final, and the historian is but a *captain in the war of time*.[6]

Notes

1. *Trans.*: A play on the word *meuble*, both 'furniture' and 'movable'.
2. D. Crivelli (1932), *La fin de la crise*. Proto-pop culture and European culture.
3. 'Could I yet have imagined that this absolutely necessary historical evolution, in determined conditions, constituted a

retreat of progress and *manufactured* men who were less than savages . . .' Engels in the *Neue Rheinische Zeitung*.

4. Letter from Charles V to ambassador Ghislain de Busbecq.
5. 'Human history is all an affair of chance.' A statement that Heidegger, on the eve of total war, renders less freely than it would seem: 'All greatness is in assault.'
6. Cf. Paul Virilio (1986), *Popular Defense and Ecological Struggles*, New York: Semiotext(e) Foreign Agents Series.

CHAPTER FIVE

Pure Power

By 1978 Virilio's little books were multiplying. In that year Editions Galilée published Virilio's fourth book, *Défense Populaire et Luttes Ecologiques,* part of which is extracted here. Again Mark Polizzotti was the translator when Semiotext(e) published an English edition in New York in 1990, translated unremarkably as *Popular Defense and Ecological Struggles.* The State and power are generally under-theorised concepts in Virilio's work but there are glimpses here of Virilio's schematic thinking in the field of the 'political', and elsewhere a development of the idea of what he calls rather confusingly, in the era of bitterly opposed camps of social democratic reformists versus Marxist revolutionaries, 'revolutionary resistance'. Whilst many students and left activists in Europe and beyond were still arguing furiously over the relative merits of Louis Althusser's 'ideological' and 'repressive' status apparatus theoreticism, or even Antonio Gramsci's forty-year-old idea of 'hegemony', Virilio's name checks were for Sun Tsu and Karl von Clausewitz. Virilio's concentration, by the late 1970s, was firmly on the terrain of war and military technology, a key question of speed and politics which would continue to occupy theoretical attention for the rest of his academic life. When Virilio was writing *Popular Defense and Ecological Struggles,* what he calls 'counter-revolution' had taken hold. By the mid-late 1970s the lessons of the political struggles in countries like Portugal, Chile and Cambodia were being hotly debated, especially the question of whether there was a need for what Virilio calls the 'military aspect' of political parties and governments of the left, in and out of power. Writing at the end of a decade when Virilio notes that, in some parts of the world at least, the legal terrain and political territory had 'disappeared' and become the 'very stakes of the struggle', *Popular Defense and Ecological Struggles* confronts head-on the questions posed by the 'Euro terrorism' of the Red Brigades and the Italian Autonomists.

'Pure Power', from *Popular Defense and Ecological Struggles*, trans. Mark Polizzotti, New York: Semiotext(e), 1990.

Western military culture always stinks of coaches and army trains in which the treasures of defeated nations are hastily piled, to be carried to museums and art galleries. While Germany bridles at 'Greek temples' made of brick, Hegel dusts off Heraclitus, seeking a new eschatology for the ancient Teutonic Order of Knights.[1]

> In History, we must look for a general design, the ultimate end of the world, and not a particular end of the subjective spirit or mind. *The sole aim of philosophical enquiry is to eliminate chance . . .* Reason is self-sufficient and contains its end within itself; it brings itself into existence and carries itself into effect . . . The World Spirit (*Weltgeist*) is the substance of history.

In a short preface, Clausewitz, for his part, turns away from any meditation on war which is not connected to concrete fact. He has never, he says, avoided logical conclusions. But 'whenever the thread became too thin, I have preferred to break it off and go back to the relevant phenomena of experience . . . ' It would obviously be a mistake, he adds, 'to determine the form of an ear of wheat by analyzing the chemical elements of its kernel, since all one needs to do is go to a wheat field to see the grown ears.'

An indirect criticism of Hegel, who gets bored seeing Livy repeat *for the hundredth time* descriptions of battles against the Volscians, occasionally limiting his narrative to: 'In this year, war was successfully waged against the Volscians.' Such historical writing is lifeless; such formulae and abstract representations make the content of the work dry. But here, the historical content is literally that of a communiqué.[2] It is *apractical* in a way that Hegel could not imagine. And if Livy endlessly resumes the litany of his commentary,[3] it is in order to link the corresponding phenomena directly to experience, to an unknown, vaster organization, a work-in-progress.

The narrative material can only function by being repeated 100 times. Through repetition, it eliminates chance and makes the

Reason in these stories a war-machine that deploys its forces by multiplying them. Thus, pure history is only the translation of a pure strategic advance over terrain. Its power is to precede and be final, and the historian is but a 'captain in the war of time'.[4]

* * *

To conduct a war is to execute a rational plan, in other words to launch an enterprise. In the West, this kind of expansion is the model for any monopoly, seeking less the accumulation of wealth than expediency.

The overall plan being clearly distinguished from its execution, the former could be confused with the uncertain and limited game of State politics, before the West offered the military enterprise – with History as general theory of information on the surroundings – the most independent space-time dimensions. The latter (execution), which Clausewitz qualifies as *a phenomenon without true intelligence*, real war, became the trial run of the scientific theory of History, of the technical limits of the enterprise's progress, its energy and uncertainty factors. Thus, to oversimplify, we could say that Cluseret and Clausewitz are operators and that Hegel is a conceptualizer, insofar as he is an initiator into a general philosophy of history.

Tracing the probable origins of strategic settlement (the Citadel-State being nothing more than an army which stops in enemy territory and sets up defensive positions), it is no longer the army that initiates war, but rather – through the perservation of conquest – all the inhabitants of the invested area. This is absolutely clear for the ancient *miles*: 'The army sets itself up as citadel and the citadel only survives by remaining an army' (Isocrates, *Orations*, 'Archidamus'). The soldier is the citizen who, within as well as without, must never know peace.

The democratic assembly (of Equals) is a military-political assembly, and not vice versa. The exercise of power by the State is a 'permanent conspiracy'[5] which marks the stages of the military revolution, the passage from the fragmentary and unsophisticated production of the war enterprise to its technological, industrial and scientific development. The historical effort of the West is thus the distribution and management of independent,

increasingly numerous human groups by the State war enterprise.

*   *   *

Harmand notes that 'the absence of reflection about the military
object in Cicero's *De Re Publica* and *De Legibus* is, *stricto sensu,*
frightening'. War, *incessant* and *mysterious activity*,[6] didn't
need to obtain conceptual autonomy in antiquity any more
than in modern times, insofar as it is the fundamental concept
of our civilization. This becomes particularly evident when
reading Sun Tsu[7] side by side with Clausewitz. Sun Tsu asks
that we never confuse *Pure Power* (the military thing) with
Domination (the State). What he means by pure power is
equally clear, and he often comes back to it: the essential thing
is to make the enemy submit without combat, 'to avoid setting
off the *mechanism*'. Open warfare must be a constant allusion to
primordial camouflage, and its only consistency must be constant change, in which no one element takes precedence for too
long.

   This could not be the case in *war begun as a perpetual mechanism of pure power*. Thus, what Sun Tsu designates as a 'war-
machine' (chapters II, V, XI) is not the 'minimum potential' from
which any military organization can exact enormous results, but
the joint dialectic that contains all of the opposing parties' operations. (Marx, in *Capital*, describes almost identically this potential mechanical growth, which occurs 'as soon as isolated events
function jointly and simultaneously', and which was a permanent
practical concern of Carnot, Napoleon, etc.[8])

*   *   *

For the western state – the military initiator which secures its
position in enemy territory – survival depends entirely on the
growth of this 'pure power', on its unlimited use. In Homeric
Greece, for example, power was divided among the various
ethnic communities, until the *notion of tyranny* – a purely military
notion of the abuse of power based on armed force – appeared.
The first tyrants came as usurpers, adventurers who had
exploited an a-national military work force (the hoplites)[9] and

had thus passed beyond the fluctuating situation previously instituted by limited pressure groups of the 'tribal prytanea'. (The latter, furthermore, continued to take part in Athenian political life in the form of interest groups and coalitions.[10])

We see these phenomena of social warfare faithfully reproduced each time the central strategic organizations are able to generalize their defence systems. At that point, research and concentration of mechanical energy become totally confused, in the Army-State, with the 'pure power' exposed by Sun Tsu. After the eclipse of siege warfare, and until the industrial revolution of armaments and means of transportation, this pure power (tyranny or dictatorship) was represented by the military-industrial proletariat, at a time when 94 per cent of all the mechanical energy produced and consumed on the earth was obtained by the physical strength of men and animals.

With military proletarianization, we approach the 'social unknown' of the army. 'Free as the wind', writes Engels about the English proletarian worker forced off his land by creditors, 'the beginning of the moral freedom indispensable to historical evolution'. In this sense, the mercenaries, long before the proletariat, brought together the class conditions necessary for 'reasonable' historical revolution. Their schizophrenic groups, spread all over Europe, were the keepers of a new mode of production, exchange and distribution.

In the seventeenth century, their treatment by men such as Louvois was directly copied from that of the Roman military proletariat: pathetic, uncertain pay, strikes, and bloody repression. The abusive Boss-State finally addressed their demands regarding salary, health care, lodging, job security. But it was the last and most important demand – the social dignity of the military condition, a demand not met by the French monarchy – that finally became (as Vauban had predicted) one of the major causes of the 1789 revolution.

The *military social body*, the army of proletarianized masses 'trailing its army-civilization all over Europe' (Balzac), replaced the body of the legitimate sovereign, before infiltrating the body politic of the State with Carnot and Napoleon.

It is precisely in this body that *civil thought* was engulfed in the nineteenth century, while military thought furthered its independence. Once the new social theories were forged, confusion became total: civil war merged with foreign war, the military model was at the centre of both reforms and revolutions, words and ideas took on multiple meanings. If Marx admires the joint manoeuvres of the army-machine, General Cluseret dreams of 'revolutionizing warfare along with the rest', of 'applying to destruction the principles of production' − such as the division of labour. He is also outraged by the bourgeois State's timidly-waged *moderate war* and its opposition to the idea of total war, which Cluseret − an old colonial firebrand − considers 'the only truly revolutionary war'.

* * *

Precisely because he could no longer doubt *the autonomy of military calculation*, Clausewitz, around 1816, noted in the margin of *Vom Kriege* − but only *after* having written the first six books: 'no less practical is the importance of another point that must be made absolutely clear, namely that *war is nothing but the continuation of State politics by other means.*' This note is therefore faithful to the spirit of the Vienna Congress, which in its declaration of 13 March 1815, condemned 'the enemy of world peace . . . Napoleon, the disruptor of civil and social relations'. The general's oft-quoted statement is but a warning and a hope. Indeed, how could Clausewitz have really foreseen, in 1816, the irresistible expansion of the concept of pure war in Europe − he who in 1807 had been led, in his plans of attack, to choose *between the good of the State and that of his army*?

Furthermore, war between nations had already been total on the sea and overseas for several centuries − notably, mobilization on the French coast had been permanent since the seventeenth century. Finally, with the French Revolution of 1789, it was *social life* between the states that began to disappear, since the enemy's *political identity* was no longer recognized. And, as we know, *that* is the primary condition for total war, whether foreign or civil.

Operational in 1794, the ocular telegraph allows, from the battlefield, for the quasi-instantaneous disruption of the political field of nations. The worldwide geostratic and statistical revolution – conceived of by Vauban and accomplished in the nineteenth century with the 'peace of great works' and the new vertical capitalism – leads directly to the revolution in transportation, information and speed – a revolution which will bring Europe to the brink of totalitarianism more surely than any battle, than any real and declared conflict.

In this context, Clausewitz also perceives the historical limitations of the new proletariat. For if, in the European war of movement (the specific form of domination of space by speed which henceforth characterizes inter-State conflicts), mass is still the major component of the machine of attack, the military proletarian nonetheless seems more and more a demanding and fragile transmission, a hazardous relay station which, for the war entrepreneur, poses the problem of its deterioration.

> Tools (soldiers) *are there to be used*, and use will naturally wear them out . . . The final product may indeed be compared to that of gold and silver mines: one looks only at the end result and forgets to ask about the cost of the labour that went into it.

The dialectic of war, delivered from passivity, demands of the military engineer an increased effort in the technical domain, *an effort centred on the suppression or replacement of the human factor in the machine's overall workings*. In this, we could see the true origin of the whole mythology of comfort, of a whole 'technical sensibility' which claims to do away with effort, whereas in reality it only seeks to transgress the limits of human energy properly speaking.

* * *

This transgression will come to pass, furthermore, since the labouring populations now produce only 1 per cent of the energy consumed on earth. What developed on the battlefields of foreign and civil wars was not only the discipline of intelligences and bodies, the elimination of individual conduct, but also the entire ethic of the industrial world and of its pseudo-revolutions. Thus, we must never lose sight of the very reason for the historic rise of the military-industrial proletariat, the 'trade union school of war'[11]: the army-State's search for pure power, for pure energy . . .

In this sense, the proletariat's determining role in history stopped with the bombing of Hiroshima.

* * *

Army-civilization reminds us of Schlegel's remark about 'that mysterious aspiring towards chaos that lies behind every ordered creation.' There is a distortion of suddenness between political activity painstakingly making its way toward reality, and the pure power of war, physical violence, which is immediately creative, always available.

History is the ordered creation of chaos through the realization of a theory of war as the geometric basis of all reality, the stabilization of all the variable magnitudes that founded and balanced the universe . . .

* * *

If certain Westerners today show less pride in their energetic superiority, we should not forget that this attitude is quite recent, and perhaps temporary. In 1924, the monk Teilhard, for example, wrote in *Mon univers (My Universe)*: 'It would be premature to suppress the vigorous – albeit overly brutal – expressions of warring force. We still need mightier and mightier cannons, bigger and bigger battleships *to materialize our aggression on the world.*'

Forty years later, Marcuse still exults: 'This economy, adapted as it is to military needs, furthers man's mastery over Nature.'

For these latter-day metaphysicians, there can be no doubt: the enemy is not only on the Eastern or Western front; it is in us and among us. It is our own nature exchanging with all of Nature (allusion to primordial camouflage). 'Everything being exchanged for fire, and fire for everything; the same as merchandise for gold and gold for all kinds of merchandise' (according to Glucksmann, speaking of Polemos as 'the thread that ties together all of *Capital*, from the first unwritten word to the last').

No one here notices that war has completely absorbed its dialectic in an absolute defence which is simultaneously the administration of an absolute attack.

The two-in-one of historical totalitarianism is realized by

nuclear deterrence, along with the 'get out of Nature' of meta-physics, which from the outset was the foundation of colonial strategy. Such is the relatively long-term collapse of the multiplic-ity of exchange systems.

'No constant civilization should consist in colonies,' says Colbert about the 'Colonial Pact'. Here, the degree of 'civilization' is absolutely assimilated to the degree of military aptitude. The 'civilized' countries, in short, are those which, facing the multi-plicity and unpredictability of violent attacks, mutually agreed to band together against risk.

A strict protocol exists in each civilization insofar as exchanges – especially violent exchanges – are concerned, an entire, intelli-gible reciprocity. Thus, from the sixteenth century on in Europe, when historical idealism is reborn, a new colonial adventure begins. Differences are drawn between those populations capable of providing war with the infrastructures of its conductivity (lit-erally, its *media*); and the subjected, underdeveloped others, chosen for their inaptitude at maintaining this level of violent exchange. Placed 'outside the laws of war', they are considered all the more inapt at every other form of exchange (economic, cul-tural, political, etc.).

This is the first realized figure of pure violence: the protocol maintained by the UN after total war, the exponential develop-ment of military science and technique, which obviously aim not toward the multiplication of violent exchanges, but toward their disappearance – *a kind of absolute colonization.*

This is the limit of historical analysis: the final image of the State is ideal, because autonomous; the cosmopolis is that which appropriates and consumes, while giving nothing back to its natural partner.

According to Sun Tsu, the mechanism of war grows like the fire that devours while spreading, *its energy producing ever-increasing speed* – no longer the speed of armies which, 'like stones rolling furiously down the mountainside', are able to regain their balance once they have reached bottom. Energy is no longer subject simply to physical laws, but also to those of metaphysics. The City-State is reorganized around the cratos, the fire that must be constantly fed and revived.[12]

A new chasm opens between the military and professional elite able to create and use complex scientific weapons, and the mass of 'ordinary citizens' assigned merely to maintain and protect the 'nuclear environment'. The machine age naturally leads to the age of central nuclear systems, which can hit the most distant targets through an operation that 'transforms every reality into diminishing energy'.

*   *   *

The Russian-American realization of global nuclear deterrence is thus, at the same time, a catastrophic process of total colonization.

In Washington, at the height of the economic crisis, James Schlesinger demanded that defence budgets for NATO members be regularly increased from 3 to 5 per cent per year. Beyond any consideration of a new strategy of deterrence, we have here a simple protection racket – safety blackmail – just as at the origin of any pact of colonial exhaustion. Elsewhere, the Portuguese military gradually brought the reality of revolutionary power to another level: that of *an army civilization*. Thus ship's captain Correia Jesuino, Minister of *Social Communication*, depicts the 'left-wing officers' as 'ethnologists studying a primitive people'. For, in his view, the Portuguese people is underdeveloped.

But the development in question here is not economic, and the captain's thought is clear: as we have seen, there is only a revolutionary historical realization for the Army-State when the concept of pure war is the basis of its organization, its own characteristics and knowledge.

Conversely, when this basic concept slackens, when the State system tries to make the military enterprise into an 'external affair', then it becomes simply a collection of 'unimportant and trivial transactions' (Tacitus, *Annals*, IV, 32), 'a narrow history, devoid of glory'.

This sheds light not only on Western nations' violent annihilation of different cultures and economies, but also (with decolonization) on the latter's spontaneous disappearance, the voluntary renunciation of enormous bodies of knowledge and expression, which have become completely inoperative for the new individuals claiming a place in History.

Pure War is neither peace nor war; nor is it, as was believed, 'absolute' or 'total' war. Rather, it is the military procedure itself, in its ordinary durability. The balance of terror, the nuclear coalition, peaceful coexistence – in short, the dissolution of the state of war and the military's infiltration into the movements of daily life – reproduce the metamorphoses of the hunter: from direct confrontation of the wild animal; to progressive control over the movements of certain species; then, with the help of the dog, to guarding semi-wild flocks; and finally to reproduction, breeding.

Domestication is the logical outcome of prey. Atrocities, blows, wounds and bloodshed, in the final account, run counter to the unlimited use of violence.

War is no longer directly identifiable with declared conflict, with battles. Since Maurice de Saxe, we know that we can wage war without fighting, through simple displacement of forces and swiftness of movement. Nonetheless, the old illusion still persists that a state of peace means the absence of open warfare, or that the military which no longer fights but 'helps' society is peaceful, and that the military institution can even be beneficial, once it stops attacking.

Partly responsible for the failure of the Paris Commune, this illusion returned in Allende's Chile and in Portugal. That is why it is so urgent to exhaustively analyze this institution, rather than hang around its outskirts, failing (voluntarily or not) to effect the most necessary de-institutionalization of all: that of the military.

That is, unless the latter, through an ultimate subterfuge, manages to simulate this very initiative. Peru or Cambodia, in this respect, constitutes a sinister forerunner: military socialism.

Notes

1. Hegel, G. W. F., 'Introduction', *Lectures on the Philosophy of World History*.
2. First ephemeris of *projected societies*, comparable to what, in the nineteenth century, the monotonous detail of secret police reports represents for sociology. 'Social – let's even say sociological – analysis is made along with the narrative, by the narrative itself,' remarks Alain about Balzac.

3. Before history as poem or mythical canto (mythification or mystification?), there is the mechanism of the trance and the persistence of those short invocations which create unanimity: 'We are not warriors. But suddenly we believe we are, and the war begins' (Leiris).

4. Lope de Vega.

5. 'Every visible power is threatened, especially when it rests on a *usurpation* that alienates both its victims and its accomplices. Thus the detective's tactics are those of the minister and the Chief of State. Power will be shady or will not be at all . . .' (Balzac, Introduction to *Une Ténébreuse Affaire*).

   Greek military power violates legality, for example, by repealing the 'religious calendars' which, in all parts of the world, limited the seasonal duration of battle (generally to twenty-four hours in ancient China). It creates a 'prytaneal calendar', thus settling the war phenomenon into an independent, temporal continuum.

6. Livy.

7. *The Art of War*.

8. *Speed and Politics*.

9. Drews, R., *The First Tyrants in Greece*.

10. Daverio Rocchi, G., *Politica de Famiglia e Politica di Tribunelle Polis Ateniese*.

11. Engels, *Théorie de la Violence*.

12. 'Thus it is on the political level of the public home, which is no longer a private home like the other since its function is precisely to represent all homes while identifying with none' (Vernant, *Mythe et Pensée chez les Grecs*).

   The West's amazing power of reproduction . . . Isn't nuclear fire simultaneously military, political, and, before long, private, thanks to the building of new plants which will provide each home with its own 'Power of nuclear consumption'?

CHAPTER SIX

The Aesthetics of Disappearance

A new decade, the 1980s, saw Paul Virilio become increasingly pro-
lific as a writer and ever more ambitious and provocative theoretically.
In the last throes of the 1970s he had written *Esthétique de la
Disparition,* one of his most important statements of position.
Published by Editions Balland in Paris in 1980, this short book also
received the more familiar Editions Galilée French publication in
1989. This late 1980s Le Livre de Poche edition featured Umberto
Boccioni's *Dynamisme d'un Cycliste* modernist painting on its pristine
white background cover and could literally fit snugly into the back
pocket, just like the fashionable Semiotext(e) books. Semiotext(e) duly
published an English translation by Philip Beitchman of the Balland
book in 1991, though not, for a change, in its 'little black book' series.
A large-format text employed a 'disappearing' cover designed by Steve
Jones and led with the quotation from Paul of Tarsus on the facing
pages of the book: 'The world as we see it is passing'. The extract which
appears here is significant for its stress on religious apparitions like the
one witnessed by Bernadette Soubirous at Lourdes. The extract is also
typical of a book which ranges across topics barely pausing to connect
the dots, employing Virilio's by-now familiar eccentric referencing
system, seemingly citing at random anyone and anything, from the
Bible, Anthony Blunt, Jules Verne and Howard Hughes to the 'special
models' (human bodies, 'fresh and in good condition') used for
research by the Renault car company. However baffling some of
Virilio's reasoning, and his diverse methods for reaching the crux of an
argument, his notion of 'the aesthetics of disappearance' has rightly
become recognized as one of the theoretical legacies of his oeuvre. He

was also developing a talent for memorable one-liners: as a professor of architecture and now a theorist of urban culture *par excellence*, in *The Aesthetics of Disappearance* he produced the gem 'architecture is only a movie'.

The Aesthetics of Disappearance, trans. Philip Beitchman, New York: Semiotext(e), 1991.

The lapse occurs frequently at breakfast and the cup dropped and overturned on the table as its well-known consequence. The absence lasts a few seconds; its beginning and its end are sudden. The senses function, but are nevertheless closed to external impressions. The return being just as sudden as the departure, the arrested word and action are picked up again where they have been interrupted. Conscious time comes together again automatically, forming a continuous time without apparent breaks. For these absences, which can be quite numerous – hundreds every day most often pass completely unnoticed by others around – we'll be using the word 'picnolepsy' (from the Greek, *picnos*: frequent).[1] However, for the picnoleptic, nothing really has happened, the missing time never existed. At each crisis, without realizing it, a little of his or her life simply escaped.

Children are the most frequent victims, and the situation of the young picnoleptic quickly becomes intolerable. People want to persuade him of the existence of events that he has not seen, though they effectively happened in his presence; and as he can't be made to believe in them he's considered a half-wit and convicted of lies and dissimulation. Secretly bewildered and tormented by the demands of those near him, in order to find information he needs constantly to stretch the limits of his memory. When we place a bouquet under the eyes of the young picnoleptic and we ask him to draw it, he draws not only the bouquet but also the person who is supposed to have placed it in the vase, and even the field of flowers where it was possibly gathered. There is a tendency to patch up sequences, readjusting their contours to make equivalents out of what the picnoleptic has seen and what he has not been able to see, what he remembers and what, evidently, he cannot remember and that it is necessary to invent, to recreate, in order to lend verisimilitude to his *discursus*.[2] Later, the young picnoleptic will himself be inclined to doubt the knowledge and concordant evidence of those around him; everything certain will become suspect. He'll be inclined to believe (like Sextus Empiricus) that nothing really exists; that even if there is existence, it cannot be described; and that even if it could be described, it could certainly not be communicated or explained to others.

Around 1913 Walter Benjamin noted: 'We know nothing of woman's culture, just as we know nothing of the culture of the young.' But the trivial parallel – woman/child – can find itself justified in the observation of Doctor Richet: 'Hysterical women are more feminine than other women. They have transitory and vivid feelings, mobile and brilliant imaginations and, with it all, the inability to control, through reason and judgement, these feelings and imaginations.'[3]

Just like women, children assimilate vaguely game and disobedience. Childhood society surrounds its activities with a veritable secret strategy, tolerating with difficulty the gaze of adults, before whom they sense an inexplicable shame. The uncertainty of the game renews picnoleptic uncertainty, its character at once surprising and reprehensible. The little child who, after awaking with difficulty, is absent without knowing it every morning and involuntarily upsets his cup, is treated as awkward, reprimanded and finally punished.

I'll transcribe here, from memory, the statements made by the photographer Jacques-Henri Lartigue, in the course of a recent interview:

Q: You've talked to me just now of a trap for vision, something like that, is that your camera?

A: No, not at all. It's before, something I did when I was little. When I half-closed my eyes, there remained only a narrow slot through which I regarded intensely what I wanted to see. Then I turned around three times and thought, by so doing, I'd caught – trapped – what I was looking at, so as to be able to keep indefinitely not only what I had seen, but also the colours, the noises. Of course, in the long run, I realized that my invention wasn't working. It's then only that I turned to technical tools for facilitating it.

Another photographer has written that his first darkroom was his room when he was a child and his first lens was the luminous crack of his closed shutter. But the remarkable thing with the little Lartigue is that he's assimilated his own body to the camera, the room of his eye to a technical tool, the time of the exposure to turning himself around three times.

He perceives a certain pattern there, and also sees that this pattern can be restored by a certain *savoir-faire*. The child Lartigue has thereby stayed in the same place, and is, nevertheless, absent. Owing to an acceleration of speed, he's succeeded in modifying his actual duration; he's taken it off from his lived time. To stop 'registering' it was enough for him to provoke a body-acceleration, a dizziness that reduced his environment to a sort of luminous chaos. But with each return, when he tried to resolve the image, he obtained only a clearer perception of its variations.

Child-society frequently utilizes turnings, spinning around, disequilibrium. It looks for sensations of vertigo and disorder as sources of pleasure.

The author of the famous comic strip *Luc Bradefer* uses the same method to transport his hero's vehicle through time: by spinning on itself like a top, the 'Chronosphere' escapes from present appearances.

In another game, the first child places his nose against the wall, turning his back on his partners, who all stay a certain distance away on a starting line. He hits the wall three times before turning suddenly on his partners. During this short period of time, the others should advance toward him, then, when he turns around, they assume an immobile position. Anyone caught moving by the first child is eliminated from the game. Whoever succeeds in reaching the wall without being detected by the first child has won, and replaces him. As in the scansion of the game of hand-ball, projected always higher and faster against the earth, a wall, or toward a partner, it seems that it is less the object that is being thrown and caught with agility than its image, projected, enlarged, deformed or erased by the player turning on himself. We may think here of the 'leap' of Mandelbrot's skein of thread[4] – the numerical result (from zero to many dimensions), depending on the rapports of distance between the observed and the observing, or what separates them.

When asked how, at an advanced age, he was able to keep his youthful look, Lartigue answered simply that he knew how to give orders to his body. The disenchantment, the loss of power over himself that obliged him to have recourse to technical prostheses (photography, easel painting, rapid vehicles . . .) have not entirely abolished the demands on his own body that he made as a child.

But we now know that unequal ageing of cellular tissues begins at a very early age, and the crystalline lens of the eye is affected precociously since breadth of accommodation declines after the age of eight until about fifty, when we become far-sighted. The nerve cells of the brain start their irreversible decline at age five. The child is already becoming a handicapped oldster; his recourse to prostheses here is really meant to be an artificial addition destined to replace or complete failing organs. The game then becomes the basic art; the contract on the aleatory is only the formulation of an essential question on the relative perception of the moving; *the pursuit of form is only a technical pursuit of time*. The game is neither naive nor funny. Begun by all from birth, it's the very austerity of its tools, its rules and its representations that paradoxically unleashes in the child pleasure and even passion: a few lines or signs traced ephemerally, a few characteristic numbers, some rocks or bones . . .

The basis of the game is the separation of the two extreme poles of the *seen* and the *unseen*, which is why its construction, the unanimity that pushes children to spontaneous acceptance of its rules, brings us back to the picnoleptic experience.

The more progress we make in the already ancient study of the *petit mal*, the more it appears to be widespread, diverse, and badly understood. In spite of lengthy polemics as to its kinship with epilepsy, with its uncertain diagnoses and with the crisis passing unperceived by those present as well as by the subject himself, it remains completely unknown by nearly everyone, and to the question: who is picnoleptic? we could possibly respond today: who isn't, or hasn't been?

So-defined as a mass phenomenon, picnolepsy comes to complement in the waking order the notion of *paradoxical sleep* (rapid-eye-movement sleep), which corresponds to the phase of deepest dreaming. So our conscious life – which we already believe would be inconceivable without dreams – is just as difficult to imagine without *a state of paradoxical waking* (rapid waking).

'Film what doesn't exist', the Anglo-Saxon special effects masters still say, which is basically inexact: what they are filming certainly does exist, in one manner or another. It's the speed at which they film that doesn't exist, and is the pure invention of the cinematographic motor. About these special effects – or 'trick photography', hardly an academic phrase – Mèliés liked to joke, 'The trick, intelligently applied, today allows us to *make visible the supernatural, the imaginary, even the impossible.*'

The great producers of the epoch recognized that by wresting cinema *from the realism* of 'outdoor subjects' that would quickly have bored audiences, Méliès had actually made it possible for film to remain realistic.[5]

As Méliès himself remarked, 'I must say, to my great regret, the cheapest tricks have the greatest impact.' It's useful to remember how he went about inventing that cheap trick which, according to him, the public found so appealing:

> One day, when I was prosaically filming the Place de l'Opéra, an obstruction of the apparatus that I was using produced an unexpected effect. I had to stop a minute to free the film and started up the machine again. During this time passersby, omnibuses, cars, had all changed places, of course. When I later projected the reattached film, I suddenly saw the Madeleine–Bastille Bus changed into a hearse, and men changed into women. The trick-by-substitution, soon called the stop trick, had been invented, and two days later I performed the first metamorphosis of men into women.

Technical chance had created the desynchronizing circumstances of the picnoleptic crisis and Méliès – delegating to the motor the power of breaking the methodical series of filmed instants – acted like a child, regluing sequences and so suppressing all apparent breaks in duration. Only here, the 'black out' was so long that the *effect of reality* was radically modified.

'Successive images representing the various positions that a living being travelling at a certain speed has occupied in space over a series of instants.' This definition of chronophotography given by its inventor, the engineer Etienne Jules Marey,[6] is very close also to that 'game against the wall' we've just been talking of. Furthermore, if Marey wants to explore movement, making of fugacity a 'spectacle' is far from his intentions. Around 1880 the debate centred on the inability of the eye to capture the body-in-motion, everyone was wondering about the veracity of chronophotography, its scientific value – the very reality it conveys insofar as it makes the 'unseen' visible, that is to say, a world-without-memory and of unstable dimensions.

If we notice Marey's subject of choice we perceive that he leans toward the observation at what seemed to him precisely the most uncontrollable thing formally: the flight of free flying birds, or of insects, the dynamics of fluids . . . but also the amplitude of movement and abnormal expressions in nervous maladies, *epilepsy*, for instance (subjects of photographic studies around 1876 at the hospital of Salpetrière).

Later, the illusionism of Méliès will no more aim to mislead us than the methodical rigour of a Claude Bernard disciple: one maintains a Cartesian discourse, 'the senses mislead us', and the other invites us to recognize that 'our illusions don't mislead us in always lying to us!' (La Fontaine). What science attempts to illuminate, 'the non-seen of the lost moments', becomes with Méliès *the very basis of the production of appearance*, of his invention, what he shows of reality is what reacts continually to the absences of the reality which has passed.

It's their 'in-between state' that makes these forms visible that he qualifies as 'impossible, supernatural, marvellous'. But Emile Cohl's earliest moving comic strips show even more clearly to what extent we are eager to perceive malleable forms, to introduce a perpetual anamorphosis in cinematic metamorphosis.

The pursuit of forms is only a pursuit of time, but if there are no stable forms, there are no forms at all. We might think that the domain of forms is similar to that of writing: if you see a deaf-mute expressing himself you notice that his mimicry, his actions are already drawings and you immediately think of the passage to writing as it is still taught in Japan, for example, with gestures performed by the professor for students to capture calligraphically. Likewise, if you're talking about cinematic anamorphosis, you might think of its pure representation which would be the shadow projected by the staff of the sundial. The passing of time is indicated, according to the season of the year, not only by the position but also by the invisible movement of the form of the shadow of the staff or of the triangle on the surface of the dial (longer, shorter, wider, etc.).

Furthermore, the hands of the clock will always produce a modification of the position, as invisible for the average eye as planetary movements; however, as in cinema, the anamorphosis properly speaking disappears in the motor of the clock, until this ensemble is in turn erased by the electronic display of hours and dates on the black screen where the *luminous emission* substitutes entirely for the original effect of the shadow.

Emphasizing motion more than form is, first of all, to change the roles of day and light. Here also Marey is informative. With him light is no longer the sun's 'lighting up the stable masses of assembled volumes whose shadows alone are in movement'. Marey gives light instead another role; he makes it leading lady in the chrono-photographic universe: if he observes the movement of a liquid it's due to the artifice of shiny pastilles in suspension; for animal movement he uses little metallicized strips etc.

With him the effect of the real becomes that of the readiness of a luminous emission, what is given to see is due to the phenomena of acceleration and deceleration in every respect identifiable with intensities of light. He treats light like a shadow of time.

We notice generally a spontaneous disappearance of picnoleptic crises at the end of childhood (in-fans, the non-speaker). Absence ceases therefore to have a prime effect on consciousness when adult life begins (we may be reminded here of the importance of the endocrinal factor in the domain of epilepsy and also of the particular role of the pituitary and hypothalamus in sexual activity and sleep . . .).

Along with organic ageing, this is also the loss of *savoir-faire* and juvenile capacities, the desynchronization effect stops being mastered and enacted, as with the young Lartigue playing with time, or using it as a system of invention and personal protection – photosensitive subjects show great interest for the causes inducing their crises and frequently resort to absence mechanisms as a defence-reaction against unpleasant demands or trains of thought (Pond).

The relation to dimensions changes drastically. What happens has nothing to do with metaphors of the 'images of time' style; it is something like what Rilke's phrase meant in the most literal sense: 'What happens is so far ahead of what we think, of our intentions, that we can never catch up with it and never really know its true appearance.' One of the most widespread problems of puberty is the adolescent's discovery of his own body as strange and estranged, a discovery felt as a mutilation, a reason to despair.

It's the age of 'bad habits' (drugs, masturbation, alcohol), which are merely efforts at reconciliation with yourself, attenuated adaptations of the vanished epileptic process. This is also the age, nowadays, of the intemperate utilization of technical prostheses of mediatization (radio, motorcycle, photo, hi-fi, etc.). The settled man seems to forget entirely the child he was and *believed eternal* (E. A. Poe); he's entered, in fact, as Rilke suggests, another kind of absence to the world. 'The luxuriance and illusion of instant paradises, based on roads, cities, the sword,'[7] to which the Judeo-Christian tradition opposes a new departure toward a 'desert of *uncertainties*' (Abraham), lost times, green paradises where only adults who have become children again may enter.

In Ecclesiastes *what is the essential is lacking*; with the New Testament *the lack is the essential*; the Beatitudes speak of a poverty of spirit that somehow could be opposed to the *wealth of moments*, to this hypothetical conscious hoarding proposed by Bachelard, to this fear 'of mini-max equilibrium by exhaustion of the stakes based on a knowledge (information, if you will), whose treasure (which is language's treasure of possible enunciations) becomes inexhaustible' (J. F. Lyotard). Images of the vigilant society, striking equal hours for everyone.

At the Arch of Triumph Award, a journalist wittily asked of the president: 'Is betting part of leisure?' The president was careful not to answer this question that pretended to assimilate lottery techniques to this *culture of leisure* proposed for more than a century to the working population as inestimable recompense for its efforts. Replying would be to admit that progress has pushed our hyper-anticipatory and predictive society toward a simple *culture of chance*, a contract on the aleatory.

New Roman circuses, at Las Vegas they bet on any and everything, in the game rooms and even in the hospitals – even on death. A nurse working at the Sunrise Hospital invented, for the amusement of the personnel, a 'casino of death' where you bet on the moment the patient will die. Soon everyone started playing: doctors, nurses, cleaning ladies; from a few dollars the stakes went up to hundreds . . . soon there weren't enough people dying. What follows is easy enough to imagine.

The basic recreation of childhood, lowered to the level of trival excitement, remains nonetheless a derivative of picnoleptic auto-induction, the dissimulation of one or several elements of a totality in relation to an adversary who is one only because of differences in perception dependent on time and appearances that escape under our very eyes, artificially creating this inexplicable exaltation where 'each believes he is finding his real nature in a truth which he would be the only one to know'.

Furthermore, number-games, like lotto or the lottery, with their disproportionate winnings, connote disobedience to society's laws, exemption from taxes, immediate redressment of poverty . . .[8]

'No power doubles or precedes the will; the will itself is this power', wrote Vladimir Jankelevitch. If you admit that picnolepsy is a phenomenon that effects the conscious duration of everyone – beyond Good and Evil, a *petit mal*, as it used to be called – the meditation on Time would not only be the preliminary job delegated to the metaphysician; relieved today by a few omnipotent technocrats, anyone would now live a duration which would be his own and no one else's, by way of what you could call *the uncertain conformation of his intermediate times*, and the picnoleptic onset would be something that could make us think of human liberty, in the sense that it would be a latitude given to each man to invent his own relations to time and therefore a kind of will and power for minds, none of which, 'mysteriously, can think of himself as being any lower than anyone else' (E. A. Poe).

With Bergsonian chrono-tropisms you could already imagine 'different rhythms of duration that, slower or faster, would measure the degree of tension or of relaxation of consciousness and would establish their respective places in the series of beings.' But here the very notion of rhythm implies a certain automatism, a symmetrical return of weak or strong terms superimposed on the experienced time of the subject. With the irregularity of the epileptic space, defined by surprise and an unpredictable variation of frequencies, it's no longer a matter of tension or attention, but of suspension pure and simple (by acceleration), disappearance and effective reappearance of the real, departure from duration.

To Descartes' sentence: 'the mind is a thing that thinks' (that is, in stable and commonly visible forms), Bergson retorted: 'The mind is a thing that lasts . . .' The paradoxical state of waking would finally make them both agree: it's our duration that thinks, the first product of consciousness would be its own speed in its distance of time, speed would be the causal idea, the idea before the idea.[9]

Even if we talk about the solitude of power as an established fact, no one really thinks of questioning this autism conferred inevitably by the function of command – which means that, as Balzac has it, 'all power will be secret or will not be, since all *visible* strength is threatened'.

This reflection radically opposes the extreme caducity of the world as we perceive it to the creative force of the unseen, the power of absence to that of the dream itself. Any man that seeks power isolates himself and tends naturally to exclude himself from the *dimensions* of the others, all techniques meant to unleash forces are techniques of disappearance (the epileptic constitution of the great conquerors, Alexander, Caesar, Hannibal, etc., is well known).

In his *Citizen Kane*, Orson Welles ignores the Freudian elements that American directors ordinarily used and designates the mysterious sled Rosebud as the apparently trivial motive for the rise to power of his hero, the key and the conclusion of the fate of this pitiless man, a little vehicle able to delight its young passenger while sliding at top speed through a snowscape.[10] After this fictive biography of William Randolph Hearst, calling out to Rosebud for help in his agony, there comes Howard Hughes' real destiny. The life of this billionaire seems made of two distinct parts, first a public existence, and then – from age forty-seven and from then on for twenty-four years – a hidden life. The first part of Hughes' life could pass for a programming of behaviour by dream and desire: he wanted to become the richest, the greatest aviator, the most important producer in the world, and he succeeded everywhere ostentatiously; overexposing his person, avid for publicity, for years he inundates the Western press with his image, with tales of his records or conquests of women.

Then, Howard Hughes disappears. He is in hiding until his death. The journalist James Phelan, who followed the billionaire's whole career, wonders about him:[11] 'Why did he allow himself to become *a man who couldn't stand being seen*? What was he looking for beyond the simple desire for acquisition?'

Master of an incomparable fortune, of a considerable technical and industrial achievement, the only purpose of his wealth, finally, was to purchase total reclusion in a dark room where he lived nude, covered with bedsores, emaciated and destitute on a pallet. Phelan concludes: what Hughes was accumulating was not money, but power.

One day, Phelan recounts, a man disguised as Mickey Mouse presented himself at the Bayshore Inn and said he had a gift for Mr Hughes. He belonged to the Disney parade on a publicity tour, and they wanted to offer a 'Mickey Mouse watch' to Hughes with this inscription: 'Legendary heros must constantly play cat-and-mouse with their public so that it will continue to believe in them, so you'll surely, once in a while, want to know the time of day?'

Now it was notoriously well known that Hughes refused absolutely to wear a watch, all the while calling himself the *Master of*

Time, which for him certainly had a precise meaning, close perhaps to Rilke's definition: to be all-powerful, to win in the game of life is to create a dichotomy between the marks of his own personal time and those of astronomical time, so as to master whatever happens and fulfill immediately what is in the offing.

Destitute billionaire, Hughes' only effort is to fake the speed of his destiny, to make his style of life a style of speed. He seems far more contemporary than Citizen Kane, emperor agonizing in his museum palace, buried in the ruins of his material goods, the baroque abundance of his collections.

For Hughes, on the other hand, *to be is not to inhabit;*[12] polytropos, like Homer's Ulysses, not occupying only one place, he desires not to be identifiable, but especially to identify with nothing. 'He is no one because he wants to be no one and to be no one you have to be everywhere and nowhere.' This taste for ubiquitous absence he'll quench, first through his use of various technical media, in surpassing what was then the most prestigious speed record: 14 July 1938, his Lockheed-Cyclone having flown around the world 'in a great circular arc', lands at Floyd Bennett Field where he had taken off on 10 July. Then he guides his plane into the hangar *to the exact point he left from*. It isn't long before Hughes recognizes that *his desire for movement is only desire of inertia, desire to see arrive what is left behind*.

Soon his only link to the world will be the telephone. Like Chateaubriand, *he locks into a narrow space his life-long hopes*. The rooms he wants to be in now are narrow and all alike, even if they are worlds apart. Not only does he thereby eliminate the impression of going from one place to another (as in the empty loop of the world record), but above all each place was such as he could have expected it to be. The windows were all shaded and the sunlight could no more penetrate these dark rooms than the unanticipated image of a different landscape.

Suppressing all uncertainty, Hughes could believe himself everywhere and nowhere, yesterday and tomorrow, since all points of reference to astronomical space or time were eliminated. At the foot of the bed where he was lying was, however, an artificial window, a movie screen. At the head there was a projector and alongside it, within reach, the controls that allowed him to project his films, always the same, eating indefinitely from the same plate.

We find here what we've always taken as a metaphor of vision, the Socratic myth of the cave (dark room), 'where those (who have been first in everything) must be brought to their term, forcing them to face the light-giving source . . . to contemplate the real which is the invisible . . .'

Hughes wanted so much to be nowhere that he could no longer stand to be visible for others and if he supported, at great expense, a harem, he never went near his protégées, it was enough to know he had the power of going there and that the young women whose pictures he had were awaiting his arrival.

It was the same with his planes and cars, parked here and there, unused for years, exposed to the weather at sundry airports. He always bought the same model of Chevrolet because he thought this particular model was especially banal.

He treated his business like his women, maverick of politics, corruptor of the American government and the CIA, playing with the world, until finally he collapsed into states approximating sleep, then death.

In his absolute impatience to see arrive what is left, Hughes – who his fellow countrymen will end up calling a 'mystic' – became a kind of *technological monk*, and there is very little different between the dark room at the top of the Desert Inn in Las Vegas and the retreat to the desert of the ancient hermits in search of the Eternal.

The Hebraic tradition manifests two kinds of lack, expressed by two deserts, emerging one from the other, *heart of everything, in its heart everything*. One is named *Shemama*, despair and destruction, and the other is *Midbar*, which is a desert not of dereliction but instead a field of uncertainty and effort. The *shemama* is, rather, polarity of the City-State (City of Ur – *Our*, light), its desert is the tragical one of laws, ideology, order, as opposed to what could have resulted from wandering.

Hughes' life, his deprivation of the present world, seem risen from the Anchorites, from those 'inhuman mortifications' that the monks inflicted upon themselves, at the end of those eremitic lives where the 'saint' seemed to recognize only madness and idiocy, in this double game of city-desert and desert-of-uncertainties — like Simeon of Emesis, who comes down from his solitude, he said, so as to *mock the world* (or to play with the world, as Hughes).

According to the chronicle, the desert had so tired him that he had attained *apatheia*, which may be translated as impassibility, and which will allow him to make a mockery of the city and its laws, by acting in it like an idiot. Always dressed in his monastic habit, he doesn't hesitate to lift his skirts in public: he's a regular at the brothel, he goes to church to disturb the liturgy. Multiplying reprehensible acts, he puts his autism to the test by acting in the city as if it were a desert and no one could see him.

Photosensitive inductor, the desert (its double aspect) is linked in every case to liberation from time: divine eternity for the Anchorite, State eternity for Caesar dreaming of turning the frontiers of his empire into a vast desert.

Christ — the inverse of Hughes — begins by a hidden life to end in public existence, confronting temptation at the juncture of these two modes, Satan offering him domination over nations (the *shemama*), as if assuming human power could only be evoked by the overview of a solitary expanse where other people are on the verge of invisibility.

The preacher in John Huston's film, *The Great Sinner*, expresses this pretty clearly: 'The Church of Christ without Christ is nothing but your own shadow, nothing but your reflection in a mirror.'

The singer Amanda Lear eliminated mirrors from her apartment, replacing them with an integrated video circuit; and so the light of her image follows after her like the most intimate of companions (like her shadow, you could say). If the ageing Castiglione had veiled the mirrors in her home to avoid witnessing the progress of her decrepitude, Amanda would not have to fear meeting her reflection, she'll just stop taping the images on the day of her choice and the screens will return her eternally young image, in an apartment where time would stop, the movable property of the living would no longer be distinct from immovable real estate. The means of communication would become a synthesizer capable of mixing body and field in her house, the video game becoming a way of playing indefinitely with everyday life, accomplishing Baudelaire's notion: 'Countless layers of ideas, images, feelings have fallen successively on your brain as softly as light. It seems that each buries the preceding, but none has really perished.'

In their intimate memoirs, erudite Germans at the beginning of the century loved to alternate methodically an account of their days and stories of their dreams, trying to create an equivalence between their waking states and oneiric universes. This style was an attempt to abrogate an abusive discrimination between waking and sleeping: 'Sleepers are in separate worlds, the awake, in the same' (Heraclitus).

German artists, who are known for their epileptic constitution, usually blur the ideal of ordinary Reason as activation of the conscious man and censor of the real, pretension to a state of wakefulness (of sentinel), in a world given as common (proto-foundation of meaning). But if you admit that each one's time has been more or less patched together and that rapid waking is as paradoxical as the dream, the reality of the passing world could in no sense seem common, and 'pure reason' would be only one of the numerous subterfuges of the picnoleptic scheme and of its *savoir-faire* – one of the sophistications that worried Bachelard: 'Applied rationalism which is only a philosophy at work, which wants to expand . . . haste of systematic thought, authoritarian propensity that no one questions . . .'

Oppressive work, accompanied from childhood on with heavy punishments, for no one is supposed to ignore Reason, as none is excused from knowing the law. To juvenile consciousness, always time's orphan, Reason supplies the *illusory recommencement of its foreign tale*, as operational language, it's the pitiful 'I knew' of the child who has recited his lesson well and so escaped punishment.

The ideal of scientific observation would therefore be a sort of *controlled trance* or, better yet, a control of the speed of consciousness. And it would be first of all as a reconstitution of picnoleptic *savoir-faire* that it could be communicated and recognized as common by each and everyone.

In his book, *Magic, Reason, and Experience*,[13] G. E. R. Lloyd, wondering about the passage from prescientific to scientific

phases in the ancient Greeks, calls our attention to the importance of the Hippocratic text on the *sacred malady* (epilepsy)
which dates from the end of the fifth century or the beginning of
the fourth century BC. The goal of the author was to show that
this malady is no more sacred than any other, that we could find
natural causes for it and therefore treat it otherwise than by
incantations or the efficacy of amulets. But what seems interesting to us here is that the epileptic process finds itself at the centre
of what nineteenth century people regarded as the advent of the
absolute dichotomy between the magical and the scientific.

However, the Hippocratic text can be understood otherwise.
To show that the divine malady is naturally explicable is to say
that the rational study of the real (the establishment of its laws
and its models) can be perfectly substituted for the epileptic ran-
domness, curing us completely of its uneven and, especially,
unpredictable frequencies.

We should remember that the divine system is also, for the
Ancient Greek, a system of events: 'The Gods are events in
motion,' which explains well enough this indecisive attitude that
contemporary scholars find naive and incompatible with the for-
mation of the scientific spirit, an ideal of science without accu-
racy where the rational project is presented as an incomplete
programme, or better yet as a simple bet on the universe where
'the real is the invisible' (Plato).

Heisenberg tells us of Einstein's irritation, rebelling at the idea
of a God playing with dice. Bachelard thought that the original
sin of reason was to have an origin. Paul of Tarsus said that 'reason
resembles death'.

If Ambrose Paré qualifies epilepsy as *retention of feelings*, in
other civilizations the attenuated adaptations of the epileptic
process, just like the accomplishment of the sexual act, are called
'little death', 'quick death'. For sleep we talk about the 'death
you come back from'. Reason, compared to death, does nothing
else but redistribute methodically the occasional eliminations of
picnolepsy.

The rational study of the real is just like the movies; the *tabula
rasa* is only a trick whose purpose is to deny particular absences
any active value.

Little by little the rational hoarding, as an expectation of the advent of what is left and a factor of non-surprise, turns our contemporaries into these characters afflicted with fly-catcher memories where whole masses of useless facts are glued together (Conan Doyle) – which makes us judge them *inferior* to those computer screens, where, in actual fact, the information of a memory without gaps, failures, absence is displayed at very high speeds, so we think.

Pascal, himself interested in the construction of this kind of fly-catcher memory, but equally afflicted by massive crises, proceeds by introducing disorder into the order in which information appears. 'What's new is not the elements but the order in which they are arranged,' he writes. Finally the discovery, the invention, that is, that which is without possible memory and therefore new, is the order in which he alone, Pascal, could put into relation those elements known to all and this in 'finally making reason yield to feeling'.[14] For he knows from experience that the faculty of feeling, that is the aesthetic emotion, is at the heart of the epileptic onset; epilepsy is provokable, it can be domesticated.

We can see here likewise the very cause of his famous wager on the existence of God, which he assimilates to a *savoir-faire*, to a theological transposition of the scientific hypothesis, comparable to the ancient Greek's approach.

The crisis, *sudden thunder in a calm heaven*, is announced by the very beauty of the sky. The epileptic isn't necessarily looking for the crisis as a factor of pleasure, but he has been warned of its coming by a very special state of happiness, a juvenile exhilaration. 'Sublime,' says Dostoevski, 'for that moment you'd give your whole life!' He is literally 'ravished', before returning, to be there again, often afflicted as he is by more or less severe lesions provoked by his fall or the sheer suddenness of the onset. The inexplicable enthusiasm precedes the accident, the shipwreck of the senses that of the body. But facilitating factors can also be of the order of distraction, the sleepiness provoked by the repetition of certain themes, or, on the contrary, by intense intellectual efforts, connected, for example, with the moment of invention, of basic discovery, as with Champillon, or with creative activity . . .

'At that moment I understood the meaning of that singular expression: there will no longer be time,' says Dostoevski.

In photosensitive subjects the processes of autoinduction of absence are called autoerotic acts, with a sexual origin. As we have seen, at puberty picnolepsy interferes with the awakening of sexual activity. Here also absence is no stranger to invention, to the crystallization of the amorous image.

If antique statuary represents the sleeper in state of erection, the fact is that he is dreaming. We had to wait for the 1940s before scholars rediscovered this phenomenon, and later, the connections between paradoxical sleep and sexual activity in men and women.

Likewise the degree of love's power and of diurnal desire is a function of the invisible recall of the state of exaltation in paradoxical wakefulness.

Michelangelo writes: 'Please tell me, O Love, if my eyes see (outside of me) true beauty or if I have it in me . . .' It is the curse of Psyche, where the external light instantaneously destroys the crystal of the love image, Eros flies, deserting the young woman as soon as she lights up her face. More simply, in the old ceremony of bundling, newly wed couples who often had never before met were advised to avoid immediate contacts and rather to sleep, that is, to dream, leaving it up to natural law to create the adhesion and 'satisfaction' of the couple.

One might contrast this traditional method with the current hyper-wakefulness of sexual information and education, one result of which is to squash anything natural in sexual actions, psychoanalysts receiving nowadays visits from rationally educated young people who nevertheless don't know how 'to go about it'.

Which reminds us also of the sword placed between Tristan and Iseult while they're sleeping – to show us that the philtre of passion has placed them in such a state of consciousness that the subterfuge of paradoxical sleep becomes useless. For them, love has created the equivalence of night and day, of rapid waking, of dream and soon of death.

We can multiply the examples and customs of dissimulation between future spouses right up to the idea of Catholic nuns wishing themselves married to Christ, who by his absolute invisibility is able to pass for a sort of absolute spouse, a new interior Eros, something that would facilitate another relation to time.

A mourning, an impression of profound unhappiness can, according to Bachelard, give us the feeling of the moment. They can, in any case, favour absence. We're afflicted and here we are visited by some tenacious sensation, affecting indifferently one of our organs of perception: in the olfactory domain, someone will sense, often for several days, a characteristic odour, connected to a far-off memory; another, seated in a garden, will see one flower among others become suddenly photogenic. The strange phenomenon lasts sometimes for a long while before everything seems *ordinary* again. You might think of Marcel Proust's reflection on the subject of the Marquise de Sévigne: 'She does not present things in a logical, causal order, she first presents the illusion that strikes us.' In the sequence of the arrival of information, Proust designates for us the stimulus of art as the fastest, since here nothing yields to sentiment, but on the contrary, everything begins with it.

In short, turned causal by its excessive speed, the sensation overtakes the logical order. Proust confirms the Sophist idea of *apate*, the suddenness of this possible entry into another logic 'which dissolves the concepts of truth and illusion, of reality and appearance and which is given by the *kairos* that one might call "opportunity"'.

What escapes from the universal and gives difference a context is the *epieikés* – that which pertains to a moment that is singular and, by definition, different.[15]

As for scientists, some today are dropping the pompous term of *basic research* for the more convenient *non-applied research*, research in which 'that which is new, the discovery, obviously does not depend on chance, but on *surprise*' (P. Joliot).

The world is an illusion, and art is the presentation of the illusion of the world. Michelangelo detested, for example, the creating of an image imitating nature or liable to resemble a living model: 'They paint in Flanders to fool our external vision . . . the beguilements of the world have robbed me of the time accorded me to worship God.' Ageing, he realized that the same duration can be utilized in diverse manners, or better yet, according to our art of seeing, the same time may serve to allow yourself to be fooled or to contemplate something other than what you think you're seeing (God, in this case, as Truth of the World).

In 1960 the painter Magritte, responding to a questionnaire, expresses the same convictions:

Q: Why is it that in some of your pictures bizarre objects appear, like the bilboquet?

Magritte: I don't think of a bilboquet as being bizarre. It's rather something very banal, as banal as a penholder, a key or the foot of a table. I never show bizarre or strange objects in my pictures . . . they are always familiar things, not bizarre but ordinary things are gathered and transformed in such a way that we're made to think that *there's something else of an unfamiliar nature that appears at the same time as familiar things.*

To look at what you wouldn't look at, to hear what you wouldn't listen to, to be attentive to the banal, to the ordinary, to the infra-ordinary. To deny the ideal hierarchy of the crucial and the incidental, because there is no incidental, only dominant cultures that exile us from ourselves and others, a loss of meaning which is for us not only a *siesta* of consciousness but also a decline in existence.

In Europe, for more than a century now, many children have seen the Virgin *appear*, and the police and religious authorities have had to take down their testimony. As for me, I am struck by the sequence of circumstances that precedes the apparition proper and where the world begins to be seen by children as illusion of the world.

Particular selection of what is seen, recording of insignificant facts that gradually transforms the true objects into a sort of background against which another designation of meaning suddenly emerges, a background which would be already a kind of *dissolving view*, reminding us of the reflection of Paul of Tarsus (but he, also, on the road to Damascus, experienced a prolonged absence which effectively altered his notion of reality), all is calm, and yet: *this world as we see it is passing away.*

As for Magritte, above, it's a question of the recording of facts, or else of 'camera shots', all you can see in the instant of the glance, isn't it only the imposture of the immediate, the untimely hijacking of a convoy of objective elements, among which operates the 'shooting' of vision?

As the meteorologist explains: 'the local level is always an uncertain objective, it's on the scale of the globe that we should envision the meteorological data, our weather's always somewhere else's weather and that's how the whole system fits together.'

Bernadette Soubirous recounts: 'I heard a noise. Looking up I saw poplars beside the torrent and brambles in front of the cave quiver as if the wind was shaking them, but all around nothing moved and suddenly I saw something white . . . and this white was . . . a white girl . . . a white girl no bigger than me. She greeted me, bowing . . .'

Sometimes visual, but also olfactory, gustatory, auditory sensations are shared by several young witnesses. But here also the children experience the particular instants that precede the passage from the familiar to the unfamiliar.

At Salette, for example, two children who didn't know each other met by chance. Mélanie is a puny little servant, miserably poor, who's considered 'withdrawn'. Maximin is himself a young man with asthmatic heredity, considered as a madcap who spends most of his time running in the mountains after his goat but who can barely be trusted to watch over the herd. The day of the apparition, the two children, who have decided to watch their animals together, are overcome by a sudden desire to sleep, and, in fact, they both fall asleep, which was unusual for them. On awakening they are worried and set out to look for the herd they were supposed to be watching, but the animals are still in the same spot, they haven't moved. And suddenly, at the spot where the children were sleeping 'a spinning globe of light, growing gradually, as if the sun had fallen there . . .'

Poor, scorned, considered as retarded, often asthmatic, these children will be, as a rule, deprived of apparitions and cured by puberty.

Bernadette Soubirous will say sadly: 'You should refer to what I first said. I could have since forgotten and others also could have forgotten . . .'

'For that moment you'd give a whole lifetime.' This is exactly what she does by hiding in a convent at Nevers where she dies at age thirty-five.

The apparitions, therefore, have been like a repetition of those surprising moments that precede the epileptic absence, but the senses that stay awake succeed in perceiving an infra-ordinary reality.

Bernadette looked characteristically pale at that moment, 'fine white muslin falling over her face', then she returned 'rubbing her eyes and her face was alive with colour once more'.

But the apparent resemblance with epilepsy stops here, for Bernadette is able to function during the ecstasy, to move, to eat even, and, upon return, she will recall what happened. Nevertheless, as her visions multiplied, the little girl feels the need to induce them by means of a personal ceremony, she acts nervous, which annoys certain witnesses, and, furthermore, she doesn't always succeed.

Later, when she leaves Lourdes to retire to the convent at Nevers, she stops at Bordeaux and 'what she found most beautiful,' she says, 'is the aquarium of the Botanical Garden, seeing the little animals swimming in the presence of a crowd of fascinated children.'

Notes

1. 'Epilepsy – *surprise* in Greek – assumes not only one form but several and we have to speak of epilepsies, from the *Grand Mal* to the *Petit Mal*. From the neurological point of view all epileptic crises result, strictly speaking, from a hyper-synchronous discharge of a population of neurons . . . The clinical way of conceiving epilepsy has changed very little over the years, except that we now distinguish the epileptic attack from epilepsy properly speaking, reserving the term rather for chronic crises.' See the text of Catherine Bousquet and her bibliography in *Macroscopies*, no. 6, p. 45.
2. From the Latin *discurrere*, to run here and there, a term that very well conveys the impression of haste and disturbance or normal mental operations in the picnoleptic.

3. Hysteria and epilepsy, specifically feminine maladies . . . Sensitive, sentimental women, great readers of novels, expert in the games of coquettry . . . (Regnard)

4. Through the constant renewal of the relations between the semblance and the mobile, occidental geometry would have proceeded to a regulation of diverse forms of representation: 'As confirmation, let's demonstrate that a complex object, for instance a spool 10 cm in diameter, made of thread 1 mm wide, possesses in some fashion, latently, several distinct physical dimensions . . .' Mandelbrot, *The Fractal Objects*, Flammarion.

5. Georges Sadoul, *Georges Méliès*, Seghers. Bibliography and bio-filmography.

6. *E. J. Marey, 1830–1904*. Monograph. for the 1977 exhibition at the Georges Pompidou Centre, Paris. 'The mechanism of our normal consciousness is of a cinematic nature,' notes Bergson, who knew Marey.

7. 'Midbar, Chemama', Shmuel Trigano, *Traverses*, no. 19. Paul Virilio, *The Insecurity of Territory*. 'The State is always the court, the city (*Urstaat*) . . .' Stock, 1976.

8. Jean Duvignaud, *The Game of the Game*, Balland.

9. As in Bernstein's joke: 'Intuition is intelligence that is speeding!' You might think of a certain restitution of *ethnological* definitions: soul, manna, potential substance, breath and energy, etc.

10. The fundamental elements of speed, of childhood, of power over destiny are already assembled here. With Orson Welles, as with many Anglo-Saxons, *the presence of absence* is a major theme.

11. James Phelan, Alain Stanké, *Howard Hughes*, International Editions, 1977.

12. 'The human space becoming that of no one becomes progression of nowhere . . . ,' *L'Insécurité du Territoire*, p. 171.

13. *Magic, Reason and Experience*, G. E. R. Lloyd, Cambridge University Press, 1979. And by the same author, *Les Débuts de la Science Grecque. De Thales à Aristote*, éditions Maspero 1974.

14. Claude Bernard, methodical thinker, whose disciple Marey

was, notes the *order* of scientific work: feeling first, then reason and experience (*Introduction à l'Etude de la Médecine Expérimental*).

15. 'Logique de la séduction', Mario Perniola, *Traverses*, no. 18.

CHAPTER SEVEN

The Overexposed City

The next major publishing enterprise of the 1980s for Paul Virilio was *L'Espace Critique*, put out by Christian Bourgeois in Paris. Taking the same title as the French series he ran for Editions Galilée, the book ranged across topics such as urban planning, 'improbable' architecture and the modern city, underlining Virilio's consistent interest in the themes of more conventional urban theory. The approach, however, is anything but conventional and references range from Benoit Mandelbrot on fractals through Paul of Tarsus (again) to Albert Einstein. When Semiotext(e) eventually published a translation into English by Daniel Moshenberg in 1991, the title had metamorphosed into *The Lost Dimension* and the English edition cover (back and front) was adorned with a bizarre artwork by Sue Ann Harkey which featured fish alongside elements of classical architecture. The book comprised five separate pieces, including a conclusion called 'Critical Space' and another essay called 'The Lost dimension'. The essay extracted here is entitled 'The Overexposed City'. Paul Virilio's long-time interviewer and friend Sylvère Lotringer utilized the concept of 'overexposed' in a quite different context, that of the extreme behaviouralist treatment of sexual deviation, in his own book of the same title, but Virilio's use of it is intended to explore the question 'architecture or post-architecture?'. The aphoristic style adopted by Virilio was becoming more evident by the sentence in this work from 1984, and cryptic queries such as this, usually unanswered in the particular text in question, permeate the work and seem to be aimed at temporarily disorienting the reader before veering off into another, tangentially related, topic. Nevertheless, in *The Lost Dimension* the reader can find the germs of Virilio's later work on 'the accident' amid much (then) futuristic musing about the 'inertia of tele-spectators at home' and the effects of the just-launched CNN (Cable News Network) twenty-four-hour news party people.

'The Overexposed City', from *The Lost Dimension*, trans. Daniel Moshenberg, New York: Semiotext(e), 1991.

At the beginning of the 1960s with black ghettoes rioting, the mayor of Philadelphia announced: 'From here on in, the frontiers of the State pass to the interior of the cities.' While this sentence translated the political reality for all Americans who were being discriminated against, it also pointed to an even larger dimension, given the construction of the Berlin Wall, on 13 August 1961, in the heart of the ancient capital of the Reich.

Since then, this assertion has been confirmed time and again: Belfast, Londonderry where not so long ago certain streets bore a yellow band separating the Catholic side from the Protestant, so that neither would move too far, leaving a chainlink no man's land to divide their communities even more clearly. And then there's Beirut with its East and West sections, its tortured internal boundaries, its tunnels and its mined boulevards.

Basically, the American mayor's statement revealed a general phenomenon that was just beginning to hit the capital cities as well as the provincial towns and hamlets, the phenomenon of obligatory introversion in which the City sustained the first effects of a multinational economy modelled along the lines of industrial enterprises, a real urban redeployment which soon contributed to the gutting of certain worker cities such as Liverpool and Sheffield in England, Detroit and Saint Louis in the United States, Dortmund in West Germany, and all of this at the very moment in which other areas were being built up, around tremendous international airports, a METROPLEX, a metropolitan complex such as Dallas/Fort Worth. Since the 1970s and the beginnings of the world economic crisis, the construction of these airports was further subjected to the imperatives of the defence against air pirates.

Construction no longer derived simply from traditional technical constraint. The plan had become a function of the risks of 'terrorist contamination' and the disposition of sites conceived of as
sterile zones for departures and non-sterile zones for arrivals.
Suddenly, all forms of loading and unloading – regardless of passenger, baggage, or freight status – and all manner of airport
transit had to be submitted to a system of interior/exterior traffic
control. The architecture that resulted from this had little to do
with the architect's personality. It emerged instead from perceived public security requirements.

As the last gateway to the State, the airport came to resemble
the fort, port or railway station of earlier days. As airports were
turned into theatres of necessary regulation of exchange and
communication, they also became breeding and testing grounds
for high-pressured experiments in control and aerial surveillance
performed for and by a new 'air and border patrol', whose anti-
terrorist exploits began to make headlines with the intervention
of the German GS.G9 border guards in the Mogadishu hijacking,
several thousand miles away from Germany.

At that instant, the strategy of confining the sick or the suspect
gave way to a tactic of mid-voyage interception. Practically, this
meant examining clothing and baggage, which explains the
sudden proliferation of cameras, radars and detectors in all
restricted passageways. When the French built 'maximum security cell-blocks', they used the magnetized doorways that airports
had had for years. Paradoxically, the equipment that ensured
maximal freedom in travel formed part of the core of penitentiary
incarceration. At the same time, in a number of residential areas
in the United States, security was maintained exclusively
through closed-circuit television hook-ups with a central police
station. In banks, in supermarkets, and on major highways,
where tollbooths resembled the ancient city gates, the rite of
passage was no longer intermittent. It had become immanent.

In this new perspective devoid of horizon, the city was entered
not through a gate nor through an *arc de triomphe*, but rather
through an electronic audience system. Users of the road were no
longer understood to be inhabitants or privileged residents. They
were now interlocutors in permanent transit. From this moment

on, continuity no longer breaks down in space, not in the physical space of urban lots nor in the juridical space of their property tax records. From here, continuity is ruptured in time, in a time that advanced technologies and industrial redeployment incessantly arrange through a series of interruptions, such as plant closings, unemployment, casual labour, and successive or simultaneous disappearing acts. These serve to organize and then disorganize the urban environment to the point of provoking the irreversible decay and degradation of neighbourhoods, as in the housing development near Lyon where the occupants' 'rate of rotation' became so great – people staying for a year and then moving on – that it contributed to the ruin of a place that each inhabitant found adequate . . .

*   *   *

In fact, since the originary enclosures, the concept of boundary has undergone numerous changes as regards both the façade and the neighbourhood it fronts. From the palisade to the screen, by way of stone ramparts, the boundary–surface has recorded innumerable perceptible and imperceptible transformations, of which the latest is probably that of the interface. Once again, we have to approach the question of access to the City in a new manner. For example, does the metropolis possess its own façade? At which moment does the city show us its face?

The phrase 'to go into town', which replaced the nineteenth century's 'to go to town', indicates the uncertainty of the encounter, as if we could no longer stand before the city but rather abide forever within. If the metropolis is still a place, a geographic site, it no longer has anything to do with the classical oppositions of city/country nor centre/periphery. The city is no longer organized into a localized and axial estate. While the suburbs contributed to this dissolution, in fact the intramural–extramural opposition collapsed with the transport revolutions and the development of communication and telecommunications technologies. These promoted the merger of disconnected metropolitan fringes into a single urban mass.

In effect, we are witnessing a paradoxical moment in which the opacity of building materials is reduced to zero. With the invention of the steel skeleton construction, curtain walls made of light and transparent materials, such as glass or plastics, replace stone façades, just as tracing paper, acetate and plexiglass replace the opacity of paper in the designing phase.

On the other hand, with the screen interface of computers, television and teleconferences, the surface of inscription, hitherto devoid of depth, becomes a kind of 'distance', a depth of field of a new kind of representation, a visibility without any face-to-face encounter in which the *vis-à-vis* of the ancient streets disappears and is erased. In this situation, a difference of position blurs into fusion and confusion. Deprived of objective boundaries, the architectonic element begins to drift and float in an electronic ether, devoid of spatial dimensions, but inscribed in the singular temporality of an instantaneous diffusion. From here on, people can't be separated by physical obstacles or by temporal distances. With the interfacing of computer terminals and video monitors, distinctions of *here* and *there* no longer mean anything.

This sudden reversion of boundaries and oppositions introduces into everyday, common space an element which until now was reserved for the world of microscopes. There is no *plenum*; space is not filled with matter. Instead, an unbounded expanse appears in the false perspective of the machines' luminous emissions. From here on, constructed space occurs within an electronic topology where the framing of perspective and the gridwork weft of numerical images renovate the division of urban property. The ancient private/public occultation and the distinction between housing and traffic are replaced by an overexposure in which the difference between 'near' and 'far' simply ceases to exist, just as the difference between 'micro' and 'macro' vanished in the scanning of the electron microscope.

The representation of the modern city can no longer depend on the ceremonial opening of gates, nor on the ritual processions and parades lining the streets and avenues with spectators. From here on, urban architecture has to work with the opening of a new 'technological space-time'. In terms of access, telematics replaces the doorway. The sound of gates gives way to the clatter of data banks and the rites of passage of a technical culture whose progress is disguised by the immateriality of its parts and networks. Instead of operating in the space of a constructed social fabric, the intersecting and connecting grid of highway and service systems now occurs in the sequences of an imperceptible organization of time in which the man/machine interface replaces the façades of buildings as the surfaces of property allotments.

*   *   *

Where once the opening of the city gates announced the alternating progression of days and nights, now we awaken to the opening of shutters and televisions. The day has been changed. A new day has been added to the astronomers' solar day, to the flickering day of candles, to the electric light. It is an electronic false-day, and it appears on a calendar of information 'commutations' that has absolutely no relationship whatsoever to real time. Chronological and historical time, time that passes, is replaced by a time that exposes itself instantaneously. On the computer screen, a time period becomes the 'support-surface' of inscription. Literally, or better cinematically, time surfaces. Thanks to the cathode-ray tube, spatial dimensions have become inseparable from their rate of transmission. As a unity of place without any unity of time, the City has disappeared into the heterogeneity of that regime comprised of the temporality of advanced technologies. The urban figure is no longer designated by a dividing line that separates here from there. Instead, it has become a computerized timetable.

Where once one necessarily entered the city by means of a physical gateway, now one passes through an audio-visual protocol in which the methods of audience and surveillance have transformed even the forms of public greeting and daily reception. Within this place of optical illusion, in which the people occupy transportation and transmission time instead of inhabiting space, inertia tends to renovate an old sedentariness, which results in the persistence of urban sites. With the new instantaneous communications media, arrival supplants departure: without necessarily leaving, everything 'arrives'.

Until recently, the city separated its 'intramural' population from those outside walls. Today, people are divided according to aspects of time. Where once an entire 'downtown' area indicated a long historical period, now only a few monuments will do. Further, the new technological time has no relation to any calendar of events nor to any collective memory. It is pure computer time, and as such helps construct a permanent present, an unbounded, timeless intensity that is destroying the tempo of a progressively degraded society.

What is a monument within this regime? Instead of an intricately wrought portico or a monumental walk punctuated by sumptuous buildings, we now have idleness and monumental waiting for service from a machine. Everyone is busily waiting in front of some communications or telecommunications apparatus, lining up at tollbooths, poring over captains' checklists, sleeping with computer consoles on their nightstands. Finally, the gateway is turned into a conveyance of vehicles and vectors whose disruption creates less a space than a countdown, in which work occupies the centre of time while uncontrolled time of vacations and unemployment form a periphery, the suburbs of time, a clearing away of activities in which each person is exited to a life of privacy and deprivation.

If, despite the wishes of postmodern architects, the city from here on is deprived of gateway entries, it is because the urban wall has long been breached by an infinitude of openings and ruptured enclosures. While less apparent than those of antiquity, these are equally effective, constraining and segregating. The illusion of the industrial revolution in transportation misled us as to the limitlessness of progress. Industrial time-management has imperceptibly compensated for the loss of rural territories. In the nineteenth century, the city/country attraction emptied agrarian space of its cultural and social substance. At the end of the twentieth century, urban space loses its geopolitical reality to the exclusive benefit of systems of instantaneous deportation whose technological intensity ceaselessly upsets all of our social structures. These systems include the deportation of people in the redeployment of modes of production, the deportation of attention, of the human face-to-face and the urban *vis-à-vis* encounters at the level of human/machine interaction. In effect, all of this participates in a new 'post-urban' and transnational kind of concentration, as indicated by a number of recent events.

Despite the rising cost of energy, the American middle classes are evacuating the cities of the East. Following the transformation of inner cities into ghettoes and slums, we now are watching the deterioration of the cities as regional centres. From Washington to Chicago, from Boston to Saint Louis, the major urban centres are shrinking. On the brink of bankruptcy, New York lost 10 per cent of its population in the last ten years. Meanwhile, Detroit lost 20 per cent of its inhabitants, Cleveland 23 per cent, Saint Louis 27 per cent. Already, whole neighbourhoods have turned into ghost towns.

These harbingers of an imminent 'post-industrial' de-urbanization promise an exodus that will affect all of the developed countries. Predicted for the last forty years, this deregulation of the management of space comes from an economic and political illusion about the persistence of sites constructed in the era of automotive management of time, and in the epoch of the development of audiovisual technologies of retinal persistence.

*   *   *

'Each surface is an interface between two environments that is ruled by a constant activity in the form of an exchange between the two substances placed in contact with one another.'

This new scientific definition of surface demonstrates the contamination at work: the 'boundary, or limiting surface' has turned into an osmotic membrane, like a blotting pad. Even if this last definition is more rigorous than earlier ones, it still signals a change in the notion of limitation. The limitation of space has become commutation: the radical separation, the necessary crossing, the transit of a constant activity, the activity of incessant exchanges, the transfer between two environments and two substances. What used to be the boundary of a material, its 'terminus', has become an entryway hidden in the most imperceptible entity. From here on, the appearance of surfaces and superficies conceals a secret transparency, a thickness without thickness, a volume without volume, an imperceptible quantity.

If this situation corresponds with the physical reality of the infinitesimally small, it also fits that of the infinitely large. When what was visibly nothing becomes 'something', the greatest distance no longer precludes perception. The greatest geophysical expanse contracts as it becomes more concentrated. In the interface of the screen, everything is always already there, offered to view in the immediacy of an instantaneous transmission. In 1980, for example, when Ted Turner decided to launch Cable News Network as a round-the-clock news station, he transformed his subscribers' living space into a kind of global broadcast studio for world events.

Thanks to satellites, the cathode-ray window brings to each viewer the light of another day and the presence of the antipodal place. If space is that which keeps everything from occupying the same place, this abrupt confinement brings absolutely everything precisely to that 'place', that location that has no location. The exhaustion of physical, or natural, relief and of temporal distances telescopes all localization and all position. As with live televised events, the places become interchangeable at will.

The instantaneity of ubiquity results in the atopia of a singular interface. After the spatial and temporal distances, *speed distance* obliterates the notion of physical dimension. Speed suddenly becomes a primal dimension that defies all temporal and physical measurements. This radical erasure is equivalent to a momentary inertia in the environment. The old agglomeration disappears in the intense acceleration of telecommunications, in order to give rise to a new type of concentration: the concentration of a domiciliation without domiciles, in which property boundaries, walls and fences no longer signify the permanent physical obstacle. Instead, they now form an interruption of an emission or of an electronic shadow zone which repeats the play of daylight and the shadow of buildings.

A strange topology is hidden in the obviousness of televised images. Architectural plans are displaced by the sequence plans of an invisible montage. Where geographical space once was arranged according to the geometry of an apparatus of rural or urban boundary setting, time is now organized according to imperceptible fragmentations of the technical time span, in which the cutting, as of a momentary interruption, replaces the lasting disappearance, the 'programme guide' replaces the chainlink fence, just as the railroads' timetables once replaced the almanacs.

'The camera has become our best inspector', declared John F. Kennedy, a little before being struck down in a Dallas street. Effectively, the camera allows us to participate in certain political and optical events. Consider, for example, the irruption phenomenon, in which the City allows itself to be seen thoroughly and completely, or the diffraction phenomenon, in which its image reveberates beyond the atmosphere to the farthest reaches of space, while the endoscope and the scanner allow us to see to the farthest reaches of life.

This overexposure attracts our attention to the extent that it offers a world without antipodes and without hidden aspects, a world in which opacity is but a momentary interlude. Note how the illusion of proximity barely lasts. Where once the *polis* inaugurated a political theatre, with its *agora* and its *forum*, now there is only a cathode-ray screen, where the shadows and spectres of a community dance amid their processes of disappearance, where cinematism broadcasts the last appearance of urbanism, the last image of an urbanism without urbanity. This is where tact and contact give way to televisual impact. While tele-conferencing allows long-distance conferences with the advantage derived from the absence of displacement, tele-negotiating inversely allows for the production of distance in discussions, even when the members of the conversation are right next to each other. This is a little like those telephone crazies for whom the receiver induces flights of verbal fancy amid the anonymity of a remote control aggressiveness.

* * *

Where does the city without gates begin? Probably inside that fugitive anxiety, that shudder that seizes the minds of those who, just returning from a long vacation, contemplate the imminent encounter with mounds of unwanted mail or with a house that's been broken into and emptied of its contents. It begins with the urge to flee and escape for a second from an oppressive technological environment, to regain one's senses and one's sense of self. While spatial escape may be possible, temporal escape is not. Unless we think of lay-offs as 'escape hatches', the ultimate form of paid vacation, the forward flight responds to a post-industrial illusion whose ill effects we are just beginning to feel. Already, the theory of 'job sharing' introduced to a new segment of the community – offering each person an alternative in which sharing work-time could easily lead to a whole new sharing of space as well – mirrors the rule of an endless periphery in which the homeland and the colonial settlement would replace the industrial city and its suburbs. Consider, for example, the Community Development Project, which promotes the proliferation of local development projects based on community forces, and which is intended to re-incorporate the English inner cities.

Where does the edge of the exo-city begin? Where can we find the gate without a city? Probably in the new American technologies of instantaneous destruction (with explosives) of tall buildings and in the the politics of systematic destruction of housing projects suddenly deemed as unfit for the new French way of life, as in Venissieux, La Courneuve or Gagny. According to a recent French study, released by the Association for Community Development, 'The destruction of 300,000 residential units over a five-year period would cost 10 billion francs per year, while creating 100,000 new jobs. In addition, at the end of the demolition/reconstruction, the fiscal receipts would be 6 to 10 billion francs above the sum of public moneys invested.'

One final question arises here. In a period of economic crisis, will mass destruction of the large cities replace the traditional politics of large public works? If that happens, there will be no essential difference between economic-industrial recession and war.

* * *

Architecture or post-architecture? Ultimately, the intellectual debate surrounding modernity seems part of a derealization phenomenon which simultaneously involves disciplines of expression, modes of representation and modes of communication. The current wave of explosive debates within the media concerning specific political acts and their social communication now also involves the architectural expression, which cannot be removed from the world of communication systems, to the precise extent that it suffers the direct or indirect fall-out of various 'means of communication', such as the automobile or audiovisual systems.

Basically, along with construction techniques, there's always the construction *of* techniques, that collection of spatial and temporal mutations that is constantly reorganizing both the world of everyday experience and the aesthetic representations of contemporary life. Constructed space, then, is more than simply the concrete and material substance of constructed structures, the permanence of elements and the architectonics of urbanistic details. It also exists as the sudden proliferation and the incessant multiplication of special effects which, along with the consciousness of time and of distances, affect the perception of the environment.

This technological deregulation of various milieus is also topological to the exact extent that − instead of constructing a perceptible and visible chaos, such as the processes of degradation or destruction implied in accident, ageing and war − it inversely and paradoxically builds an imperceptible order, which is invisible but just as practical as masonry or the public highways system. In all likelihood, the essence of what we insist on calling urbanism is composed/decomposed by these transfer, transit and transmission systems, these transport and transmigration networks whose immaterial configuration reiterates the cadastral organization and the building of monuments.

If there are any monuments today, they are certainly not of the visible order, despite the twists and turns of architectural excess. No longer part of the order of perceptible appearances nor of the aesthetic of the apparition of volumes assembled under the sun, this monumental disproportion now resides within the obscure luminescence of terminals, consoles and other electronic nightstands. Architecture is more than an array of techniques designed to shelter us from the storm. It is an instrument of measure, a sum total of knowledge that, contending with the natural environment, becomes capable of organizing society's time and space. This geodesic capacity to define a unity of time and place for all actions now enters into direct conflict with the structural capacities of the means of mass communication.

Two procedures confront each other. The first is primarily material, constructed of the physical elements, walls, thresholds and levels, all precisely located. The other is immaterial, and hence its representations, images and messages afford neither locale nor stability, since they are the vectors of a momentary, instantaneous expression, with all the manipulated meanings and misinformation that presupposes.

The first one is architectonic and urbanistic in that it organizes and constructs durable geographic and political space. The second haphazardly arranges and deranges space-time, the continuum of societies. The point here is not to propose a Manichaean judgement that opposes the physical to the metaphysical, but rather to attempt to catch the status of contemporary, and particularly urban, architecture within the disconcerting concert of advanced technologies. If architectonics developed with the rise of the City and the discovery and colonization of emerging lands, since the conclusion of that conquest, architecture, like the large cities, has rapidly declined. While continuing to invest in internal technical equipment, architecture has become progressively introverted, becoming a kind of machinery gallery, a museum of sciences and technologies, technologies derived from industrial *machinism*, from the transportation revolution and from so-called 'conquest of space'. So it makes perfect sense that when we discuss space technologies today, we are not referring to architecture but rather to the engineering that launches us into outer space.

All of this occurs as if architectonics had been merely a subsidiary technology, surpassed by other technologies that produced accelerated displacement and sidereal projection. In fact, this is a question of the nature of architectural performance, of the telluric function of the constructed realm and the relationships between a certain cultural technology and the earth. The development of the City as the conservatory of classical technologies has already contributed to the proliferation of architecture through its projection into every spatial direction, with the demographic concentration and the extreme vertical densification of the urban milieu, in direct opposition to the agrarian model. The advanced technologies have since continued to prolong this 'advance', through the thoughtless and all-encompassing expansion of the architectonic, especially with the rise of the means of transportation.

Right now, vanguard technologies, derived from the military conquest of space, are already launching homes, and perhaps tomorrow the City itself, into planetary orbit. With inhabited satellites, space shuttles and space stations as floating laboratories of high-tech research and industry, architecture is flying high, with curious repercussions for the fate of post-industrial societies, in which the cultural markers tend to disappear progressively, what with the decline of the arts and the slow regression of the primary technologies.

Is urban architecture becoming an outmoded technology, as happened to extensive agriculture, from which came the debacles of megalopolis? Will architectonics become simply another decadent form of dominating the earth, with results like those of the uncontrolled exploitation of primary resources? Hasn't the decrease in the number of major cities already become the trope for industrial decline and forced unemployment, symbolizing the failure of scientific materialism?

The recourse to History proposed by experts of post-modernity is a cheap trick that allows them to avoid the question of Time, the regime of trans-historical temporality derived from technological ecosystems. If in fact there is a crisis today, it is a crisis of ethical and aesthetic references, the inability to come to terms with events in an environment where the appearances are against us. With the growing imbalance between direct and indirect information that comes of the development of various means of communication, and its tendency to privilege information mediated to the detriment of meaning, it seems that the *reality effect* replaces immediate reality. Lyotard's modern crisis of grand narratives betrays the effect of new technologies, with the accent, from here on, placed on means more than ends.

The grand narratives of theoretical causality were thus displaced by the petty narratives of practical opportunity, and, finally, by the micro-narratives of autonomy. At issue here is no longer the 'crisis of modernity', the progressive deterioration of commonly held ideals, the proto-foundation of the meaning of History, to the benefit of more-or-less restrained narratives connected to the autonomous development of individuals. The problem now is with the narrative itself, with an official discourse or mode of representation, connected until now with the universally recognized capacity to say, describe and inscribe reality. This is the heritage of the Renaissance. Thus, the crisis in the conceptualization of 'narrative' appears as the other side of the crisis of the conceptualization of 'dimension' as geometrical narrative, the discourse of measurement of a reality visibly offered to all.

The crisis of the grand narrative that gives rise to the micro-narrative finally becomes the crisis of the narrative of the grand and the petty.

This marks the advent of a disinformation in which excess and incommensurability are, for 'post-modernity', what the philosophical resolution of problems and the resolution of the pictorial and architectural image were to the birth of the 'enlightenment'.

The crisis in the conceptualization of dimension becomes the crisis of the whole.

In other words, the substantial, homogeneous space derived from classical Greek geometry gives way to an accidental, heterogeneous space in which sections and fractions become essential once more. Just as the land suffered the mechanization of agriculture, urban topography has continuously paid the price for the atomization and disintegration of surfaces and of all references that tend towards all kinds of transmigrations and transformations. This sudden exploding of whole forms, this destruction of the properties of the individual by industrialization, is felt less in the city's space – despite the dissolution of the suburbs – than in the time – understood as sequential perceptions – of urban appearances. In fact, transparency has long supplanted appearances. Since the beginning of the twentieth century, the classical depth of field has been revitalized by the depth of time of advanced technologies. Both the film and aeronautics industries took off soon after the ground was broken for the grand boulevards. The parades on Haussmann Boulevard gave way to the Lumière brothers' accelerated motion picture inventions; the esplanades of Les Invalides gave way to the invalidation of the city plan. The screen abruptly became the city square, the crossroads of all mass media.

From the aesthetics of the appearance of a *stable* image –

present as an aspect of its static nature – to the aesthetics of the *dis*appearance of an *unstable* image – present in its cinematic and cinematographic flight of escape – we have witnessed a transmutation of representations. The emergence of forms as volumes destined to persist as long as their materials would allow has given way to images whose duration is purely retinal. So, more than Venturi's Las Vegas, it is Hollywood that merits urbanist scholarship, for, after the theatre-cities of antiquity and of the Italian Renaissance, it was Hollywood that was the first Cinecittá, the city of living cinema where stage-sets and reality, tax-plans and scripts, the living and the living dead, mix and merge deliriously.

Here more than anywhere else advanced technologies combined to form a synthetic space-time.

Babylon of filmic de-formation, industrial zone of pretence, Hollywood was built neighbourhood by neighbourhood, block by block, on the twilight of appearances, the success of magicians' tricks, the rise of epic productions like those of D. W. Griffith, all the while waiting for the megalomaniacal urbanizations of Disneyland, Disney World and Epcot Center. When Francis Ford Coppola, in *One from the Heart*, electronically inlaid his actors into life-size Las Vegas built at the Zoetrope studios in Hollywood (simply because the director wanted the city to adapt to his shooting schedule instead of the other way around), he overpowered Venturi, not by demonstrating the ambiguities of contemporary architecture, but by showing the 'spectral' characters of the city and its denizens.

The utopian 'architecture on paper' of the 1960s took on the video-electronic special effects of people like Harryhausen and Tumbull, just at the precise instant that computer screens started popping up in architectural firms. 'Video doesn't mean I see; it means I fly', according to Nam June Paik. With this technology, the 'aerial view' no longer involves the theoretical altitudes of scale models. It has become an opto-electronic interface operating in real time, with all that this implies for the redefinition of the image. If aviation – appearing the same year as cinematography – entailed a revision of point of view and a radical mutation of our perception of the world, infographic technologies will likewise force a readjustment of reality and its representations. We already see this in 'Tactical Mapping Systems', a videodisc produced by the United States Defense Department's Agency for Advanced Research Projects. This system offers a continuous view of Aspen, Colorado, by accelerating or decelerating the speed of 54,000 images, changing direction or season as easily as one switches television channels, turning the town into a kind of shooting gallery in which the functions of eyesight and weaponry melt into each other.

If architectonics once measured itself according to geology, according to the tectonics of natural reliefs, with pyramids, towers and other neo-gothic tricks, today it measures itself according to state-of-the-art technologies, whose vertiginous prowess exiles all of us from the terrestrial horizon.

Neo-geological, the 'Monument Valley' of some pseudo-lithic era, today's metropolis is a phantom landscape, the fossil of past societies whose technologies were intimately aligned with the visible transformation of matter, a project from which the sciences have increasingly turned away.

CHAPTER EIGHT

The Imposture of Immediacy

By 1984 Paul Virilio was also considered very much a theorist of the image. And in the French context the image was frequently conflated with the cinema. The famous Cahiers de Cinéma editions in Paris published Virilio's next book in that Orwellian year entitled *Guerre et Cinéma 1: Logistique de la Perception*. It was put out in a series alongside works by the likes of André Bazin and François Truffaut, key figures identifiable with French cinema. The English version came out with Verso in London and New York in 1989 with the slightly abridged title *War and Cinema: The Logistics of Perception*. Translated from the French by Patrick Camiller, the English edition had a cryptic preface written specially by Paul Virilio in 1988 called 'The Sight Machine' in which he clarified the '1' in the title of the French edition: 'The first volume seeks to show the recent origins of this project and to follow the twists and turn of its development. A subsequent book will look more closely at the latest results in this domain.' As Virilio made clear in the preface, the project was 'the logistics of *military* perception' and his aim was to investigate the systematic use of cinema techniques in the conflicts of the twentieth century, but the 'subsequent book' was never written. Instead, the photographically illustrated *War and Cinema* had to suffice, and it became one of Paul Virilio's better-known books. The short piece extracted here is typical of this mid-period Virilio theorization of what he has called the ecology of the image. The theme of the whole book, the history of photography into cinema, recalls obliquely another of French theory's lost classics: namely Bernard Edelman's *Ownership of the Image*, first published in 1973 in French as *Le Droit Saisi par La Photographie*, where the law relating to photography and cinema played a critical role in Edelman's attempt to show the role of the subject in law. Edelman's work was certainly well known to Virilio who, for his part, concentrated on the interdependence of fast-changing technologies of war and cinema.

'The Imposture of Immediacy',[1] from *War and Cinema*, trans. Patrick Camiller, London: Verso, 1989.

Once the optical telegraph came into operation in 1794, the remotest battlefield could have an almost immediate impact on a country's internal life, turning upside down its social, political and economic field. The instantaneity of action over a distance was already an accomplished fact. Since then, as many people have noted, geographical space has been shrinking with every advance in speed, and strategic location has lost importance as ballistic systems have become more widespread and sophisticated. This technological development has carried us into a realm of factitious topology in which all the surfaces of the globe are directly present to one another.[2]

After the war of movement of mechanized forces, the time came for a strategy of Brownian movement, a geostrategic homogenization announced at the end of the last century in Mackinder's theory of the single 'World Island' into which various continents are supposedly contracting. (One is reminded of the war in the Malvinas, whose remoteness did not dampen the British ardour for Antarctic contraction.) With the great universal or colonial exhibitions, it was no longer necessary for people to travel to distant lands; the faraway could be presented to them as such, on the spot, in the form of more or less obsolescent scale models. The transport revolution made itself felt less in the desire for exoticism than in a new endogeny. In breaking open one's normal surroundings through a lightening trip to dreamlands, one could conjure away the trip and not even know one was travelling.

The Disney Corporation (which the French have consulted for the ghostly Universal Exhibition of 1989) took over the idea for Disneyland and then for EPCOT (the Experimental Prototype of the Community of Tomorrow). Walt Disney, speaking on 15 November

1965 at a memorable press conference held in the great lounge of Orlando's Cherry Plaza, described EPCOT as 'a new town of revolutionary design where we will try to solve *the communication and environmental problems posed for inhabitants of the cities of the future*'. Disney died suddenly thirteen months later, after the bulldozers had begun work on the 11,000 hectares of Florida swampland purchased in 1964, an area larger than that of San Francisco.

It is significant that Disney's successors decided to solve the 'communication problems' of the city of the future by erecting the 'Showcase of the World'. Here past, present and future are telescoped together, and the five continents, represented by assorted visual relics of monuments and real objects, lie overlapping on the narrow shoreline of an artificial lake. The buildings and the perfectly copied cars and trains are a fifth of the normal size – a scaling down that Disney saw as the essence of *dream creation* – and 'cinema knowledge' here repeats the strategist's negation of dimensions.

When the offer of a trip 'Around the World in Eighty Minutes' shone in lights outside cinemas in the 1930s, it was already clear that film was superimposing itself on a geostrategy which for a century or more had inexorably been leading to the direct substitution, and thus sooner or later the disintegration, of things and places. In 1926, in the Paramount 'Hall of Nations' in New York, Adolf Zukor had the idea of bringing under one roof a collection of representative material from ruins around the world, as if to assemble the last witnesses of a physical universe that had vanished into the special effects of communication machines. Rich Americans like John D. Rockefeller Jr followed this example by incorporating genuine pieces of architecture from medieval churches or castles into modern architectural structures, while the funerary handprints of stars left in the concrete sidewalk of Grauman's Chinese Theatre in Hollywood already prefigured the 'human negatives' of the atomic age.

Despite the massive accumulation of documents, publicity and films, young army recruits still say in response to questions that they cannot *imagine what a war would be like*. They are like that rookie in a fine chapter of Clausewitz's *On War* who, before facing the battlefield for the first time, looks at it from afar in astonishment and 'for a moment still thinks he is at a show'. The soldier then has to leave the calm of the surrounding countryside and to move ever closer to what might be regarded as the epicentre of battle, crossing one zone after another in which the intensity of danger continually increases. To the accompaniment of roaring cannons, whistling shells and quaking earth, more and more of his comrades collapse round him, dead or suddenly maimed . . . 'beneath that steel storm in which the laws of nature appeared suspended, the midwinter air quivered as in the scorching days of summer and its flicker set stationary objects dancing to and fro.'[3] Here the static sense of the world has come to an incomprehensible end. 'Beyond a certain threshold,' Clausewitz remarks, 'the light of reason moves in a different medium and is reflected in a different manner.'[4] Once his customary faculties of perception and reasoning have let him down, the soldier has to display that military virtue which consists in believing that he will come through it all. To be a survivor is to remain both actor and spectator of a living cinema, to continue being the target of subliminal audiovisual bombardment or, in the colloquial language of French soldiers, to 'light up' (*allumer*) the enemy. It is also to try to postpone one's own death, that last technological accident or 'final separation of sound and image' (William Burroughs).

During the Second World War, while still a child, I experienced first-hand the fierce flight of strategic bombing and, later, witnessed a series of land battles in the company of a former artillery liaison officer, a survivor from the 1914–18 war who taught me how easily a tested mind could cut through such a subliminal barrage, could locate and materialize in space the atmospheric dimensions of a battle, and could anticipate what the different parties intended to do. To cut a long story short, my old friend jubilantly described the *scenario* of battle which I, being a newcomer, saw only as its *special effects*. Young American GIs advancing to dangerous battlefield positions used the most eloquent expression: 'We're off to the movies.'

After 1945, this cinematic artifice of the war machine spread once more into new forms of spectacle. War museums opened all over liberated France at the sites of various landings and battles, many of them in old forts or bunkers. The first rooms usually exhibited relics of the last military-industrial conflict (outdated equipment, old uniforms and medals, yellowing photographs), while others had collections of military documents or screenings of period newsreels. It was not long, however, before the invariably large number of visitors were shown into huge, windowless rooms resembling a planetarium or a flight (or driving) simulator. In these *war simulators*, the public was supposed to feel like spectators-survivors of the recent battlefield. Standing in near-total darkness, they would see a distant, accurately curving coastline gradually light up behind the vast plane of a panoramic windscreen, which then displayed a rush of events indistinctly represented by dim flashes, rough silhouettes of aircraft and motor vehicles, and the glimmer of fires. It was as if news-reels had been too 'realistic' to recapture the pressure of the abstract surprise movements of modern war; and so, the old diorama method, with its enhancement of the visual field, was brought into service to give people the illusion of being hurled into a virtually unlimited image. If one thinks of the cinema-mausoleums or atmospheric cinemas of the 1930s, one can see in this a new outflanking of immediate reality by the cinematic paramnesia of the war machine. Shortly afterwards, in the 1950s, the grandson of the famous conjuror Robert Houdin invented the immediately popular 'Son et Lumière', a kind of open-air museum in which the past is reinjected into real places (temples, castles, landscapes) by means of projectors, sound equipment, artificial mist and, more recently, laser graphics. Similarly, in the American 'freedom-lands' one can see 'Old Chicago' collapse and rise again from the flames every twenty minutes, or join in the Civil War and escape by the skin of one's teeth through the gunsmoke as the opposing sides open fire. Because of their overexposure in time, the material supports thus lose out to artificial lighting and become no more than a crepuscular threshold. The audience itself no longer knows whether the ruins are actually there, whether the landscape is not merely simulated in kaleidoscopic images of general destruction.

The sites chosen for museums of the Second World War remind us that these fortress-tombs, dungeons and bunkers are first and foremost camerae obscurae, that their hollowed windows, narrow apertures and loopholes are designed to light up the outside while leaving the inside in semi-darkness. In his pencil-like embrasure, the look-out and later the gunner realized long before the easel painter, the photographer or the film-maker how necessary is a preliminary sizing-up. 'You can see hell much better through a narrow vent than if you could take it in with both eyes at once', wrote Barbey d'Aurevilly, evoking the sort of squint necessary in taking aim and firing. This action, like the seductive wink so fashionable in the 1930s, increased the depth of the visual field while reducing its compass. As recent experiments in anartho-scopic perception have shown,

> It is not enough to know that one is looking through a crack; it is also necessary to see the crack and in certain circumstances the observer may even invent it. In any case, it has been proved that the form of the aperture influences the perceptual identification of objects, and that visual tracking is a constitutive element in anarthoscopic perception of a moving shape.

More simply, the soldier's obscene gaze, on his surroundings and on the world, his art of hiding from sight in order to see, is not just an ominous voyeurism but from the first imposes a long-term patterning on the chaos of vision, one which prefigures the synoptic machinations of architecture and the cinema screen. In the act of focusing, with its proper angles, blind spots and expo-sure times, the line of sight already heralds the perspectival van-ishing-line of the easel painter who, as in the case of Dürer or Leonardo, might also be a military engineer or an expert in siege warfare.

The nineteenth-century development of viewfinders precisely allowed the view to be 'found' and 'snapped' for military pur-poses, within interpretative codes for fixing the three-dimen-sional identity of two-dimensional images. This introduced a new reading of the battlefield, but also considerably increased the impotence and obscenity of the military decision-maker, now in ever greater danger of being tracked down and elimi-nated. Thus, in order to escape two-dimensional observation from anchored reconnaissance balloons 400 or 500 metres up, the army began to bury its strongholds and outworks in a third dimension, throwing the enemy into a frenzy of interpretation.

Invisible in its sunken depths, the camera obscura also became deaf and blind, its relations with the rest of the country now depending entirely on the logistics of perception, with its technology of subterranean, aerial and electrical communication. Already, what I have called the problem of the 'third window' – how to light the surrounding world without seeing it – posed itself in a most acute way.[5] From now on, strategy is concealed in the special effects of signals and communications:

> Located in deep shelters that open onto communication trenches, the projectors invented by General Mangin can send messages over a distance of more than eighty kilometres. The light from a powerful oil-lamp is concentrated in a telescope by means of a concave mirror. This telescope is fitted with a moveable shutter, so that one can obtain either a constant beam or a short burst or a long burst corresponding to the dot and dash of the Morse code. (*Ecole du Génie Français*, 1887)

The inner walls of the central command posts became screens covered with gridded maps whose ceaseless animation abstractly logged the slightest movement of troops in what were still proximate theatres. About 1930, some countries, including Britain, wound down their conventional means of defence and concentrated on research into perception. This reorientation led to the development of cybernetics and radar, as well as advancing the sciences of goniometry, microphotography and, as we have seen, radio and telecommunications. Thus, during the Second World War, the military commands and war cabinets no longer needed to set up their bunkers near the field of battle, but were able to remain in Berlin or London, in command centres which bore a passable resemblance to huge theatre-halls, for a war which had already become a Space Opera.

No longer having any real extension in space, these centres of interaction received an endless mass of information and messages from the most scattered points and radiated it back into their own, defined universe. In a sense, they may be said to have taken over the inertia of the old *Kammerspiel*, with its subjection to the pressure of time. But in these aseptic chambers so overwhelming was the sense of *negative charge*, so bare the visual and acoustic representation, that Hitler decided to introduce sound effects into his control-room at Bruly-le-Pesch when he was planning Operation Sealion. For the miniaturization of technological power, reducing space and time to nothing, was incompatible with the expansive imagination of the Nazi *Lebensraum* and could only be countered with artificial depth and grandiosity.

Notes

1. Dietrich Bonhoeffer.
2. P. Virilio (1977), *Vitesse et Politique*, Paris.
3. Ernst Jünger, *In Stahlgewittern* (translated here from the French edition, *Orages d'Acier*, Paris, 1970).
4. In *Cahiers du Cinéma* (no. 311), Samuel Fuller argued that it was impossible to film the Normandy landing because you couldn't decently film yards of intestine on a beach. Apart from the fact that dead people do not take well to being photographed (see the pictures of assassinations or traffic accidents), Fuller's witticism suggests that military-industrial films cannot *decently* be horror films, since in one way or another they are intended to embellish death. Moreover, the Allied landing acutely re-posed the problem of documentary realism. Today everyone knows that there were not yards of intestine on the Normandy beaches and that the landing was a remarkable and technically difficult operation – not because of German resistance (which was virtually non-existent), but because of the adverse weather and the complicated Normandy countryside. Thus, *in order to make up the numbers*, the Allied commanders threw their men into operations like the storming of Hoc Point, which were as suicidal as they were spectacular. In 1962, when Zanuck made his fictitional documentary with fifty stars, 20,000 extras and six directors, the action took place on the Ile de Ré or in Spain, where the beaches were 'grander' than those of Arromanche. This immortalization of a battle that had never happened ensured that *The Longest Day* was a great box-office success.
5. P. Virilio (1975), *Bunker Archéologie*, Paris.

CHAPTER NINE

The Last Vehicle

In the autumn of 1986 a conference in New York brought together a number of European scholars including Jean Baudrillard and Paul Virilio to (literally) 'Look Back on the End of the World' where the 'world' was never more than an image and a regulative idea, a normative concept for planning and implementing a global society. The symposium was divided into three parts: Phantasms of the End of the World, which featured Baudrillard; Concepts of the End of the World; and Beyond Apocalypse, which featured Virilio. Virilio's contribution to the international seminar is reprinted in its entirety here. Semiotext(e) published the proceedings of the conference, translated by David Antal, in 1989 in the Foreign Agent series with all of the participants named on the front cover and two of their number, Christoph Wulf and Dietmar Kamper, listed as the actual editors of the volume. Although the editors agreed that 'it was not the physical end of the world' that they were all anticipating at the conference, they were convinced that 'it was the imaginary end', relying on the evidence of a (mid-1980s) obsession with the last moment and the 'great acceleration of all the trends pointing to the destruction of existing conditions', a culture which seemed to indicate 'the inevitable end of the world'. The editors further claimed that the 'contributors to this volume are intent on furthering and accelerating the fundamental thought processes involved so as to conceive of an extraterrestrial vantage point and develop a historical type of anthropology and cosmology'. Virilio plays, in his contribution, with the idea of 'the last', but his part in the conference project was considerably less apocalyptic than many others, especially Jean Baudrillard who famously proclaimed in New York that 'time can slow as it nears its end' and 'the year 2000, in a certain way, will not take place'.

A longer version of Virilio's 'The Last Vehicle' was later published as one of the chapters in *L'Inertie Polaire* published in 1990 by Christian Bourgeois.

'The Last Vehicle', from *Looking Back on the End of The World*, trans. David Antal, New York: Semiotext(e), 1989.

Tomorrow learning space will be just as useful as learning to drive a car. (*Wernher von Braun*)

In Tokyo there is a new indoor swimming pool equipped with a basin of intensely undulating water in which the swimmers remain on the same spot. The turbulence prevents any attempt to move forward, and the swimmers must try to advance just to hold their position. Like a kind of home-trainer or conveyor belt on which one moves in the direction opposite that of the belt, the dynamics of the currents in this Japanese pool have the sole function of making the racing swimmers struggle with the energy passing through the space of their mutual encounter, an energy that takes the place of the dimensions of an Olympic pool just as the belts of the home-trainer have been replacing stadium race-tracks.

The person working out in such cases thus becomes less a moving body than an island, a pole of inertia. Like a theatre set, everything is focused on the stage, everything occurs in the special instant of an act, an inordinate instant offering a substitute for expanses and long stretches of time. Not so much a golf course but a video performance, not so much an oval track but a running simulator: space is no longer expanding. Inertia replaces the continual change of place.

Moreover, one observes a quite similar trend in museographic presentation. Being too vast, the most spacious exhibitions have recently been subject to temporal reduction in inverse proportion to their overall dimensions: twice the amount of space to cover means twice as little time that one can spend at any one place.

The acceleration of the visit is measured by the area of the exhibition. Too much space, too little time, and the museum welters in useless expanse that can no longer be furnished with works of art. In any case, probably because the latter still tend to sprawl, to make a show of themselves, to pour themselves into these vast and utterly uninviting surfaces, just like the grand perspectives of classical period.

Whereas our monuments were once erected to commemorate significant works that can now be viewed for long periods by visitors interested in the past, they are presently simply ignored in the excessive zeal of the viewer, this 'amateur' who seems to have to be forced to fixate for more than only a moment, for the more impressive the size of the volumes presented, the quicker he tries to escape.

We are talking about the monument of a moment in which the work tends to disappear without a trace more than expose itself. The contemporary museum vainly attempts to assemble and present these works, these pieces that one ordinarily views only from a distance in the atelier, at the workplace, in these laboratories of a heightened perception that is never the perception of the passer-by, this passing viewer distracted by his exertion. With regard to this perspective of retention, of the restriction of the time to pass through, of passing by, we should point out yet another project. It concerns a miniaturized reconstitution of the state of Israel where 'in complete safety and with a minimum of physical movement, visitors can marvel at the exact copy of the Holocaust museum, a small section of the wailing wall, and the miniaturized reconstitution of the Sea of Galilee created with a few cubic metres of water from the original'. Seizing this opportunity, the directors of this institution could perhaps complete it by exhibiting electronic components, products of Israeli industry. This extraterritorial manifestation could be sited in Douarnenez, on Tristan da Cunha as soon as this group of islands is finally ceded by France to the Hebrew state.

Even if this utopia does not really come to be, it nevertheless reveals in exemplary fashion this *tellurian contraction*, this sudden 'overexposure' now befalling the expansion of territories, the surfaces of the vastest objects, and the nature of our latest displacement. Displacement in place, the advent of an inertia that is what has always been the 'still-frame' for the film as far as the landscape through which we walk is concerned. Also the advent of a final generation of vehicles, of means of communication for distances that have nothing in common with those associated with the revolution of transport anymore – as if the conquest of space ultimately confirmed the conquest of the mere *images* of space. If in fact the end of the nineteenth century and the beginning of the twentieth experienced the advent of automotive vehicle, the dynamic vehicle of the railroad, the street, and then the air, then the end of this century seems to herald the next vehicle, the audiovisual one, a final mutation: static vehicle, substitute for the change of physical location, and extension of domestic inertia, a vehicle that ought at last to bring about the victory of sedentariness, this time an ultimate sedentariness.

The transparency of space, of the horizon of our travels, of our racing thus ought to be followed by this *cathodic transparency*, which is only the successful realization of the discovery of glass some 4,000 years ago, of iron 2,000 years ago, and that 'glass showcase', that puzzling object that has constituted the history of urban architecture from the Middle Ages down to our own times or, more precisely, down to the most recent realization of this *electronic glass case*, that final horizon of travel of which the most developed model is the 'flight simulator'.

That is also made obvious by the latest developments in amusement parks, those laboratories of physical sensations with their slides, catapults, and centrifuges, reference models for training and flight personnel and for astronauts. In the opinion of the very people responsible, even vicarious pleasure is becoming collective experimentation with mere mental and imaginary sensations.

In the previous century the leisure park became the theatre of physiological sensations to a working population for which many different physical activities had become things of the past. Thereafter, the leisure park prepared to become the scene of mere optical illusions, the place for a generalization of simulation, fictitious movements that can create in each person an electronic hallucination or frenzy – 'loss of sight' following upon the loss of physical activities in the nineteenth century. Analogous to dizziness and the unusual calling of gymnasts, it is nevertheless true that the 'panoramas', 'dioramas', and other cinematographies smoothed the way toward the 'panorama', to 'Géode', a hemispheric movie anticipated by Grimoin-Sanson's 'balloon cinerama'. They are all old forms of our present audiovisual vehicles, whose forerunners were made more precise by the American *Hale's Tours*; after all, a few of them were actually funded by the railroad companies between 1898 and 1908. Remember that these films, which were shot on a panoramic platform either from a locomotive or from the rear of the train, were ultimately shown to the public in halls that were exact imitations of the railroad cars of that epoch. Some of these short films were made by Billy Bitzer, the future cameraman of D. W. Griffith.

At this point, however, we must return to the origins of kinematic illusion, to the Lumière brothers, to the 1895 film *L'entrée d'un Train en Gare de La Ciotat*, and above all to the spring of 1896, when the very first travelling shot was invented by Eugène Promio.

> In Italy that I first had the idea of shooting panoramic film. When I arrived in Venice and took a boat from the train station to the hotel, on the Grand Canal, saw the banks recede from the skiff, and I thought that *if the immovable camera allowed moving objects to be reproduced, then one could perhaps also invert this statement and should try to use the mobile camera to reproduce immovable objects.* So I shot a reel of film, which I sent to Lyon with a request to hear what Louis Lumière thought of this experiment. The answer was encouraging.

To comprehend the significance of this introduction of the 'mobile camera' or, to put it another way, the first static vehicle, we must again look back at the course of history. Disregarding for the moment Nadar's 'aerostatic negatives' (1858), which were indeed the origin of cinematic weightlessness, one must wait until 1910 to find the first 'aeronautic film', taken on board a Farman aeroplane. The now traditional 'travelling vehicle', which was mounted on tracks and which is inseparable from the contemporary cinema, came about four years later during the shooting of *Cabiria* by Giovanni Pastrone. For memory's sake, let us also mention the trains of AGIT PROP between 1918 and 1925 and the use of train travel in the work of Dziga Vertov. He joins Moscow's film committee in the spring of 1918, waiting until 1923 in order to promote the founding of a 'cinematographic automobile department' that would provide cars in emergencies if needed to film important events. The cars are thus predecessors of the mobile video productions of television. With this use of transport, this combination of the automotive and the audiovisual, our perception of the world inevitably changes. The optical and the cinematic blend. Albert Einstein's theory, subsequently to be called the special theory of relativity, appears in 1905. It will be followed about ten years later by the general theory of relativity. To make them more understandable, both take recourse to the metaphor of the train, streetcar, and elevator, vehicles of a theory of physics that owes them everything, or, as people will see, almost everything. The revolution of transport will coincide with a characteristic change of arrival, with the progressive negation of the time interval, the accelerated retention of the time of passage that separates arrival and departure. Spatial distance suddenly makes way for mere temporal distance. The longest journeys are scarcely more than mere intermissions.

But if, as already shown, the nineteenth century and a large part of the twentieth really experienced the rise of the automotive vehicle in all its forms, this mutation of it is by no means completed. As before, except now more rapidly, it will make the transition from the itinerancy of nomadic life to inertia, to the ultimate sedentariness of society.

Contrary to all appearances, the audiovisual vehicle has indeed prevailed since the 1930s with the radio, television, radar, sonar, and emerging electronic optics. First during the war, then, despite the massive development of the private car, after the war, during peace, during this 'nuclear peace', which will experience the *information revolution*, the telematic informatics that are tightly linked with the various policies of military and economic deterrence. Since the decade from 1960 to 1970, what really counts does not occur through the customary communication channels of a given geographic region (hence the deregulation of rates, the deregulation of transport in general), but rather in ether, in the electronic ether of telecommunications.

From now on everything will happen without our even moving, without us even having to set out. The initially confined rise of the dynamic, at first mobile, then automotive, vehicle is suddenly followed by the generalized rise of pictures and sounds in the static vehicles of the audiovisual. Polar inertia is setting in. The second screen that can suddenly be turned on substitutes itself for the very long time intervals of displacement. After the ascendance of *distance/time* in the nineteenth century to the disadvantage of space, it is now the ascendence of the *distance/speed* of the electronic picture factories: *the statue follows upon the continual stopping and standing still.*

*   *   *

According to Ernst Mach, the universe is mysteriously present in all places and at all times in the world. If every mobile (or automotive) vehicle conveys a special vision, a perception of the world that is only the artefact of the speed at which it is displaced within its terrestrial, aquatic, or aerial milieu, then, vice versa, each of those visions, those optical or acoustical images of the perceived world, represents a 'vehicle', a communication vector that is inseparable from the speed of its transmission. All this since the telescopic instantaneousness of the image's rectification in the passive lenses of Galileo's telescope down to our modern 'means of telecommunications', our active optics of videoinformatics.

The dynamic vehicle can thus no longer be clearly distinguished from the static vehicle, the automotive no longer from the audiovisual. The recent priority of arrival over departure, over all forms of depature and, accordingly, over all forms of travel and trajectories realizes a mysterious conspiracy – inertia of the moment, of every place and every instant of the present world, which ultimately allies itself closely with the principle of inseparability, thereby completing indeterminateness in the sense meant in quantum theory.

Even when one witnesses the attempt in Japan today to combine two vehicles technologically by systematically installing video landscapes in the elevators of skyscrapers or by showing feature films during long plane flights as done in commercial air travel, this momentary link will nevertheless inevitably lead to the elimination of the least efficient vector regarding the speed of dispersion. The contemporary forward race of high-speed trains, supersonic aircraft, as well as the deregulation affecting both show better than any other preview that the threatened vector, the threatened vehicle, is really that of terrestrial, aquatic, and aerial automotility.

The era of intensive time is thus no longer that of means of physical transport. Unlike earlier, extensive time, it is solely that of telecommunications, in other words, walking in place and domestic inertia. Recent developments in both the automobile and Formula One racing prove it. Since the high performance of the audiovisual cannot seriously be improved upon, people go about altering the performance of the racing car, the rules of racing, the weight of the vehicles, and the fuel reserves. They even go so far as to reduce the power of the engines, which is really the limit! Lastly, the dynamic land vehicle and the most symptomatic one of this sporting involution is the dragster (and the hot rod), the motto of which could be 'How can I get nowhere, or at least as close to it as possible (400, 200 yards), but with increasing speed?'

The extreme emphasis on this intensive competition may eventually have the finish line and starting line combined in order to pull even with the analogous feat of live television broadcasting. As far as the domestic car is concerned, its development is the same in every respect, for the automobile has a kind of self-sufficiency about it that is developing increasingly into a separate piece of property. Whence this move, this duplication of accessories, furniture, the hi-fi chain, radio telephone, telex, and videomobile that turn the means of long-haul transport into a means of transport in place, into a vehicle of ecstasy, music, and speed.

If automotive vehicles, that is, all air, land, and sea vehicles are today also less 'riding animals' than *frames* in the optician's sense, then it is because the self-propelled vehicle is becoming less and less a vector of change in physical location than a means of representation, the channel for an increasingly rapid optical effect of the surrounding space. The more or less distant vision of our travels thereby gradually recedes behind the arrival at the destination, a general arrival of images, of information that henceforth stands for our constant change of location. That is why a secret correspondence between the static structural design of the residential dwelling and the medially conveyed inertia of the audiovisual vehicle becomes established with the emergence of the *intelligent dwelling* – what am I saying? – with the emergence of the intelligent and interactive city, the teleport instead of the port, instead of the train station and the international airport.

In answer to a journalist's indiscreet question about her address, a well-known actress responded: 'I live everywhere!' Tomorrow, with the aesthetics and logic behind the disappearance of the architectonic, we will live everywhere, that is a promise. All of us, like the animals of the 'video zoo', which are present only by virtue of a single image on a single screen, here and there, yesterday and the day before, images recorded at places of no importance, excessive suburbs of a cinematic development that finally takes audiovisual speed as it relates to the interior design of our dwellings and puts it on the same footing as what the speed of automobiles has long been for the architecture of our cities and the layout of our countries.

The 'immobile simulators' will then replace the flight simulators. Behind our cathode glass cases we become teleactors and teleactresses of an animated theatre whose recent developments in sound and light shows already herald this, although it is repeatedly used by people ranging from André Malraux and Léotard to Jack Lang only on the pretext of saving our monuments.

It is thus our common destiny *to become film*. Especially ever since the person responsible for the Cinéscénie du Puy-du-Fou, Philippe de Villiers, became secretary for culture and communication and announced his intent to institute 'scenic walks through areas being preserved as historical sites' in order to enhance the attractiveness of our historical monuments and thereby compete with the imported 'Disneyland' near Paris or 'Wonderworld' near London.

In the footsteps of the theatrical scenography of the *agora*, *forum*, and church square as traditional places of urban history there now follows *cinescenography*, the sequenced mutation of a community, region, or monument in which the participating population momentarily changes into actors of a history intended to be revived. It does not matter whether it is the war in Vendée with Philippe de Villiers or the centuries-old services of the city of Lyon with Jean-Michel Jarre. Even the predecessor of the current minister of culture has paid tribute to this phenomenon by tapping the budget for funds (earmarked 'Salamandar') to finance the production of an interactive videotape of a tour through the *châteaux* of the Loire. It is 'light and sound' at home, and it turns the earlier visitors from a bygone age of tourism into video visitors, 'tele-lovers of old stones', whose record collections and discotheques now have not only Mozart and Verdi but Cheverny and Chambord as well.

*   *   *

As noted in a poem entitled 'La Ralentie', by Henri Michaux, 'One does not dream any more; one is dreamed of, silence'. The inversion begins. The film runs in reverse. Water flows back into the bottle. We walk backwards, but faster and faster. The involution leading to inertia accelerates. Up to our desire, which ossifies in the increasingly distinct medial distancing: after the whores of Amsterdam in the display windows, after the striptease of the 1950s and the peepshow of the 1970s, we have now arrived at videopornography. The list of mortal sins in the Rue Saint-Denis is confined to the names of the new image technologies like BETACAM, VHS, and VIDEO 2000 in the expectation of erotic automatism, of the vision machine.

The same is happening with military confrontation. After the home trainer for the pilots in the First World War, the swivel chair for training pilots in the Second World War, and NASA's centrifuge for future astronauts, which is a reality test for the ability or inability to become accustomed to weightlessness, we have for ten years been witnessing the development of increasingly sophisticated and powerful simulators for the advocates of supersonic flight. Projection domes up to nine yards in diameter and more; a geode for a single man, the most developed of which will have a field of vision of up to almost 300 degrees because the pilot's helmet will comprise an optical system for expanding the retina. To enhance realism even more, the person who practises here will don inflatable overalls that simulate the acceleration pressure related to the earth's gravity.

The essential is yet to come, though, for tests are being run on a simulation system that is derived from the oculometer and that will finally liberate us from the spheric video screen. The presentation of the images from aerial combat will be projected directly into the pilot's eyeballs with the aid of a helmet fitted with optic fibres. This phenomenon of hallucination approaches that of drugs, meaning that this practice material denotes the future disappearance of every scene, every video screen, to the advantage of a single 'seat' [*siège*], in this case, though, a *trap* [*siège/piège*] for an individual whose perception is programmed in advance by the computing capabilities of a computer's motor of inference. Before this future model of a static vehicle is invented, I think it would be appropriate to reconsider the concept of energy and the engine. Even though physicists still distinguish between two aspects of energetics – potential and kinetic energy, with the latter setting off motion – one should, eighty years after the invention of the travelling in the movies, perhaps add a third, the *kinematic* energy resulting from the effect that motion and its more or less great velocity has on ocular, optic, and optoelectronic perception.

In this sense, the contemporary industry of simulation seems like a realization of this latter energy source. The computational speed of the most recent generation of computers approximates a final type of engine: the cinematic engine.

But the essential would not yet be said if we did not return to the primacy of time over space, a primacy best expressed today by the primacy of arrival (which is momentary) over departure. If the profundity of time is greater today than that of the field, then it means that earlier notions of time have changed considerably. Here, as elsewhere, in our daily and banal life, we are in fact switching from the extensive time of history to the intensive time of momentariness without history – with the aid of contemporary technologies. These automotive, audio-visual, and informatic technologies all operate on the same restriction, the same contraction of duration. This earthly contraction questions not only the extension of the countries but also the architecture of the house and the furniture.

If time is history, then velocity is only its hallucination that ruins any expansion, extension, and any chronology. This spatial and temporal hallucination, which is the apparent result of the intensive development of cinematic energy – of which the audio-visual vehicle would be the motor today just as the mobile vehicle and, later, the automotive vehicle were for kinetic energy yesterday – these synthetic images, ultimately displacing the energies of the same name that were invented in the previous century.

Let us not trust it. The third dimension is no longer the measure of expansion; relief, no longer the reality. From now on the latter is concealed in the flatness of pictures, the transferred representations. It conditions the return to the house's state of siege, to the cadaver-like inertia of the interactive dwelling, this residential cell that has left the extension of the habitat behind it and whose most important piece of furniture is the *seat* [*siège*], the ergonomic armchair of the handicapped's motor, and – who knows? – the *bed*, a canopy bed for the infirm voyeur, a divan for being dreamt of without dreaming, a bench for being circulated without circulating.

CHAPTER TEN

Candid Camera

By the late 1980s Virilio's own self-styled labelling of himself as a critic of the art of technology was becoming more and more appropriate. Also, what once seemed to be an idiosyncratic approach to technological change was becoming much more recognizable as Virilio in action. By the turn of the decade Virilio could quite rightly be described as one of France's leading contemporary intellectuals. The book *La Machine de Vision* published in Paris by Editions Galilée in 1988 was typical of the 1980s prototype 'Virilian' work on the technologies of perception and the history of seeing, which threatened to reconfigure art history before petering out somewhat in the 1990s. Published in English in 1994 jointly by the British Film Institute and Indiana University Press, with a translation by Julie Rose, *The Vision Machine* contained five chapters, one of which was actually called 'The Vision Machine' and another playfully entitled 'Candid Camera'. The latter is the short essay reprinted in full here. The title 'Candid Camera' echoed the name of the long-running light entertainment television show in Britain in the 1960s which featured unsuspecting citizens 'caught' on camera who were urged, when the trick was ultimately smugly revealed by the presenter, to 'Smile – you're on *Candid Camera*!'. In contrast, this piece by Virilio is a serious look at the history of 'regimes of the visual', especially photography. The book as a whole finds Paul Virilio the 'old painter', as he still likes to see himself today, ranging over tiny details from the history of painting, engraving and architecture from the eighteenth century through the era of photography and cinematography in the nineteenth century and the beginning of the twentieth century, to the age of videography, holography and infographics of the late twentieth century and beyond. Virilio's last book of the 1980s promised a new logistics of the image to go with the logistics of perception of his earlier projects.

'Candid Camera', from *The Vision Machine*, trans. Julie Rose, London and Bloomington: British Film Institute/Indiana University Press, 1994.

At the *Second International Video Festival* in Montbéliard in 1984, the Grand Prix went to a German film by Michael Klier called *Der Riese* (*The Giant*). This was a simple montage of images recorded by automatic surveillance cameras in major German cities (airports, roads, supermarkets . . .). Klier asserts that the surveillance video represents 'the end and the recapitulation' of his art. Whereas in the news report the photographer (cameraman) remained the sole witness implicated in the business of documentation, here no one at all is implicated and the only danger from now on is that the eye of the camera may get smashed by the odd thug or terrorist.

This solemn farewell to the man behind the camera, the complete evaporation of visual subjectivity into an ambient technical effect, a sort of permanent pancinema which, unbeknown to us, turns our most ordinary acts into movie action, into new visual material, undaunted, undifferentiated vision-fodder, is not so much, as we have seen, the *end of an art* – whether it be Klier's or 1970s video art, television's illegitimate offspring. It is the absolute culmination of the inexorable march of progress of representational technologies, of their military, scientific and investigative instrumentalisation over the centuries. With the interception of sight by the sighting device, a mechanism emerges that no longer has to do with simulation (as in the traditional arts) but with substitution. This will become the ultimate special effects of cinematic illusion.

In 1917, when the United States entered the war against Germany, the American review *Camera Work*[1] ceased publication with a final issue on Paul Strand. This involved trotting out yet again the contrived polemic against 'the absolute objective incompetence of photography as inspired by painting, the confusion perpetuated between the photograph and the painted picture by the use of lighting, emulsions, retouching and various other tricks of process, all consequences of the eccentric relations kept up between the two modes of representation, the absolute necessity of *rejecting pictorialism as an avant-garde process.*'[2]

In reality the debate derived especially from the fact that, like most technical inventions, photography delivers a hybrid. Thanks to Nicéphore Nièpce's correspondence, we can trace the hybridization process relatively easily. To start with, there was the substantial art heritage (such as the use of the camera obscura, tonal values and the negative as in etching and engraving). The recent invention of lithography then gave Nièpce the idea of selective permeability in the image base when exposed to a fluid . . . Then, of course, there was the industrial application of lithography and the power of the lithograph to be mechanically reproduced. Science also came into it ultimately, since Nièpce was using the same instruments as Galileo, the lens of the microscope or refracting telescope. The pictorialists were interested in the first of these three applications and there is not a lot of difference between Nièpce's photographic work and theirs. It is this dependence that Strand, in the middle of the war, hoped to erode by insisting that the photograph was first and foremost an objective document, hard evidence.

That same year, under General Patrick's orders, Edward Steichen took over the direction of the American Expeditionary Force's aerial photographic operations in France. Approaching forty, with a background as a painter-photographer, Steichen was one of the masters of pictorialism. He was also a true francophile, and had visited France numerous times from 1900 onwards to meet Rodin, Monet and a few of the other greats.

With a force of fifty-five officers and 1,111 enlisted men, Steichen was to organize aerial-intelligence image production 'like a factory', thanks to the division of labour (the Ford car assembly lines were already in operation in 1914). Aerial observation had in fact stopped being episodic from the beginning of the war; it was not a matter of images now, but of an uninterrupted stream of images, millions of negatives madly trying to embrace on a daily basis the statistical trends of the first great military-industrial conflict. Initially neglected by the military hierarchy, after the Battle of the Marne the aerial photograph was also to come to lay claim to a scientific objectivity comparable to that of medical or police photography. As a professional effort it was already nothing more than the interpretation of signs, the development of visual codes prefiguring contemporary systems of digital-image restoration. The secret of victory – *predictive capability* – would henceforth reside in high-powered performance in reading and deciphering negatives and films.

Vaguely lumped in the same category as spies, civilian filmmakers and photographers were generally kept out of military zones. The job of presenting the war in a personal way to those left behind was, essentially, left to painter-photographers, illustrators and engravers working on newspapers, almanacs and illustrated magazines. These were flooded with fictional documents, cleverly touched-up photos, more or less authentic tales of dazzling individual acts and heroic battles from a bygone era.

When the war was over, Steichen holed himself up in his house in the French countryside, utterly depressed. There he burned all his previous work, swearing never to touch a brush again, to forsake everything that smacked of pictorialism *for the redefinition of the image as directly inspired by instrumental photography and its scientific processes*. With Steichen and a few other survivors of the Great War, the war shot become that of the American Dream; its images soon merged with the equally disidentified images of the great industrial sales-promotion system and its codes in the launching of mass consumerism, of proto-pop culture . . . President Roosevelt's declaration of 'peace of the world'.

But Steichen claimed to have only been able to carry out his military mission properly thanks to his knowledge of French art (the Impressionists, the Cubists and especially the work of Rodin). There is nothing paradoxical about this statement. As Guillaume Apollinaire wrote on the subject of Cubism in about 1913, *the main aim of the new art is to register the waning of reality*: an aesthetic of disappearance had arisen from the unprecedented limits imposed on subjective vision by the instrumental splitting of modes of perception and representation.[3]

At the end of the Great War, the cannons may well have stopped smoking, but the intense phonic and optical activity continued unabated. The *steel storms* of a war which, according to Ernst Jünger, *hoed into places more than people*, were succeeded by a media conflagration that continued to spread, regardless of fragile peace treaties and provisional armistices. Immediately after the war Britain decided to abandon classic armaments somewhat and to invest in the logistics of perception: in propaganda films, as well as observation, detection and transmission equipment.

The Americans prepared future operations in the Pacific by sending in film-makers who were supposed to look as though they were on a location-finding mission, taking aerial views for future film productions. John Ford was one. From on board a freighter, Ford meticulously filmed the approaches and defences of all the major Eastern ports. Not surprising, Ford found himself appointed as head of the OSS (Office of Strategic Services) some years later. He took practically the same risks as servicemen in order to film the Pacific War (losing an eye in the Battle of Midway in 1942). Among other things, what Ford would retain of his military career were those almost-anthropomorphic camera movements that anticipated the optical scanning of video surveillance.

On their side, defeated, ruined and temporarily disarmed, the Germans had no intentions of giving up. Not yet having the famous Luftwaffe, and no longer having fighter planes, they used light touring planes for observation. Colonel Rowehl recounts: 'We took advantage of a break in the clouds or else we just took pot luck that the French or the Czechs wouldn't pick us up; some- times we trailed an ad for chocolate behind us!' Month after month, without being disturbed in the slightest, they recorded the progress of the defence of the sombre Polish Corridor and, a little while later, of the construction sites along the Maginot Line. While the heavy cement-and-steel infrastructures, roads and railway lines of the next decade's battlefield were being laid, as in a negative, the tinny film-makers' planes committed them to memory in anticipation of the war to come.

One of the first results of this continuation of the First World War through other means – military means of a truly scenic kind

– was the invasion of the picture show by the accidental images of the newsreel.

Already at the beginning of the century, particularly in the United States, scraps of newsfilm lying about the cutting-room floor were no longer systematically swept up, 'lost scenes' to be automatically incorporated into any old bit of junk that could be salvaged by the garbage collection or, at best, the cosmetics industry. These began to be seen as 'viewing matter', recyclable within the film industry itself. Once that happened, *background reality* resurfaced, with blazing fires, storms, cataclysms, assassination attempts, crowd scenes . . . but, above all, a mountain of material of military origin. These authentic documents, often judged at the time to be of no immediate interest, suddenly cropped up in the middle of feature films. Such subliminal sequences were inserted wherever editing would allow. These were bombings and magnificent shipwrecks, but also photos of combatants, unknown soldiers transformed into chance extras whose ultimate talent was to reveal to astute members of the audience how impoverished the performances and special effects of the period piece really were; as though military or other facts gave themselves up more generously to the sleepwalker's eyes of automatic cameras, or to the curiosity of unskilled photographers, than to the masterly contrivances of the top pros, the elite of career film-makers.

Soon after the Second World War, by a curious reversal, I found I just could not wait for these casual shots to appear on the screen, with all their incomparable emotional impact, whereas scenes played by the stars of the moment seemed like 'time out' to me, boring. I will never forget, either, when Frank Capra's famous *Why We Fight* series was screened in the main auditorium of the Gaumont Palace Theatre and seeing, for the first time, colour sequences of movie-camera machine guns in which that old *kinêmaatos* magic appeared in all its primitive simplicity.

While busy shooting *Napoléon* (1925–7), Abel Gance scribbled in his notebook: 'Reality leaves a lot to be desired . . .', whereas the film critic André Bazin, going through montages of old newsreels, is glad he never became a film-maker. Reality, he reckons, will outdo any mere director every time and with inimitable flair, too. In fact, the ever-increasing use of scraps already posed a problem for the future of the picture show which was not, as Méliès had supposed, the 'seventh art', but rather an art that took something from all the other arts – architecture, music, the novel, theatre, painting, poetry, etc. In other words, all former modes of perception, reflection and representation. Like them, therefore, and despite its apparent novelty, it found itself subject to a swift, ineluctable ageing process. What happened to cinema was no different from what had happened to painting and the traditional arts when the Futurists and Dada burst on the scene at the beginning of the century. Jean Cocteau understood this only too well. In 1960, just before his death he declared: 'I'm giving up making films since technological progress means anyone can do it.'

That is exactly what it is all about. In popularizing a futurist vision of the world, the cinematic features of the man of war, following on those of the documentary school, encouraged cinemagoers more and more to reject all former registers: actors, scriptwriters, directors and designers either had to get out of the way of their own accord or agree to be mown down by the camera's so-called objectivity.

Once a photographer in French aerial reconnaissance and perfectly accustomed to accidental vision, the director Jean Renoir made his actors rehearse for hours on end till they had learned to forget all conventional references. 'Do it as if you've never seen it done, as if you've never done it before, the way in real life, in reality, one does everything for the first time!'

Rossellini would go one step further, incorporating the casual war shot into the script and into the shoot itself. *Roma, Città Aperta* was made with a simple documentary film-making permit, not easy to get from the allied military authorities. 'The entire film was a re-enactment of a news film,' wrote Georges Sadoul, and that is precisely why it was such as huge hit.

Stroheim had already said: 'Capture, don't reconstruct'. Rossellini was to apply the radical theories of the old *art vivant* to film. He was against composition in editing with its *pathetic little aesthetic jots, truths that have had their day and no longer have anything to do with reality . . . The film-maker must gather as many facts as possible in order to create a total image: he must film cold so that everyone is equal before the image.*[4]

None of this was new, and Italian Neo-realism can only be considered an avant-garde phenomenon to the extent that it operated in the murkiest area of the documentary: that of *propaganda fide*, war propaganda, a transit zone between virtuality and some kind of reality, between potential and action. Here the cinematic is no longer content to give the viewers the illusion that some kind of movement is being performed in front of them; it gets them interested in the forces behind its production, in their intensiveness. Reverting to its (technical, scientific) essence, under cover of objectivity, it turns its back on an art based on simulation and breaks with an aesthetics of sensitive perception that still depended, in the picture show, on the degree, nature and importance of the cinemagoer's past aesthetic experiences, memory and imagination.

Let's not forget that Rossellini had made numerous films for Mussolini and that after the Allied victory he still wrote scripts, more or less secretly, for propaganda films, notably on behalf of Canada, which was then on the brink of civil war.

Eighty years after Rodin's plea in support of arts that were in the process of disappearing, it was cinema's turn to require witnesses, and not merely ocular but existential witnesses at that, cinemagoers becoming an increasingly rare and sceptical breed.

For many film-makers the aim therefore became to create a convincing world and thus accentuate the instantaneity-effect in the spectator, the illusion of being there and seeing it happen.

Eric Rohmer said: 'With cinema, observation does not mean Balzac taking notes; it is not beforehand, *it is here and now.*'

A specialist in criminal law, the American documentary film-maker Fred Wiseman, whose films are no longer financed and distributed by state television, *claims he makes films so he can observe because new technology allows him to do so.* As for editing, he says it makes him feel like he is *sitting in a plane.*

On the other side of the camera, however, all this visual gadgetry only amounts to telesurveillance for Nastassja Kinski, spying on her every transformation as an actress, second by second:

I sometimes wonder if films are not more of a poison than a tonic, in the end. If these little flashes of light in the night are really worth all the pain. When I cannot get that moment of truth where you feel yourself opening up like a flower, I absolutely loathe the bloody camera. I can just feel this black hole eyeing me, sucking me in, and I feel like smashing it to smithereens.[5]

For Edward Steichen, in the most banal way possible, the First World War resolved the question posed by Paul Strand in *Camera Work* concerning 'the avant-garde' in photography. The image is no longer solitary (subjective, elitist, artisanal); it is solidary (objective, democratic, industrial). There is no longer a unique image as in art, but the manufacture of countless prints, a vast panoply of imagery synthetically reproducing the natural restlessness of the spectator's eye. *Camera Work* only ran to 1,000 copies, with only a dozen full-page photographic reproductions, stuck in by hand, in each issue, whereas Steichen kept about 1.3 million military prints whch wound up in his personal collection after the war. Furthermore a large number of these photographs were exhibited and sold as products of Steichen's authorship and as his property, that exotic art estate which war photographers, paradoxically maintain to this day. This applies to photographers in Hitler's PK or the *British Army Film and Photographic Unit*, as well as the big modern agencies. Steichen also ended up as Director of the Photography Department of the Museum of Modern Art in New York, this last appointment simply translating a persistent ambiguity in reading and interpreting the photographic document.

In January 1940 the British Ministry of Information, formed in September 1939, published a memorandum reviewing the position of the official army photographic units. This memorandum actually amounted to a long-awaited revolution, putting an end to press use of military photographs that were seen to be too lifeless, too technical and therefore ineffectual for a population called on to furnish an unprecedented war effort. Clearly it was a question of knowing how to reach and mobilise the millions of people who had become habitués of the picture houses (most people went to the pictures on average once a week), the readers of the big illustrated magazines, ordinary, everyday visionaries for whom daily life was now no more than a film mix, a reality with endless superimpositions.

At the end of 1940, inspired by Hitler's initiatives of the 1930s, the Ministry 'persuaded' picture-theatre managers to include shorts of five to seven minutes in their programmes. These were veritable commercial breaks ahead of their time, and they paved the way for the distribution of documentary pseudo-films. Roger Manvell chuckled at the time in *Film* that while they were being screened 'the audience could change its seats and buy its chocolate'.[6] In any case, the movement had been launched and the public's craving for *cinéma du réel* only became more and more compulsive.

Faced with Hitler proclaiming that *the function of the artillery and infantry will be taken over in the future by propaganda*, John Grierson, that veteran pioneer of a cinema liberated by the *candid camera*, felt moved to write in *Documentary News Letters*, March 1942, that through propaganda: 'We can give [the citizen] a *leadership of the imagination* which our democratic education has so far lacked. We can do it by radio and film and a half a dozen other imaginative media.' But most feature-film directors were already making *semi-documentary films*, thereby achieving the fusion-confusion desired in the first instance by the Ministry of Information.

From the outset of the war, a significant British colony had left Hollywood. Actors, scriptwriters, photographers and directors rushed home to serve their country, then under threat of Nazi invasion. Thanks to people like Leslie Howard, the Special Branch (Propaganda) would finally twig that artists who had just won the battle for the New Deal in the United States and raised the morale of a whole nation in the grip of economic depression, had the power, with their particular talents, to do likewise in time of war, stirring the masses to unsuspected heights and finding as yet unguessed shortcuts to victory. Cecil Beaton was among them.[7]

A London gentleman and Hollywood photographer, society portraitist, consummate traveller, most intimate friend of Greta Garbo, *Vogue* contributor, etc., Beaton, like Steichen in 1917, was nearly forty when the Second World War broke out. He was to do the same thing, only the other way round. Where Steichen had abandoned pictorialism and his visits to Rodin twenty years earlier, only to end up in in the Holywood dream factory, Beaton started from a position of extreme Hollywood sophistication only to discover finally in sculptor Henry Moore's portraits of miners his own personal way of photographing a media war that was no longer restricted to the battlefield proper. Its hold now suddenly extended from the physical to the ideological and the psychological.

Beaton's idea was simple: like Moore's miners, committed to daily heroics, men and women at war, from all walks of life, no longer had anything in common psychologically with their peace-time selves. The camera, therefore, ought to be able to capture this difference, this personal transformation which was obvious from the look on people's faces, in their attitudes. A few years earlier, new kinds of film and especially cameras like the Leica, Rolleiflex or Ermanox had become available, offering exposures of well under a second. So Beaton set out armed with his faithful Rollei and a few primitive flash-bulbs to conduct what he called his *private war*. This master of appearances travelled to appearance's outer reaches to catch there, off-guard, with only the bare essentials, technically speaking, the personal energy of the war's thousands of actors, famous or unknown, in an ultimate and unconscious return to basics for the *living art of photography* as defined some 100 years earlier by Nadar:

> The theory of photography can be taught in an hour, preliminary technical notions in a day . . . What cannot be taught is the moral intelligence of the subject, or the instinctive tact that puts you in touch with the model, allowing you to size them up and to steer them towards their habits, their ideas, according to each person's character. This enables you to offer something more than the ordinary, accidental plastic reproduction that the humblest laboratory assistant could manage. It enables you to achieve the most familiar, the most positive resemblance: a speaking likeness. This is the psychological side of photography. I don't think that is too ambitious a term.

From the wounded lying in hospital to munitions workers and the very young pilots of the RAF, aware of their impending doom; from bomb-blasted London to the Libyan desert and Burma, Beaton went all over the various battlefields as official war photographer for the Royal Air Force. But he never showed them. This caused friction with a military propaganda outfit that was somewhat out of date in its brief '*to establish photographically* the most colossal demonstration of force, to attempt the impossible . . . not just photograph one plane but sixty plans at once, not one tank but 100!'

Beaton's most original endeavour remained unknown for a long time. He himself would continue to wonder how he managed to take his war pictures. 'My most serious work,' he said of them, just before his death in 1980, 'work that made everything I'd done before passé; I've never known what part of me it could possibly have come from.'

Edward Steichen, on the other hand, though over sixty, went off once more to war. In the United States the British Documentary Movement had enjoyed considerable influence from the beginning of the 1930s. Paul Strand now headed the famous New York School. The former photographer had become a film producer and director in the same intellectual line as Joris Ivens, who would become involved in the amalgamation of reportage, old newsreels and fictional documents like *Why We Fight*, as well as Robert Flaherty and Fred Zinnemann, the young German anti-fascist émigré.

Steichen was no longer interested in giving the public instrumental photographic shots or, conversely, bad special effects. He, too, was convinced of the need to reveal the human drama of *the just war* as accurately as possible to the American people for whom the Second World War was still just a war of machines, of mass production. Having won over the sceptics, Steichen took shots of everything from armament factories to the great aeronaval units of the Pacific Fleet. Under his command, freshly trained teams of military photographers were essentially detailed to give an account of daily life on board the *Saratoga*, the *Hornet*, the *Yorktown* . . . Steichen had never really had a chance to see men at war in 1917; he now discovered that they were adolescents worn out before their time by the crushing weight of the industrial arsenal, the new giganticism in equipment. Roosevelt died in April 1945, taking the old American Dream with him; Steichen's units took their last photographs in Hiroshima in September. With the nuclear flash (at 1/15,000,000th of a second), the fate of military photography once more began to look grim.

On the eve of the Korean War, significantly, Steichen was appointed director of the Photography Department of the Museum of Modern Art in New York.

Photographers, the group who had contributed so much to the Allied victory against the Nazis, were soon to precipitate America's defeat in Vietnam. The hopes and inner harmony of those who had fought *the just war* had long ceased to light up soldiers' faces from within, but what the *subjective photo* now revealed was truly alarming. John Olsen and his cohorts showed piles of American corpses, soldiers out of their minds on drugs, the mutilation of children and civilians caught up in the terrorism of *the dirty war* (with well-known consequences for American public opinion).

Once the military twigged that photographers, steeped in the traditions of the documentary, now lost wars, image hunters were once again removed from combat zones. This is perfectly apparent with the Falklands war, a war that has no images, as well as in Latin America, Pakistan, Lebanon, etc. Representatives of the press and television, witnesses now suddenly regarded as a pest, are locked up or just plain murdered. According to Robert Ménard, the founder of 'Reporters Sans Frontières', in the year 1987 around the globe 188 journalists were arrested, fifty-one expelled, thirty-four assassinated and ten kidnapped.

The last big international agencies are in serious trouble, while magazines and newspapers are busy replacing the great photo-essays of the likes of London, Clemenceau, Kipling, Cendrars or Kessel, with a revival of the old media terrorism, a brand of *investigative journalism* still best typified by the Watergate scandal and the *Washington Post*'s campaign.

Having become the latest form of psychological warfare, terrorism imposes new media skills on its diverse protagonists. The military and secret services extend their control: General Westmoreland can attack 'information run riot' and sue the television channel CBS; in Europe there is the British government's raid on the *New Statesman* weekly, among other things. Terrorists themselves, in a bout of role reversal, indulge in *a savage documentary genre*, offering the press and television degrading photos of their victims, who are often reporters or photographers, or doing video-location recces for sites that will become the scenes of their future crimes.

In 1987 the experts in charge of the 'Action Directe' file had to wade through more than sixty cassettes seized at the group's hideout in Vitry-sur-Loges. Specifically, they were seeking those bearing on the assassination of Georges Besse, Renault's managing director.

Notes

1. *Camera Work*, the celebrated review published in New York by Alfred Stieglitz from 1903 to 1917, circulated the work of pictorialists such as Kühn, Coburn, Steichen and Demachy.
2. See Allan Sekula (1975), 'Steichen at war', *Art Forum*, December, and also Christoper Phillips (1981), *Steichen at War*, New York: Harry N. Abrams.
3. We may also wonder what Rodin meant, since he only liked working with destructible, extremely malleable material like clay or plaster; there's a strange similarity between his work and the modelling of the battlefield of the Great War over which reconnaissance planes used to fly, keeping a close eye on the geological metamorphoses of bomb-damaged landscapes.
4. Robert Rossellini, *Fragments d'une autobiographie*, Paris: Ramsay.
5. *Studio*, 7.
6. Roger Manvell (1977), *Film*, Harmondsworth: Pelican Books, p. 96.
7. In 1981 the Imperial War Museum in London published a remarkable album, *War Photographs 1939–1945*, featuring 157 of Beaton's photographs previously scattered throughout the press (*The Sketch*, *Vogue*, *Illustrated London News*, *Life*, etc.).

CHAPTER ELEVEN

Environment Control

The 1990s began, for Paul Virilio at least, with inertia. 'Polar inertia' to be exact, an accelerated modernity where everything happens at the speed of light without the need to go anywhere. Here we have a condition of 'pathological fixedness' according to Virilio – a generalized coming of 'seated man' or, even, 'couched man'. Virilio was not to guess then that later in the 1990s there would emerge a group of DJ remixers called Sofa Surfers in the European city of Vienna whose name would unconsciously trump his own original idea. Christian Bourgeois in Paris published *L'Inertie Polaire* in 1990, a book which contained five chapters, including an essay actually entitled (in the English from the French) 'Polar Inertia' and another christened, tantalizingly, 'Kinematic Optics'. Sage, in its groundbreaking 'Theory, Culture and Society' social theory series, published an English translation of the whole book by Patrick Camiller as *Polar Inertia* in London in 2000. A photograph taken by Sophie Virilio at what looks like a fairground adorned the cover. The jacket proclaimed the book's questioning of the simplicities of the 'globalization' thesis. The extract reprinted here is the fourth of those five chapters. It finds Virilio recalling his major phenomenological mentor Maurice Merleau-Ponty, at whose feet Virilio had sat in the early 1960s at the university of the Sorbonne. Merleau-Ponty has been in and out of international philosophical fashion ever since but Virilio has consistently returned to the legacy of those influential lectures he heard when he was a young(ish) student. Here he 'applies' Merleau-Ponty to the question of how temporal speed-up has, since the nineteenth century, 'illuminated' the world around us through photography. In the book's diverse but strangely connected chapters, Virilio in typically non-linear, jump-cut thinking looks back on events of the 1980s like Tiananmen Square in Beijing, China and what he sees as the 'illumination' of such events in the media.

'Environment Control', from *Polar Inertia*, trans. Patrick Camiller, London: Sage, 2000.

I am not looking for anything. I am here. (Philippe Soupault)

What are the implications for the transparency of air, water and glass, for the 'real space' of the things surrounding us, when the 'real-time' *interface* supersedes the classical *interval*, and distance suddenly gives way to power of emission and instant reception? What happens, in the end, when classical optical communication is replaced by electro-optical *communication*?

If repeated use of the prefix 'de-' (as in decentralization, de-regulation, deconstruction, etc.) has set its seal on the times, we may perhaps add another term – *derangement*: not only of sense-appearances but of transparency itself, a 'transparency' with nothing beyond, which has nothing in common with the density of any material or even of the earth's atmosphere.

If transparency may be defined as 'that which light can easily pass through', or as 'that which allows us clearly to perceive objects through its very density' (a window-pane, for example), it changes its nature with the new concept of *real-time interface*, since now it is the transparency not of light rays (solar or electrical) but only of the speed of elementary particles (electron, photon . . .) propagated at the very speed of light.

Light remains the only discloser of sense-appearances; but now it is its *speed* which discloses or makes things visible, to the detriment of sunlight or the artificial light of electricity.

Transparency, then, no longer just refers to the appearance of objects that become visible at the moment of looking. Now, suddenly, it refers to the appearances instantly transmitted over a distance – which is why we have suggested speaking of the *trans-appearance* of real time, and not just the transparency of real space. 'Live' transmission of the appearance of things is now superseding the old real-space transparency of air, water or lens glass.

In fact, this move beyond the direct transparency of materials is principally due to the emergence of a new, *active optics* through the recent development of optical electronics and radio-electrical vision, to the detriment of the previously supreme *passive optics* of telescope, microscope or camera lenses. In other words, it is mainly due to the application of wave optics right beside classical *geometrical optics*. Thus, much as a non-Euclidean or topological geometry is now available alongside Euclidean geometry, the passive optics of the geometry of camera or telescope lenses now has right beside it a 'tele-topological' *active optics* of electro-optical waves.

Furthermore, in parallel to the instant transmission of a radio-like 'video signal', optical properties have recently become attached to computers through the digitalization of transmitted images. The optical correction of appearances is no longer just a matter of the geometry of camera lenses, but now involves point-by-point (pixel-by-pixel) calculation of the picture through a computer linked to the transmitter, digitalization offering a better definition of appearances, as in the most recent 'adjustable optics' telescopes where the lens does not have to be flawless because the *calculation speed of computer graphics* achieves the optical correction of light rays. Here again we see the supremacy of the speed of light over the illuminating capacity of its rays.

On the one hand, the speed of electrons and photons indirectly lights up what remains distant, thanks to video reception of the broadcast appearances (videoscopy being a great improvement upon classical telescopy). On the other hand, the speed of electronic pixel calculation accelerates the definition or clarity of the picture, overshadowing the optical quality even of the soft lenses of new telescopes. Thus, it is less light than speed which helps us to see, to measure and therefore to conceive the reality of appearances.

Now acceleration is useful not so much for easy movement over distance as for clear vision or apperception, high definition of reality entirely depending upon speed of transmission of appearances, and not just on transparency of the atmosphere or various materials.

To grasp the real importance of the 'analyser' that speed, especially audiovisual speed, now represents, we must again turn to the philosophical definition: 'Speed is not a phenomenon but *a relationship between phenomena*.' In other words it is the very *relativity* or transparency of the reality of appearances, but a 'spatio-temporal transparency' that here supersedes the spatial transparency of the linear geometry of optical lenses – hence the term *trans-appearance* to designate the transmitted electronic appearances, whatever the space interval separating them from the observer. This subject or *subjugated* observer thus becomes inseparable from the observed object, because of the very immediacy of the interface, of the aptly named 'terminal' that perfects the extension and duration of a world reduced to man-machine commutation, where the 'spatial depth' of perspectival geometry suddenly gives way to the 'temporal depth' of a *real-time perspective* superseding the old real-space perspective of the Renaissance.

*   *   *

Let us now look at a few technological examples of this new *real-time optics*. Researchers at NASA and the Ophthalmology Institute at Johns Hopkins University, Baltimore, have recently developed a pair of revolutionary spectacles: two miniature lenses fitted to a frame transmit images by optical fibre to two-minute video cameras fitted at the height of the imperfectly sighted patient. The electronically processed image is then sent back to the spectacles, which have screens instead of corrective lenses. This optical-electronic system, soon to be marketed in the United States, automatically adjusts images to the particular sight of the wearer, who thus has a bright and clear-seeming image before his or her eyes.

This system, which has been tested on remote-controlled robots, is one by-product of military research into the 'vision machine' of the future. In fact, recent work on the automation of perception has the declared aim of replacing immediate with indirect, *assisted* perception, where the speed of electrons will be of greater advantage than the light of the sun's rays or electric bulbs.

Thus, while the spectacular research of a Scott Fisher at NASA is developing an *interactive* virtual environment helmet (that is, a portable simulator akin to the one on board fighter aircraft), these video spectacles are more modest testimony to the coming transformation of ocular optics into a truly everyday electro-optics. The look of direct vision is thus ceding to a real-time, radio-electrical *industrialization of vision* capable one day of standing in for, if not supplanting, our observation of the environment. The direct light of the sun, candles or electric lamps will gradually make way for the not just artificial but indirect light of electronics or photonics, following the example of those windowless Japanese apartments that are *bathed in sunshine* by means of optical fibres.

In the next century, said Timothy Leary, whoever controls the screen will control consciousness – and indeed, contrary to a widespread belief, the very first interactivity is not the remote control or the touch-operated screen but the inter-visibility of various filming devices, what we might call *opto-activity*. This links up or merges three kinds of image: the virtual image of consciousness, the ocular and optical image of the look, and the electro-optical or radio-electrical image of video computing.

This is the point of our proposed concept of *trans-appearance*, rather than just transparency.

The indirect light of various electro-optical (and electro-acoustic) prostheses competes with the direct light of classical optics. The customary distinction between natural and artificial light is then coupled with an unaccustomed one between direct and indirect light.

For whereas the light radiating from an electric lamp or the sun gives rise to *ordinary* transparency, the indirect light of electrons, photons and various devices gives rise to an *extra-ordinary* transparency in which the real time of the image prevails over the real space of vision, and instantly transmitted appearances supersede the usual illumination of places.

This light-acceleration function is clearly displayed in *light-intensifying* cameras or binoculars, where rare nocturnal photons are multiplied to give considerable increase in ambient brightness.

Thus, the time-frequency of light has suddenly become the determining factor in the apperception of phenomena, to the detriment of the space-frequency of matter. From now on, the speed of light has the upper hand over sunshine or ordinary lighting.

*   *   *

But let us return to the origins of this situation – to photography.

In his conversations with Paul Gsell, who thought he had irrefutable evidence of the photography of movement, Auguste Rodin objected: 'No, it is the artist who is truthful and photography which is false. For in reality *time does not stop*, and if the artist succeeds in producing the impression of a gesture performed over several instants, his work is certainly much less conventional than a scientific image in which time is suddenly suspended.'

This key statement, later taken up by Maurice Merleau-Ponty,[1] is worth some consideration. The time in question here is the usual linear time of *chronology*, which never stops but keeps flowing on. But the really new contribution of photosensitive techniques – which Rodin seems not to have noticed – was that they defined no longer a passing time but rather an exposure time which 'surfaces' (if we may dare put it like that) and thus succeeds the time of classical historical succession.

The time of 'taking photographs' is thus from the start *light-time*. The *time* interval (plus sign) and the *space* interval (minus sign: with the same name as the film's inscription surface) are inscribed only thanks to *light*, to that third kind of interval whose zero sign indicates absolute speed.

The exposure time of the photographic plate is therefore nothing but *exposure of the time* (space-time) of its photosensitive material to the speed of light, that is, to the frequency of the photon-bearing wave.

Thus, the sculptor Rodin also does not see that it is only the *surface* of the negative (negative interval) which stops the *time* of the representation of movement. When the instant photogram permitted the invention of the cinematographic sequence, *time no longer stopped*. The reel of recorded film, and later the 'real-time' video cassette of constant surveillance, illustrate this invention of *continuous light-time* (the most important in science since the discovery of fire) in which *indirect* light supersedes the direct light of the sun or the Edison lamp, as the latter itself once superseded daylight.

From the eighteenth and nineteenth centuries on, time is thus no longer so much a problem of more or less rapid *ageing*; it is above all a question of more or less intensive *lighting* – the famous Age of Enlightenment obviously well deserving its name.

This seems to be the main philosophical contribution of Nièpce's invention, but also, above all, of that *snap-shot* which eventually made possible Marey's chronophotography and the later emergence of real-time technologies in which two times (the real and the deferred) take over from the customary three, with the future appearing in the computer and systems programming of the 'vision machine'.[2]

By way of confirming the emergence of this *light-time*, let us note that picture-taking became shorter and shorter between the hours-long pose of early photography and the invention of the snap-shot. Similarly, in the cinema, the reduction in the through-time of one frame (from 17 f.p.s. to 24 f.p.s. and then 30 f.p.s.) was for many years – until television really began to take off – offset by *spatial elongation* of the film and therefore of its projection. This spatial elongation has been combined with temporal short-ening, from early flash cinematography to present-day video-clips.

For more than 150 years, then, temporal speed-up has led to advances in what still and moving photography represent. It is the 'light of time' – or, if you prefer, the time of *speed-light* – which has illuminated the world around us, to such a point that it seems to be no longer a mere 'means of representation' akin to painting, sculpture or theatre, but a veritable 'means of informa-tion'. Hence the forward surge of information technology – from the days of electronic calculators to the 'computer-generated image', the digitalized video or radio signal, and 'high-resolution vision' (or high-fidelity sound), where the only unit of measure is the 'bits per second' designating the quantity of information con-veyed by a 'message', and *the image is left as the most sophisticated form of information*. Let us recall that the true measure of time is not, as most people think, the number of years, months or hours that have passed, but the alternation of day and night, the order of daytime and its absence. Even if calculation (whether astro-nomical or economic) is a kind of *foresight*, even if the totting up of ephemeris and calendar days has signposted human history, it is no less true that shadow and light are at the very origin of *time information*, the yardstick of duration that is not only quantifiable but also qualifiable. Thanks to the theory of Shannon and a few others, we can see that there are actually two kinds of information: *knowledge* information and *organization* information.

Now, in both these cases, the intervals of passing time have grown ever more precise – from the hours of the sundial or marked candle to the minutes and seconds of our quartz watches. Today, however, the measure of time is no longer just figures on a dial; it is also images displayed on the screens and monitors of 'real time'. The old pendulum movement and clockwork mechanisms, as well as the throbbing of quartz watches, are thus giving way to the movement of the shutter, as cameras and their monitors become so many 'precision watches' or model light-clocks.

The old chronometric system of before, during and after will thus probably be superseded by a 'chronoscopic' system of underexposed, exposed and overexposed.

In the time of succession, duration is paradoxically considered as a series of instants *without any duration*, after the manner of the geometric line conceived as a sequence of points without any dimension. But to this it is now necessary to oppose the concept of exposure time, which ultimately leads us to think of all the (physiological and technological) 'picture-taking' procedures as so many *intakes of time*.

This 'lighting up' of the relativist concept of temporality would lead us into a fundamental revision of the status of the different magnitudes of space and time, such that the light interval overrides the classical intervals of extension and duration. To the daylight of astronomical time should logically be added the daylight of technological speed: from the chemical daylight of candles through the electrical daylight of the Edison lamp (the same Edison who invented the kinetoscope) to the electronic daylight of computer terminals, that deceptive indirect light propagated at the speed of light waves, those transmitter-receivers and other visual generators of duration which still and moving photography and video-computer graphics represent alongside traditional timepieces.

*   *   *

This *indirect light* is ultimately the result of the fusion of optics and kinematics, a fusion which now embraces the whole range of ocular, graphic, photographic and cinematographic representations, making each of our images a kind of *shadow of time* – no longer the customary 'passing time' of historical linearity but the 'exposed time' which (as we said) surfaces. This is the time of Nièpce's photographic developing, the time of the Lumière brothers' cinematographic resolution of movement, but now above all *the time of videographic high definition* of a 'real-time' representation of appearances which cancels the very usefulness of passive (geometric) optics in favour of an active optics capable of causing the decline of the direct transparency of matter. What is inordinately privileged by this process is the indirect (electro-optical) transparency of light or – to be even more precise – of the light of the speed of light.

Thus, after the nuclear disintegration of the space of matter which led to the political situation we know today, the disintegration of *the time of light* is now upon us. Most likely, it will bring an equally major cultural shift in its wake, so that the depth of time will finally win out over the depth of spatial perspective inherited from the Renaissance.

* * *

'There is no longer any distance. You are so close to things that they no longer affect you at all,' wrote Joseph Roth in 1927.[3]

One can well imagine the importance this had for the planning of space: whereas it used to be just a question of arranging our environment to house our bodily activities, the point now is to *control* that environment through interactive online techniques.

In fact, there is an inversion of the classical architectural organization. Instead of various domestic functions being successively distributed around the space that is used for living, all the occupant's activities are concentrated at a single-point remote control so that he or she does not have to move about. 'Meeting at a distance', the paradox of home-based work, becomes through interactivity, 'gathering at one point that which is kept at a distance'. Obviously the user occupying these absolute 'restrooms' is the one who constitutes this point, or centre, of inertia, and so they have nothing in common with the distribution of tasks in the traditional domestic set-up.

The individual's *centre of intensive time* therefore becomes the organizing centre of the home. The 'milieu' of the occupant's present time becomes the preponderant milieu of the habitat, to the detriment of any spatial concentration. Successive fragmentation suddenly gives way to the control of simultaneity, the emergence of a directing centre in the shape of a remote-control or even verbally controlled device, if the system is sufficiently developed to respond to his master's voice.

Rather as in the space environment described by Ludwig Boltzmann, where the living being's weightless present becomes the sole temporal referent replacing both future and past – and also, we should not forget, the sole inertial referent in the environment control of the intelligent home – the *self-referent* dominates all external references and the endogenous holds sway over the exogenous.

Some readily speak here of a strengthened individualism, but it really involves a transfer of the space-time of human residence, a transfer from the 'extensive' domain of external references (mass, area, climate, etc.) to the solitary intensive realm of the *self-reference of a being present here and now*. Instantaneous remote action upon the environment suddenly takes over from the customary action through communication.

'To inhabit energy' (heat, light, etc.) or 'to be inhabited by energy' then becomes a cruel dilemma for the user, but above all for the architect responsible for the synchronism or diachronism of the space and time of strictly human action.

'This house has become my own body and its horror – my own heart,' cried the architect Varelli in Dario Argento's film *Inferno*. And indeed, if the real-time milieu of the user's *intensive present* definitively gains the upper hand over the milieu of real space, architecture suffers a disturbing regression. Where spatial depth used to play a part in rationally organizing the home from floor to ceiling (through the distribution of hallways, corridors and staircases), 'temporal depth' (of real-time immediacy and ubiquitousness) undermines and dissolves that rational organization. From the order of *succession*, we suddenly pass to the disorder of *simultaneity*. Here again, the time of succession gives way to the time of exposure. Even if the general volumetry of the building remains unchanged in order to house the occupant's body, it loses its ergonomic foundation, its organic relationship to action, necessary movement and distinctively human animation. For the practical efficiency of the intelligent home rests upon the *omnipresence* and *omnivoyance* of a resident who no longer even needs to be there to operate the various instruments, a telephone call being enough for his slightest wish to be met.

Here is the lattest twittering of such home-based interactivity.

> Thomson presents SECURISCAN, a computer-run system that can be remotely programmed and interrogated, a combination of comfort and security that allows automation and monitoring of the basic household chores as well as protection of home and person. An electronic exchange receives information coming in from the peripherals. The owner's remote-control device is accepted and his home welcomes him with a synthesized voice, but an intruder sets off alarms and warning lights while the exchange notifies the police.

This general exchange has built into it a household function manager which, in response to a simple telephone call, can switch on the heating, lighting or even the garden sprinkler. 'This standard model,' we learn from the publicity, 'can always have other functions added to it. In particular, since SECURISCAN detects breakdowns and major hazards (gas or water leaks, etc.), *it may also prove an excellent home-nurse.*'[4]

Finally, let us note that this mechanical domestic is cordless and operates at high frequencies.

If extension or distance is no longer a limit to power, present being is no longer so much here and now as *potential* – that is, 'potential' *in absolute speed*.

Here we find the insoluble problem facing the architect and town planner: namely the paradoxical *generalized* (real-time) arrival which now supersedes the limited (real-space) arrival of physical movement from one point to another.

In fact, while this type of movement is still evidently one constant in the volumetric arrangement of built space, the latter's customary necessity is more and more yielding to environment control pure and simple.

Already in the nineteenth century, the appearance of block lifts and escalators or moving walkways helped to *relativize* access to both height and area, as these prostheses complemented in fixed property what the railway, underground and motor car had achieved in the movable domain.

In this final part of the twentieth century, however, the situation is reversed: the famed new *mobility* of public and private transport is giving way to the *immobility* of transmission, to that home inertia which some already call 'cocooning'.

Just as Paul Morand's 'man in a hurry' could no longer invest in anything that took too long, so the man 'under stress' from the contemporary environment shuts himself away not just at home but *inside himself*. Like a motor-disabled person, the occupant of these *endogenous zones* concentrates on his ego not out of egoistic individualism but because of the cruelly demanding schema of temporality governing his action, or rather his interaction with a 'human milieu' that is no longer a place [*un lieu*], to the very extent that his main activity is temporal.[5]

* * *

A Polish architect who had been seriously injured in a traffic accident once explained to me that at the moment when the Warsaw bus hit his taxi he had a feeling of 'spherical projection'; the world seemed to rush upon him, in the manner of a 3-D film. As a magnet attracts metals, so did my friend's body suddenly attract the surrounding space of buildings, windows and cars – even the unhealthy curiosity of passers-by when he came round again.

To find oneself at the centre is always a trying experience. It is well known that to be the object of public attention and expectation causes a kind of fright and quickened heartbeat, and yet this is an exceptional situation which occurs only at rare moments in a lifetime. In environment control, however, the *stage* is there at every moment of one's life, all day and all night.

At the interactive centre of the 'home pilot' system, the occupant is rather like a car driver in the midst of heavy city traffic: reflex activity is more important than reasoning, and stress prolongs the moments when he is powerless to change things or to move forward – for example, when the traffic has slowed down or the road is blocked. The intelligent home presents the same kind of trials. Far from being the acme of domestic comfort, the new *domotics* involves a special kind of temporary or permanent disablement whose only parallel is the situation following a traffic accident, except that here the 'paralysis' is actually intended.

Already with the spread of electrification in the 1930s, electric light produced curious reactions among people used to the oil lamp. A peasant woman once explained to me: 'The really funny thing when I flick the switch is that *the light comes on behind me.*' She had been used to lighting a lamp or candles and bringing the flame to the table or mantelpiece, so that for her the technical surprise of electricity was not the greater brightness but *the physical gesture of bringing light*.

What changes through electronic environment control, however, is not just one familiar gesture but the whole ergonomics of behaviour, with the possible exception of the acts of eating, washing, dressing or going to the toilet.

The only parallel to this sudden gestural rarefication is the katalavox, tetravox or other electronic prosthesis employing the paralytic's own voice, or similar devices used by F-16 or Mirage 2000 fighter pilots. (In fact, the able but *overequipped* air force pilot resembles in every feature the *equipped invalid*, the paraplegic or tetraplegic able to use some residual bodily function [a cheek or the tip of his tongue] to steer him around the home environment.)

The blind or paralysed person is now the model for the 'sight-disabled' or 'motor-disabled' occupant of the intelligent home.

If space is what prevents everything from being in the same place, domotics means that there is no longer any domestic space or stage, but only domestic time, a kind of usual temporality rarefied in the extreme.

Absolutely everything rushes at the occupant. The real-time interface (the remote control) dresses the user in interactive space in a kind of *data suit*. Instead of just having a few familiar portable objects such as a watch or a walkman, he is *invested with the power* to control his domestic environment.

Rather as an instrument panel shows how a vehicle's engine is performing, the user's energy and motor body triggers the reflex operation of the classical architectonic functions. However the rooms and spaces are arranged or distributed, the architectonic ensemble interacts with *the finger and eye*, sometimes just with the voice.

Here it is (electro-magnetic) speed which governs the architecture, as (electric) light illuminates its spaces. In the end, people are not so much *in* the architecture; it is more the architecture of the electronic system which invades them, which is *in* them, in their will to power, their reflexes, their least desires, every hour of the day and night.

How is it possible to live from day to day with such a chimera on one's back? How can one use such a potential *without collapsing into one's own ego*, just as astrophysicists promise for the solar system?

As a boomerang returns to its thrower, so does the intelligent home go back to its source in *present being*. The disorder of its passions, the brusqueness of its reflexes are all that organize the space-time of residence. When one knows the bad effects that zapping has on how films are constructed, it is not hard to imagine the damage done by environment control to architectonics. Similarly, when one observes the harm caused by raging drivers, one can imagine the secret dramas, the *parking accidents*, of the home automation of the future.

'Deconstruction' is, to be sure, the order of the day, but certainly not in the way that some contemporary architects think. *Deconstruction is the result of the new primacy of real time over space*, of instant interactivity over customary activity, and of the 'trans-appearance' described above over the very appearance of things.[6]

To control the environment, then, is not so much to furnish or inhabit it as to be *inhabited* or engulfed by the domestic organs that populate it. Rather as air conditioning succeeded the thermal comfort of walls, the whole of a building will tomorrow come as a package conditioned by domotics, the domotics that is merely the borrowed name of the deconstruction of the old domestic residence.

The 'tele-present' occupant of telematic restrooms is in the position of a miracle-worker. To the *omnivoyance* of the sudden trans-appearance of things is added another divine attribute, namely remote *omnipresence*, a kind of electro-magnetic telekinesis. Thus, the house is literally haunted by its occupant's spirit or will to power, as the occupant is in turn constantly preoccupied by his building.

As the power of his will supplants the old distances that had to be covered, and even the dimensions of the built space, the user of this immediate dwelling becomes the energetic director or motor of an environment that may just as easily be close as distant. There is a kind of *reciprocal bewitchment* here between the individual and the place that houses him, a bewitchment made possible simply through the feat of speed performed by a radio or video signal.

The example of Scott Fisher's virtual environment helmet is particularly revealing of this dramatic change. In the 'portable simulator' (fashioned after a motorcycle helmet), a complete virtual environment featuring architectural volume, cockpit, control room, instrument panel, and so on, is reconstituted through computer technology, so that the wearer can take instant action by means of captors which equip his hands (the data glove), his feet, or indeed his whole body (the data suit). Thus, the man can take or move *virtual objects* with his *quite real hands*, thanks to a fictitious image of the surroundings that appears on his simulator helmet screen.

The situation is similar with our real environment control: the distances and times that usually separate various functions are abolished through the virtues of domotics. That which used to make up the very reality of space, and of the use of space, now vanishes. Human use no longer gives constructed space its characteristic quality, for *the remote-control device virtualizes measurable distance between things*. In order to 'realize' environment control of the interactive dwelling, it is necessary to 'derealize' classical architectonic space. Thus the difference becomes minute, less than minute, between the software-generated *virtual environment* where one acts with a body equipped with nerve impulse detectors, and the architect-produced *real environment* where one instantly acts over a distance by means of zapping or purely vocal commands.

Derealization of a simulated environment where one *really* acts will therefore go together with 'realization' of an actually built environment where one acts virtually by means of electro-magnetic waves.

For future missions to Mars, Fisher is also preparing a *robot technician* with the latest interactive technology. An earthling based at NASA headquarters will be equipped with a data suit and a helmet relaying live vision of the Martian surface; *he will then be able to remote-guide a vehicle several light-years away on the red planet.*

The robot's video-sight will certainly be his own, as will the hands steering the instrument about. And when it cautiously moves around on the burning soil of Mars, it will be the feet of its human remote-guide that allows it to do so.

Literally possessed by its operator, Scott Fisher's robot will be the *double* of the human technician working it at a distance. Humans will no more tread the soil of the distant planet than people on earth will actually have to walk around their intelligent home.

As action and remote action, presence and tele-presence, become so tightly entangled with each other, the intensity of mechanical transmission signals and the intensity of human nervous impulses also tend to merge into one, effacing not only sidereal (or terrestrial) space but even the spatial extension of the animal body. For *bodily energy* is transferred to the machine – or, to be more precise, locomotion commands are transferred from one 'body' to another, from one machine to another, *without any contact at all with any surface.* The 'man-machine' interface eliminates all physical supports one after the other, thus achieving a constant *weightlessness* between individual and place. The famous 'real time' here helps to erase both real space and all the bodies it contains, to the dubious benefit of a total virtualization of lived space and time.

It should not be forgotten, however, that the drawback of this weightlessness is spatial and temporal disorientation, a sweeping deconstruction of the real environment. 'Above' and 'below' become equivalent like 'past' and 'future', the sudden reversibility putting the body back at the *centre* of the surrounding world.

We are thus heading towards a situation where the key feature will be control over ego-centric (introverted) space, not, as in the past, the arrangement of exo-centric (extroverted) space. As self-reference supplants the classical reference of some 'horizon line', individuals will no longer refer to anything other than their own weight-mass or polarity.

* * *

'Coma is a state in which relations with the outside world are lost,' explains Professor Lemaire, head of the intensive care unit at Henri-Mondor Hospital in Créteil. 'After three minutes without brain oxygenation, irreversible lesions appear which may go as far as brain death. In other cases, only the higher functions of memory, speech and motivity are affected, but the vital functions are preserved. That is what is called a vegetative state.'

Domestic interactivity, involving a progressive loss of relations with the external environment, is thus technically *a form of coma*. But it is a 'coma' that does not end in brain death and all the associated ethical problems; it only leads to the 'vegetative state' of home inertia, a 'habitable coma' that is the exact opposite of the 'habitable circulation' of the traditional block of flats.

Already in the late 1970s, the American craze for the sensory deprivation box and the all too famous *camera silenta* of German prisons heralded this blind-pulling on the body of the individual. Some held the view that this illustrated the coming of a police state or the rise of individualism, but it pointed more to a shift in personal time away from the extensiveness of immediate action to the intensiveness of sensations, where certain delinquent or pathological situations prefigured the generalization of such behaviour.

'They don't want to die, they want to be dead,' a British psychiatrist explained at the time.

Today the situation has evolved still further and given rise to even more disturbing symptomatic reactions. 'We wanted to live intensely as long as possible, knowing that death was the only possible outcome,' Norbert Tallet's girlfriend stated to the examining magistrate of Libourne in January 1989, after she and Tallet had committed a long series of more or less gratuitous attacks.

This transfer – or, to be more precise, this *transfer accident* – from extensive personal time to intensive personal time illustrates the new and last figure of death: no longer the big sleep or disappearance, but the full blossoming of the individual's powers. Rather as the 'rising to extremes' characterizes mass warfare in Clausewitz's theory, so does 'rising power' now characterize civil peace in a mass society where *instant switching* (and drugs) wreak such havoc.

This sudden shift in personal time is imperceptibly leading our species towards dramatic destruction of the physical environment, but also towards a deconstruction of domestic space in which the tempting myth of 'absolute shelter' will soon be a tangible reality. Not only will there be no need to *go out* to work, have fun or do the shopping, but it will be unnecessary to *go in*, since the intelligent home will have no opening, no entrance door. Instead, a kind of hood will cover the locomotive body, as the barrel of a sarcophagus or the cell of a cabin houses, or rather covers, the body of a mummy or pilot equally well.

Environmental control, whether close or distant, is thus leading our societies towards a final technological hybrid whose ergonomic archetype is the seat or 'throne' capable of turning itself into a bed, an invalid's litter.

In the extra-vehicular activities of the American space shuttle, we can see the same shift in the centre of gravity: from the astronaut's body to a jet-propelled seat that replaces man's natural motivity as soon as he leaves the spaceship to move around in weightlessness.

With the primacy accorded to the 'real time' of interactivity over the real space of customary activity, are we moving towards home activity on earth analogous to the activity of astronauts moving around in high orbit? Unfortunately, this probably is the case, since the *general inrush* of data and images is finally placing us in the same position of inertia – a domestic inertia that radically alters our relationship to the world, our relations with the *real* (terrestrial or extra-terrestrial) environment.

We should be in no doubt: whereas *limited inflows* used to require some upward physical movement in the act of rising and going out, or movement from near to far in the act of travelling, the decline of such activity represents for the human species a shift as great as that involved in the passage to an *upright gait*. The difference is that there is no longer 'positive evolution' to a new type of motivity, but, rather, 'negative behavioural involution' leading towards a pathological fixedness: the coming of *seated man* or, worse still, *couched man*.

Notes

1. Maurice Merleau-Ponty, *L'Oeil et l'esprit*, Paris: Gallimard, p. 78.
2. See the final chapter of Paul Virilio (1994), *The Vision Machine*, London: British Film Institute.
3. *Die Flucht ohne Ende*, Munich 1978.
4. Quoted [and retranslated] from sales publicity issued in 1989.
5. Paul Klee.
6. See Paul Virilio (1991), *The Lost Dimension*, New York: Semiotext(e).

CHAPTER TWELVE

Desert Screen

The 'first' Gulf War in 1991 engendered a mass of theorizing and pontificating from the world's public intellectuals. Paul Virilio's particular contribution to this speculative enterprise is a good deal more cautious than many others, including his friend and compatriot Jean Baudrillard, who (quite understandably from his own pataphysical perspective) proclaimed that the 'gulf war did not take place'. Editions Galilée published *L'Ecran du Désert* by Paul Virilio in Paris in 1991. The book consisted of Virilio's chronicles (originally published in French newspapers and magazines) of the various stages of the Gulf War from August 1990, before the 'crisis' became a war, to June 1991 when it was (apparently) all over, including the text of an interview recorded with J.-C. Raspiengeas, in January 1991. The book was divided into three parts corresponding to the stages of the conflict: 'Desert Shield', 'Desert Storm' and 'Desert Screen'. Continuum books published *Desert Screen: War at the Speed of Light*, an English translation by Michael Degener, in London and New York in 2002 with a preface and new postscript interview with Virilio by American political science professor James Der Derian. The extract reprinted here is part of the original foreword to the book by Virilio. The significance of the Gulf War mark 1 to Virilio was its being the 'first total electronic war. Broadcast live, via satellite'. By the time the preface to the English translation was written by Der Derian in February 2001, the neo-conservatives in the Bush Republican government were already preparing to finish off the project begun in Iraq in 1991. Translator Michael Degener offered a brief postscript of his own as the book went to press in February 2002, emphasizing just how prescient Virilio had been in 1990–1. The second Gulf War duly followed in March 2003 only a few months after *Desert Screen* had seen the light of day. 'War at the speed of light' was already becoming a media cliché by the end of hostilities.

Desert Screen, trans. Michael Degener, London: Continuum, 2002.

From the potential war to the probable city

To say that the City and War go hand in glove is a euphemism. The city, the *polis*, is constitutive of the form of conflict called WAR, just as war is itself constitutive of the political form called the CITY. Even if tribal conflicts, the turmoil of nomadic and prehistoric origins, represented a tactical prefiguration of the conflict organized by sedentary societies, we must await the rise of urban civilization for real war to emerge from the historical development of the city.

Indeed, before being its actual perpetration, the political conflict is first its economic preparation, I would even say its strategic premonition. But this sort of military anticipation will first be associated with the management of the 'theatre of operation', with this training ground where war will actually take place.

Where the hunter's snares and traps anticipated the movement and the fall of game, war will anticipate, in its turn, the movement of troops, their momentum, their course and finally their halting in place. From this arises the decisive importance of the urban territory, of its limits and its ways of access like a 'training field for manoeuvres', to this strategic thinking that was confused from the start with the political reasoning of the leader of the city, at once mayor and military leader, 'strategist'[1] of the ancient city.

If there are three major epochs of real war – the tactical and prehistorical epoch consisting of limited violence and confrontations; then the strategic epoch, historical and purely political; and finally, the contemporary and transpolitical logistical epoch, where science and industry play a determining role in the destructive power of opposing forces – there are also three great types of weapons that progress in importance through the course of the ages, in the age-old duel between offensive and defensive forces: weapons of obstruction (ditches, ramparts, bastions, armour and fortresses of all sorts); weapons of destruction (lances, bows, cannons, machine-guns, missiles, etc.); and finally, weapons of communication (lookout towers and signals, information and transport carriers, optical telegraph, wireless telephone, radar and satellites, among others).

For each of these weapons a particular type of confrontation dominates: the war of siege for the first , the war of movement for the second and the all-out blitzkrieg [*guerre éclair et totalitaire*] for the last.

Moreover, for each of the decisive weapons, there was, in its time, a specific 'mode of deterrence'. The city surrounded by a fortified ring long deterred attacks by siege, up to the invention of artillery capable of destroying its walls. The war of movement, which succeeded techniques of encirclement, reached its limit with the innovation of strategic bombing equipped with atomic weapons.

And thereupon followed the nuclear deterrence between the East and West in the wake of the destruction of the cities of Hiroshima and Nagasaki.

Before analysing further the recent development of the new 'real-time' weapons of communication, arising from what, during the course of the Cold War, were long called 'counter-value[2] strategies', let us return again to the very origin of the 'political war' – that mode of war of which Clausewitz made himself the apostle and theoretician. An important fact prevails: if the synoecism of the tribes composing the Greek city led finally to rites of autochthony,[3] that is, to the means for integrating strangers, it is because the nascent city (Athens, as it happens) first defined itself by reference to the latent threat of civil war. This stasis[4] (metastasis) will later explain the advent of the rights of citizens[5] and the rise of the political-citizen as soldier-citizen, a free man who could initiate an *agon* and therefore give up his life for his rights, the no-man's land of neighbouring territories being the place of non-rights, the space of exile, of ostracization.

Just as the enclosure of the city protected it from its external enemies, so also was it fortified against the enemy within, clans whose politico-military unity threatened to explode at any moment. This double challenge to the urban order explains the appearance of the public place (*agora, forum*), at once a 'political stage' for democratic confrontations and a 'staging ground' for the mobilization of soldier-citizens before they would head out, united, to defend the gates and walls of the urban fortification.

A double construction of a theatre of military operation: first, on the ramparts and beyond, at the foot of the walls of the city – on this glacis that would later become the suburb, the exterior [*la banlieue*], the place of exclusion [*le lieu des bannis*] from the rights of the citizen – and second, in the heart of the city, with its *agora*, the staging ground of politics, where the battle of ideas and interests would be both concrete and metaphorical.

The later invention of the ghetto (in Venice and elsewhere) would eventually reproduce, like an echo, this phenomenon of panicked anticipation of internal war, by the management of the most populated neighbourhoods for those excluded and for those to be promoted in the future.

With the obstruction of, and later the accession to, first ownership, and then the right to vote based on census taxation, and then full citizenship, the foreigner would be put through a sort of filter that would most often prove to be a dead end, in the form of pogroms and other programmes for eliminating supernumerary groups perceived as a danger to the stability of the connective tissue of the city. Internal and external, not only within and outside the enclosure of the law, of *nomos*,[6] but interior and exterior to citizenship, that is, the active participation in the militia of citizen-soldiers who could not allow the inclusion of questionable 'comrades' – questionable because they possessed nothing to defend but their own hides, which were not worth much in the epoch of slavery.

Thus the strategic and political importance of the *miles*,[7] the ancient 'citizen-soldier' who defended his possessions, his family and the entire city, as well as his own person. And from this that chant of the *agon* where the citizen found himself already dead within the sphere of rights and law, those 'rights of the citizen' that, in surpassing him as an isolated individual, made of him a participant in the large, fundamentally political, body of the city. Thus the ghetto was, like the *agora* or the *forum*, a two-sided coin: on the one hand, a place of retreat and exclusion from the social fabric; and, on the other, a space of relative liberty for the like/unlike, foreigners as potential enemies on the way to assimilation or complete exclusion.

The sphere of the elect [*lieu d'élection*] of the city state of free men was therefore also a sphere of exclusion [*lieu d'éjection*], the engine of the pneumatic[8] democratic life that was predictably selective in the very measure to which this democracy was of the minority, the Greek city state having been a sort of island of the political in an ocean of servitude and tyranny in the ancient world.

*   *   *

Today, even if God may still need men, war does not, or just barely . . . as victims. Consider, for example, chemical weapons or the neutron bomb, which eliminate humans, the animal, but carefully preserve material objects. In fact, the metastasis so feared by the ancients has taken place. The decomposition of the social (what Leonardo Sciascia called a sicilianization, by virtue of the proliferation of clans, of sects) progresses as the enlarged family of the agrarian mode of production gives way to the nuclear family of the urban petite bourgeoisie, and finally to the contemporary form commonly called monoparental. Thus, as the city increases through the course of the ages, so the unity of the people has decreased. Henceforth useless, or nearly so, as a 'producer' (skilled or non-skilled worker . . .) or as 'destroyer' (soldier, conscript . . .), the supernumerary man of the enormous megalopolis is forced to give up his status as citizen to the dubious advantage of increasingly sophisticated substitute material: automated machine tools operated by remote control, or war machines automatically controlled by computer.[9]

In this epoch military-industrial and scientific logistics prevail over strategic doctrines and truly political arguments – war being no longer the continuation of politics by other means, according to Gorbachev. The era opens as weapons of instantaneous communication come to dominate, thanks to the rise of globalized information networks and telesurveillance. In effect, in the logistical era of war, and contrary to the strategic era that preceded it, the power of destruction has been transferred from the armed population to weapons systems, mass killers excluding the mass of killers of the past: the soldiers of the second year of the republican calendar,[10] the soldiers of Napoleon's old guard or the allied soldiers of the last two world wars, and this beginning with the terrorist innovation of an atomic weapon capable of precluding political war ecologically, by endangering the very survival of the human race.

We enter thus into both a third era of war and a new stage of the city, or more exactly of the post-industrial meta-city. The relatively recent end of classical deterrence between the East and West, with its geopolitical uncertainties, results in the urgent necessity of reinterpreting the doctrines of military engagement, going all the way back to the most distant origins of history.

If, as Michelet asserted, each epoch dreams the next, each conflict of historical importance tends to imagine that which follows. We saw this with the First and Second World Wars leading into the era of atomic deterrence; and we will see it tomorrow with the end of the equilibrium of terror and the inauguration of a nuclear proliferation, the inception of a sudden multiplication of the 'deterrence of the strong by the weak' of which the Gulf crisis is a harbinger.

If weapons of obstruction were initially established by the city state within its ramparts, and the ghetto within the limits of a reserved quarter, and if weapons of destruction, from the age of artillery until that of the atomic bomb, were created to surpass the urban limit spread around its content, the railroad and automobile extending this dissolution, with the development most recently of 'weapons of mass communication', the political definition of the image of the city again becomes problematic.

A crucial question presents itself to those currently in power: if early warning satellites – but also telecommunications satellites – have led to the impossibility of a surprise attack on opposing territory and have thus contributed to the disarmament that is abolishing the deterrence of the strong by the strong – all the while promoting the interpenetration of different points of view throughout the world – what type of 'military' interdiction, or even just 'police' interdiction, will these weapons of instantaneous communication give rise to in the face of the proliferation of chemical or atomic weapons? The appearance of a deterrence of the strong by the weak is no longer limited to France, or Great Britain or Israel, but is rather generalized, as Iraq, Pakistan and the constantly growing list of other countries are preparing to avail themselves of the ultimate weapon.

Are we about to witness a return to inertia, to the blockade and therefore to a stage of siege, as in the most distant past of the city? If we consider the role played by the United Nations throughout the course of 1990 – this is what seems most likely – we can see that all of the Security Council resolutions, which imposed embargoes first by land, then by sea and then by air, were all heading in this direction.

The bipolar deterrence between the NATO bloc and the Warsaw bloc, with its allies in the third world, was succeeded by the conception of a polar deterrence in which the UN would play the role of a worldwide pseudogovernment, with France even going so far as to propose to the Security Council the launching of 'blue satellites'[11] to guarantee world peace.

And so, following upon the great wars of movement and the advent of a *total war* involving the progressive militarization of science and the economy of nations, we would be providing for a paralysis: a polar inertia of a *total peace* guaranteed by the UN.

This would mark a return to the point of departure of history, where the 'state of siege' would again find its strategic primacy, no longer on the level of the city state, of the threatened region or nation state, but, this time, on the level of the entire world – while the recent development of a protectionist ideology of ecology is heading in the direction of a definitive supremacy of a 'global security' over the political defence of nations. We have, however, a certain reservation with regard to what might appear to some as an 'end to history': with the logistical importance accorded to weapons of mass communication over that of weapons of mass destruction, the logic of war becomes paradoxical. Everything depends henceforth on verisimilitude or the lack thereof, information and disinformation renewing the duel between arms and armour.

Listen to the words of Emile Gaboriau, a writer from that nineteenth century which saw the rise of the first great press agencies: 'As concerns the news: distrust what seems most likely, always begin by believing what seems most unbelievable.'

And so the era of illusion is about to make its debut. The topical character of the city of free and equal men assembled in a public place is to be succeeded by a teletopical metacity where the public image 'in real time' will probably supplant the quite real space of cities of the republic. Harbingers of a serious conflict of interpretation between democracy and dromocracy, where the post-industrial implementation of an absolute speed (that of electromagnetic waves) will abolish the progress that arose from the accessibility to the public of relative speeds since Greco-Latin antiquity. In *The Constitution of the Athenians*, a text dating from 429 to 424 BC, we find something on the subject:

> I would say first that it is just that in Athens the poor and the people count more than the nobles and the rich: for it is the people who make the navies work and who give to the City its power. And this counts as well for the pilots, the rowing masters, the second-in-command, the lookout, and those who build the ships. It is to all of these that the City owes its force, much more than to the hoplites, or nobles, or gentlemen.[12]

In maritime democracy, contrary to Lacedemonian democracy, the power of Athens is first of all that of its vessels and not solely of its citizen-infantry – consider the importance of Piraeus and the fortification of 'long walls' between Athens and its port. Democracy, the constitution of the Athenians, is therefore also dromocratic, since those who run the navy govern the city. Contrary to traditional autocratic regimes, the division of public power is comparable to that of the power of physical displacement (such as was not the case with the ancient cavalry, in particular the *equite romani*[13]).

It would be the same in the republic of Venice, which will, appropriately, inaugurate the island of the *Ghetto Nuovo* with its apartments of approximately ten storeys. With the division of riches and especially of spoils, the Athenian democracy, like the Venetian republic, will also be founded upon the division of the speed of triremes or galleys.[14] The considerable political and cultural power of these great historic cities will thus derive literally from the propulsive capacity of a people engaged in the great movement of the acceleration of history (read Fernand Braudel!).

All of this will continue up to our day, with not only the impact of the 'labour force' of the proletariat engaged in the industrial revolution but also in the ultimately misunderstood transportation revolution that will favour the democratization of rapid movement, not only public transportation, thanks to railroads (following seafaring) and to the railroad station (following the port), but also private transportation, with the domestic automobile.

It is relative speed, on the one hand, with seafaring, the train, the car, the plane (the airport following the train station), that will permit the progressive development of an industrial democracy; while absolute speed, on the other hand, with telecommunications and tele-command (the teleport following the airport), will finally give rise to the latest of revolutions: the communications revolution that will abolish, along with distances, the very necessity of physical movement of whatever sort . . .

Can we democratize ubiquity, instantaneity; in other words, can we democratize inertia? Such is indeed the question that presents itself today to politics, to those who tomorrow will build the 'Mediate City' [*Cité Médiate*]. After the unfortunate invasion of the private automobile, will generalized automation bring us back, through the bias of an absurd individualism, towards autocracy? A post-industrial and post-urban autocracy whose golden boys and other traders would have proven to be the clinical symptoms? Far more threatened by the 'excess speed' of tele-technologies than by the excess wealth of an apparently triumphant capitalism, will democracy finally prevail as some imagine, or on the contrary, it is simply going to disappear?

The answer to these questions is being worked out, beginning today, not only according to the civic and political plan of the rights of people to come, but especially, it would seem, according to the military and logistical plans of the war to come.

Notes

1. Virilio's use of the word is alluding to the Greek term for military leader, *strategos* [Tr.].
2. This refers to the deterrence doctrine that targeted populations as opposed to military targets (counter-force strategies) [Tr.].

3. See Nicole Loraux (1979), 'L'autochtonie, une topique athénienne', *Les Annales*, January–February.
4. The word *stasis* in Greek refers to taking a defiant *stand* in a civil uprising [Tr.].
5. The French phrase *droit de cité* preserves more closely the definitional role of the *polis* in determining citizens' rights [Tr.].
6. *Nomos* is Greek for 'law' or 'custom'. Virilio is developing here the derivation of the word *nomos* from its root *nemo* [νέμω], which entails notions of habitation and the delimitation of territory [Tr.].
7. The Roman foot soldier [Tr.].
8. Deriving originally from the Greek word *pneuma*, 'wind' or 'spirit', this term's primary meaning in French is 'spiritual' [Tr.].
9. In the autumn of 1990, a computer was installed in the Pentagon in Washington in order to manage the Gulf Crisis. The name of this *deus ex machina*: the 'inertial center'.
10. The reference is to the second year of the French Revolutionary calendar, which was the official calendar of France between 24 November 1793 and 31 December 1805 [Tr.].
11. An allusion to the blue helmets worn by UN peacekeepers [Tr.].
12. This text of pseudo-Xenophon can be found in L. Canfora's book, *La Démocratie comme Violence*, Desjonquères, 1989.
13. Roman cavalry [Tr.].
14. The trireme was an ancient Greek vessel with three rows of oars [Tr.].

CHAPTER THIRTEEN

The Data Coup d'Etat

After the series of short newspaper chronicles of the first Gulf War, the next major publishing venture for Paul Virilio in the 1990s was a new book called *L'Art du Moteur* put out by Editions Galilée in Paris in 1993. 'The art of the motor' as an English-language label summed up very well Virilio's focus for his elusive approach to technology, and a chapter with this title concluded the book. It found Virilio fascinated, understandably, by the development of technologies such as Global Positioning System or GPS. If any technology of the 1990s was tailor-made for Virilio this was it. He regarded it as 'the event of the decade' and expressed wide-eyed fascination with the idea that through this technology the United States was marketing a watch which 'does not tell the *time*; it tells you *where* you are', a confirmation for Virilio that the world would from now on be lived in real time. An English translation of the whole book was soon produced by Julie Rose and published by the University of Minnesota Press in Minneapolis in 1995 with the explicit title *The Art of the Motor*. The extract reprinted here is one of seven chapters of the book. On the back jacket, a quotation from Brian Massumi praised Virilio as a 'brilliant, complex and wonderfully idiosyncratic thinker whose work is most deserving of the increased attention it is receiving in the English-speaking world'. However, such praise and specific intellectual recognition was still relatively rare. By the mid-1990s, when the English translation of *L'Art du Moteur* appeared, it was still possible for book series on past and present theorists to completely ignore Paul Virilio as a thinker whilst including much lesser figures in their A–Z of key names. Virilio, as if by knee-jerk reaction, embarked on a concentrated period of original publishing in the French language which was to secure his place in such series by the beginning of the next century.

'The Data Coup d'Etat', from *The Art of the Motor*, trans. Julie Rose, Minneapolis: University of Minnesota Press, 1995.

Speak while you remain silent, remain silent while you speak. (Proverb)

Since movement creates the event, the real is *kinedramatic*. The communications industry would never have got where it is today had it not started out as an *art of the motor* capable of orchestrating the perpetual shift of appearances.[1]

It has been doing this ever since a record in manufacturing and distribution was attained in 1814, when John Walter II, the owner-editor of the *Times* in London, installed the first really effective stream press with a capacity of 1,000 pages an hour. This was soon replaced in 1827 with the Cowper and Applegarth press, which could print 5,000 pages an hour on both sides. The first rotary press was in action in 1848, followed ten years later by a machine that could run off 20,000 pages an hour. At the end of the century, composition also got faster, thanks to Ottmar Mergenthaler's invention of the linotype.

We might also remember that the *Times* gained another three hours on its competitors by sending papers directly to the country by rail from Euston Station. Great Britain's press amounted to 250 million franked copies a year around 1810; ten years later, the figure was 300 million.[2]

After the shipwrecks and derailments of maritime and rail acceleration, the collisions and crashes of the car and the plane and the steam press, and then the rotary press and the rotary image press of cinematic illusion, wave trains would come along and produce their own specific catastrophes through radio and video signals. News is dynamite, information explodes like a bomb, opinion polls or war propaganda are time bombs, we even have epidemics, for, as lawyer Gisèle Halimi recently wrote, 'Nothing is more contagious than the processes of liberation.'

Lord Beaverbrook, the grand patron of the British press, was also director of military aeronautics in 1940. His motto: 'Wherever I find things organized, I disorganize them.'

Already under the Second Empire, Pascal Grousset, editor of *La Marseillaise*, compared his successful rag to 'a torpedo boat launched full-speed at the armour-plating of the imperial ship'. A little while later, among the organs of the popular press busily abusing republican liberties to make money out of the economic crisis as well as out of scandal and the pillorying of legal entities, publications such as *Le Père Peinard* and *L'En Dehors* went as far as providing readers tempted by anarchy and crime with recipes for explosive cocktails, and even blithely suggested targets. Completely conscious of the reciprocal relationship between events and the press, the anarchists then invented 'politics in action'. One such anarchist, Jules Bonnot, a great innovator in the crime line, took to thumbing his nose at the heads of the Paris criminal investigation department through the intercession of the press.

During the siege of the building where he was to meet his doom on 28 April 1912, Bonnot wrote, 'I am famous. Renown trumpets my name to the four corners of the globe. Enough to make those who go to great lengths to get themselves talked about green with envy.' Similarly, on the eve of the Great War, the entire bellicose press would incite patriots to assassinate Jean Jaurès – which was duly carried out on 31 July 1914. Nearly a century later, TV presenter and former legionnaire Charles Villeneuve could still compare TV channel TF1 to 'a nuclear aircraft carrier equipped with a tactical nuclear weapon: the Tele-Vision Show.'(!) No doubt about it, *only the vectors* change with time. 'Eliminating distance kills,' René Char once said. When you endlessly increase the liberating power of the media, you bring what was once hidden by distance and the secret – which was distant and naturally foreign to each one of us – far too close; you then run the risk of reinventing, here and now, some kind of *barbarism* (*barbaros* = foreigner, one who does not speak the language). In other words, you run the risk of *inventing the enemy*.

Since *the minds of armed men always waver*, the ancient Greeks accorded the benefit of a certain blindness to bards whose itinerant song was supposed to keep them informed about the appearances of a world where what happens – the surprise, the accident, the eruption of the unforeseen, all that cannot be immediately perceived in the invisible movement of time, *that escapes even the gaze of old men who have seen several generations come and go* – gets mixed up with the ubiquitous tyranny of those rumour-mongers, the vindictive gods, who stir up hatred and unhealthy dreams and lurk in all things though nothing is known of them except by hearsay . . .[3]

A few millennia later, one realizes that our own era, impious as it may be, has never stopped tarting up the power of its communication tools with the menacing attributes of a theocracy, and that the miraculous credibility of the media, now under a cloud, was perhaps nothing more than one of the last avatars of a once superhuman infallibility. At the beginning of the nineteenth century, the major American newspapers were still able to present themselves not merely as sources of information but as 'the gospel truth' and as censors in the social, economic, and political realms. The *New York Tribune* (200,000 copies a day in 1860) was nicknamed 'The Great Moral Organ'. F. Luther Mott ranked it second *only to the Bible!*

From time immemorial, the 'gods' have always been cast as vectors: thus the Egyptians usually translated the name of the god Thoth (who invented language and writing) as Hermes. Hermes then becomes the mediator whose job it is to convey messages and negotiate changes and transitions, but also, equally, to guide, mislead, redirect, and lead astray (a tradition maintained by numerous incarnations of the volatile and polymorphous Greco-Roman Hermes-Mercury). Implicated in the 'secret of the gods', the first media thereby invested in hermeticism. Written correspondence that gets in before the event by overcoming distance could effectively look like the 'it had to happen' of the *fatum*. In a passage in *The Iliad*, Proitos sends Bellerophontes to Lycia in order to do away with him, entrusting him with 'signs of disastrous meaning, many lethal marks that he wrote in a folded tablet, and told him to show them to his father-in-law, to ensure his death'. Cryptograms reserved for a small circle of initiates who could communicate regardless of distance, riddles, semantic signals carved into a tree, a rock, designating a rendezvous, marking a route, awaiting a stray nomad.

When the use of language or writing spreads and comes to

guarantee democratic laws, an antidote immediately appears in the form of new epistolary codes. Plutarch cites the Spartans' secret methods of correspondence. But cryptography, strictly speaking, in the sense of the substitution of numbers, words, or symbols, was of Semitic origin. The prophet Jeremiah is said to have been among the first to use a cryptographic system, well before reigning powers like the deified caesars used permutations in simple applications.

From the message's secret as appropriation of the divine *fatum*, things took certain decisive turns: the military regimes of ancient Greece, such as Sparta's timarchy, were based on an arithmetical division of goods (spoils) and a geometric division of space (colonization). The change in the scale of war with the end of local combat and the emergence of the great Hellenic states would require an essential division of information and would soon lead to a *theory of mediatization*.

In one generation, Herodotus's *history* (*historia*), which still held to the Homeric tradition, gave way to the *super-journalism* of Thucydides, recounting the wars he took part in. Brushing aside the enigma of divine intervention, Thucydides focuses on eyewitness accounts, ensuring their exactness by a system of information cross-checking combined with serious critical analysis.

The history of Greece, however, preserves a strong emotional charge in which the military necessity for democratic cohesion makes itself felt.

You cannot effectively improvise a citizen any more than you can become a killer on your own. There must be common rituals, a certain trancelike state, for one to manage to leave one's body, to become one's own double, to pass from one's own *identity to identification* with some *warrior who has already died in the City*.

Because it is easier to fool a crowd than it is to fool a single person, the forming of *public opinion* in Greece is associated with the military trance. Public opinion, Plato tells us, will be 'an *intermediate state* between knowledge and ignorance, touching on the vast majority of things'. He adds that 'the visible world is the domain of opinion'. Socrates will be anxious about the education of Greek children – an education based on Homer's epics and the songs of the bards, with their quota of crime, incest, violence, hate, revenge, and family atrocities and having no cathartic effect whatsoever as far as he is concerned (quite the opposite – no more, anyway, than the tragic theatre that comes after). *Able to move everyone on the spot*, the minstrels of tragedy wander from city to city, bringing the multitudes together in theatres like the one at Epidaurus, which already held 14,000 to 15,000 seats. There, what is declaimed, sung, imagined, attacked, becomes *the domain of the visible* for all present. The secret, the intimate, personal truth are now considered a break with communication, all democratic truths having now to be found in common, to become collective, through theatre, just as in the assembly or court of law. Plato makes an objective statement about this: *You can easily imitate appearances, but not reality.* Just as a magician can quickly, very quickly even, '*make* the sun and the stars in the heavens, the earth, himself, and other animals and plants'. It's all done with mirrors.

What we have on the ancient theatre stage is already actual *plagiarism of the visible world*. The first mass media, designed to crack open the secret and educate public opinion, are just a trick effect of reality, a mise-en-scène with changing sets, disguises, machinery, and *dei ex machina*. In the *Republic*, Plato also notes that democracy certainly has its 'charms'; it is, he says, 'a veritable hodgepodge of constitutions', a shop window in which the whole heterogeneous kit and caboodle of optical illusions lie piled up 'like one of those many-coloured garments that women and children just adore'. *But*, the philosopher asks in conclusion, *are there any states of existence that are not perverse?*

On the battlefield, the disciplinary logistics of the new democratic armies are also supposed to pull off this excessive incorporation of parts into a whole capable of a common movement, are they not? Suggestions and hallucinations mushroom, war machines multiply, fiercely blazing mirrors induce blindness or fire, and when 'glorious Hector reaches out to take his son . . . , the child shrank back crying against the breast of his girdled nurse, terrified at the sight of his own father, frightened by the bronze and the crest of horse-hair, as he saw it nodding grimly down at him from the top of his father's helmet' (*The Iliad*, VI).

In Greek antiquity, whenever democracy pits itself against the tyranny of a small or single group, the democrats always claim to be replacing brute physical force with a moral force allowed by a mass mediatization that flies in the face of the very concept of reality. So it is only natural that in the city-states where this kind of cinetheatrics are big, certain faux philosophers and sophists begin to develop increasingly perverse techniques of persuasion from the fourth century BC on: that *ancient eloquence* that was so little concerned with what was true or false regardless of the issue, happy just to hurry events along and offer information about the instability of the world.

Sophists such as Plato's Thrasymachus, who chased young men and diverse profits, was a false rhetorician and occasional informer and yet excelled in 'whipping up the crowds and then calming them down again *as if by magic*'. For Lucian, eloquence is like theatre or the tribunal; it is 'a battle against the inertia of images *that one could make people see but that would have no movement or signs of life*'. Seneca thought the fact of being compressed into a verse or saying gives thought *the force of a projectile hurled by some vigorous arm*. Eloquence is less a means of communicating than a communication weapon in which the energy of delivery information is often combined with that of denunciation, of attack. No one knew better than Thrasymachus how to hurl or refute an accusation, Plato again notes. Archaeological sites are littered with vestiges of such democratic eloquence – with *ostrakons*, the remains of vast numbers of votes that often called for irrevocable decisions, potshards, carved shells on which the kinedramatic destiny of the *polis* was written, day by day, along with the necessity, for each and every person, *of being wherever the others are*, at the same point in space: the *agora*, theatre stadium, or assembly . . . Ostracism has often been called '*the reverse vote*' and is certainly a carry-over from athymie and primitive stoning, collective murder. But we might also wonder if the old tyranny was now appropriate to the endlessly expanding city, to urban chaos in general, whether it was able to maintain its effectiveness there. At the 'policing' level, mass communication was effective in other ways once it became a system of general incrimination.

A bit like *politically correct* language, that so-called (*culturally sensitive*) verbal rigour from which American democracy is now suffering and which reeks of lynching, 'in this moribund system that leads to anarchy while claiming to resist the reduction of the many to the few' (Emerson), antiquity's denunciatory eloquence was not aimed at punishing crimes or attacks on the *polis*. It was aimed at outstripping these, at getting a jump on crime thanks to an obsessional vigilance in the form of a *permanent statistical opinion poll*.

Ostracizing a group or a person means 'turfing out' an undesirable, one who through ambition, personal genius, or services rendered becomes too 'heavy' and so risks putting a spanner in the works of the democratic machine, in the manner of Hercules, excluded from the argonauts' ship because he weighed too much and might have caused the ship to come to grief.

In the United States in 1890, the results of a census were analyzed by means of punch cards, a process that already allowed faster and more sophisticated statistical evaluation. In the French elections of 1992, 100 years later, the role of *televised polls* was more impressive than ever. There was even a plan to keep broadcasting poll results right up to the last minute under the pretext of *democratizing information*, though this would have been illegal. René Rémond, among others, actually spoke of election polls as a *'first round'*.

As another stab at a future *cathodic democracy*, in certain constituencies the smart card, designed to count votes electronically and thus speed up the publication of results, was tried out for the first time.

Each new regime remains unrecognizable when it emerges since it preserves certain traits of the preceding regime, much as a son looks vaguely like his father. We have thus, without realizing it, gone from simple statistical management to a new phenomenon of *representation*, the virtual theatricalization of the real world.

We had to wait for the fusion/confusion of information and data processing to obtain the fusion/confusion of *the secret of speed* – initially, with the first military decoders to become operational during the Second World War. These ancestors of our computers and software systems were also heirs to the obsessional vigilance and providence of ancient democracies . . . After this, with real-time transmission and transcription of the message or image, we would be tempted to compensate for any erratic behaviour on the part of the public and to finally achieve higher *success rates* (the power to correctly predict) than what the classic methods of statistics allow in the areas of economics, military action, industry, and, eventually, even politics.

If the destiny of the city-state depended on each person's obligation to be where the others were, then for the victims of multiple solitude, the televised poll is now a mere pale simulation of the ancient rallying of citizens, of their movement to the urns and the final result.

As we have seen, the gap between the speed of prognosis and the slowness of the actual political act is endlessly narrowing, already causing some to confuse the latter with the premature displaying of results on the television screen. After *war games* and other reflex games, they may as well legalize *binary political simulators*, the electronic home vote that could act instantaneously, a 'hodgepodge of constitutions' now turned into a *cathodic shop window display: democratic software* whose 'politically correct' programmes only a handful of initiated informers would control. The principle of this new interactive game has been on the drawing board for a long time. American president Richard Nixon gave it his enthusiastic support back in the early 1970s.

Tennyson claimed that, along with a touch of anarchy, democracies bear within them the seeds of their own doom and the probability of a return to tyranny. Similarly, the anarchic carving up of representational techniques, in provoking the implosion of the visible world, which was once the domain of public opinion, inexorably catapults us into this final phase of political *mediatization* – which becomes, once more, the privilege of smaller and smaller groups, keepers of that ultimate strange brew composed of the speed of light (the secret) and the exorbitant eloquence of figures, messages, and images (information).

Notes

1. Karl Kraus employs the term 'kinedramatic' in *Nachts* (*By Night*), originally published by Herbst, 1918. See Karl Kraus (1965), *Beim Wort Genommen*, Munich: Kösel Verlag, p. 340.

2. Many of the points discussed here are based on the following works: Charles Ledré (1958), *Histoire de la Presse*, Paris: Arthème Fayard; Jean Morienval (1934), *Les Créateurs de la Grande Presse en France*, Paris; Eugène Hatin (1859–61), *Histoire Politique et Littéraire de la Presse en France*, Paris.

3. According to *The Iliad*.

CHAPTER FOURTEEN

From Sexual Perversion to Sexual Diversion

By the mid-1990s Virilio had already completed another full-length book called *La Vitesse de Libération*. Editions Galilée published it in Paris in 1995. An English translation by Julie Rose was speedily put out by Verso in London and New York in 1997 with the odd title of *Open Sky*. Virilio told Sylvère Lotringer in interview that someone had already taken the preferred English-language title, which would have been 'Escape Velocity'. This did indeed become the title of the last chapter of the book. The French title had seen Paul Virilio self-consciously reintroduce the word speed into his work twenty years or so after *Speed and Politics*. 'Liberation speed,' explained Virilio to Lotringer, 'is the speed you need to reach orbit'. For Virilio in the late 1990s, looking back on his burgeoning discourses on a rapidly accelerating modernity, the two important velocities seemed to be 'the speed-limit' or 'light-speed, which allows for telecommunications' and also 'liberation speed, which permits man to free himself from his world and escape Earth'. It is the latter that is a major focus of *Open Sky*. It is notable too that by this period Virilio is talking about his idea of the generalized accident, or accident of accidents, a notion that is to dominate his future thinking. The notion of 'cyber-monde' is more obvious as electronic media proliferate at a rapid pace in this part of the decade. These are the years, after all, where the internet and mobile phone technologies, once nowhere, suddenly seem to be everywhere. Inevitably cybersexuality is one of the most discussed aspects of cyberculture, and Virilio, who writes and talks relatively rarely about the erotic dimension of being a 'tele-spectator', cannot resist an idisosyncratic intervention on love, speed and sex. The extract reprinted here is one of nine chapters in a book which also includes the much discussed and anthologized piece 'The Third Interval'.

'From Sexual Perversion to Sexual Diversion', from *Open Sky*, trans. Julie Rose, London: Verso, 1997.

They think they are happy because they are not moving. (Tristan Bernard)

With cybersexuality, you no longer divorce, you disintegrate. Proprioceptive reality suddenly becomes improper; it is all done with reciprocal distancing.

So, what is being set up is a discreet, furtive conjunction not based on attraction any more but on mutual rejection and repulsion. Thanks to copulation between partners who are already no longer 'joined together', the aesthetics of disappearance is in turn vanishing in the face of the ethics of the essential disappearance of one's 'nearest and dearest' – the spouse, the lover – to the benefit of this 'furthest' (and not so dear) that Nietzsche once urged us to love.

After the seduction of simulation comes the disappointment of substitution: the woman-object of all desire, all fantasy, suddenly yields to the *object-woman*. This inversion, the symptom of a vast explosion of tangible reality, is merely the effect of crossing the 'time barrier'; the barrier of this limit-time of the speed of electromagnetic light-waves that disqualifies not only the relative speed of the living being but all matter, all effective presence of other people. The result is a panic-stricken disjunction already clearly demonstrated by the scale of divorce and the exponential growth of single-parent families. To prefer the virtual being – at some remove – to the real being – close-up – is to take the shadow for the substance, to prefer the metaphor, the clone to a substantial being who gets in your way, who is literally on your hands, a flesh-and-blood being whose only fault is to be there, here and now, and not somewhere else.[1]

The great mutation of remote-action teletechnologies will, in fact, only have helped tear us away from the dimensions of the world as we know it. Whether steam engine (train) or combustion engine (automobile, aeroplane), the acceleration of techniques of propulsion will have caused us to lose touch with tangible reality. The aviator waxes nostalgic: 'The plane tears you away, makes you live dangerously, offers you happiness, brings you back when it's good and ready! The plane is the only thing I've ever really loved' (Claude Roy).

At the foot of the wall of time, of this *global* time that has superseded *local* time, there is indeed another explosion, another supersonic **bang** that signals the loss of reality of the man or woman one none the less claims to be meeting up with or to love.

As with the nozzle on the jet engine of a machine capable of breaking the sound barrier, everything comes together in long-distance love, thanks to the power of ejecting others, to this ability to ward off their immediate proximity, to 'get off on' distance and make headway in sensual pleasure the way jet propulsion propels the jet. So, just as the supersonic aircraft's take-off enables it to *overfly* Mother Earth and the geography of the continents, so the 'remote manipulation' of jet-propelled love allows partners to *overcome* their reciprocal proximity without risk of contamination, the electro-magnetic prophylactic outdoing by a long shot – and how! – the fragile protection of the condom.

What was till now still 'vital', copulation, suddenly becomes optional, turning into the practice of remote-control masturbation. At a time when innovations are occurring in artificial fertilization and genetic engineering, they have actually managed also to interrupt coitus, to short-circuit conjugal relations between opposite sexes, with the aid of biocybernetic (teledildonic) accoutrements using sensor-effectors distributed over the genital organs.

'*The deepest thing in man is his skin,*' Paul Valéry once claimed. This is where the very latest perspective comes in: the *tactile perspective* of so-called 'touching at a distance' (tactile telepresence), which now puts the finishing touches on the classic perspectives of sight and hearing. And we cannot begin to understand the outrageousness of cybersexuality without this *paradoxical cutaneous perspective*.

In donning the DataSuit, *the individual slips into information*; his body is suddenly endowed with a second skin, with a muscle and nerve interface that fits over his own cutaneous layer. For him, for both of them, information becomes the sole 'relief' of corporeal reality, its unique 'volume'.

With this 'overwear', literally woven out of electronic impulses coding and decoding each of their emotions, partners in virtual love engage in a cybernetic process in which the operator console is no longer satisfied just to synthesize images or sounds. From now on, it orchestrates sexual sensations.

We have had *chemical suppressants*, psychotropic drugs. Here is the *electronic suppressant* – only, the desired effect is the reverse. It is now no longer a matter of damping down a momentary madness, but of whipping madness up, driving it to a frenzy. And this frenzy is contagious, transmitted instantaneously. They say that old priest of the American psychedelic movement, Timothy Leary, made long-distance love with a Japanese woman living in Tokyo.

At the heart of this cyberculture, the same old law operates as always in the technical arena: the *law of least action*.

After the transport revolution, which once promoted the honeymoon in Venice or somewhere, the age of the revolution in *amorous transport* is upon us, largerly fostered by the development of the tools of the instantaneous transmission revolution.

The virtual consummation of the *act of the flesh* being to turned-on couples what the virtual community already is to a lay society of **internet** subscribers, we will in the near future see a phenomenal divorce rate.

Indeed, if industrial technologies have progressively favoured the decline of the *extended* family of the rural world and promoted the *bourgeois*, and then the *nuclear*, family (so aptly named) at the time of the last century's urban expansion, the end of the supremacy of physical proximity in the megalopolis of the post-industrial age will not content itself with promoting a boom in the *single-parent* family. It will go on to provoke an even more radical gap between men and women, thereby directly threatening the future of sexual reproduction. Parmenides' great divide between masculine and feminine principles will widen further as a result of the very performance of love at a distance.

*   *   *

Let us turn now to the reasons for the amazing privileging of sexual reproduction in the evolution of the animal species, when parthenogenesis seemingly offered a more economical alternative. At the end of a long project, doctors Stephen Howard and Curtis Lively of Indiana University have recently come to the conclusion that the commingling of genes which all sexual reproduction implies allows the risk of extinction to be reduced to a minimum where species are faced with various infections, but especially, where they are faced with predictable mutations of the species. Now, there is just one single mutation that nature overlooked: the mutation of bio-technology.

With the development of the technosciences of the living organism – research on the human or procreant genome – which we are seeing today, the biosphere and technosphere are merging thanks, on the one hand, to the feats of nanotechnologies, and to those of computer science, on the other; and we can only expect further drifts before too long, further noisy mix-ups in genetic information. One of the most amazing examples of this is not the *test tube baby* of in-vitro fertilization but in fact, and sooner than you think, *love experienced at a distance*, thanks to telesexual interactivity.

We are here touching (so to speak!) on a paradox which consists in our *coming together at a distance* in future for exchange.

Let us examine for a moment what is lost, or at least in danger of being completely forgotten, in the practices of cybernetic sexuality, which even threatens to attack sexual reproduction itself, the desire for procreation already largely cauterized by our way of life.

Today, if immediate proximity is still clearly defined by *being here present*, tomorrow this situation risks becoming dangerously blurred or actually disappearing, taking with it the old rule of socializing: *You can tell a man by the company he keeps.*

But before going any further, we need to go back a moment over the role of mating dances in the animal kingdom and the courtship manoeuvres and 'engagements' that were once the prelude to 'nuptials' between spouses who would then 'found a line' with their offspring.

Traditionally, weddings were marked, on the one hand, by the voyage, the auspicious distancing that either preceded or followed the ceremony, and so kept alive the memory of the biological risks of the spouses' possible consanguinity.[2] And, on the other hand, by the actual *act of flesh*, a coupling which guaranteed that the marriage had indeed been consummated, copulation ensuring the legal reality of the contract.

But now nuptial rites are in turn feeling the impact of a way of life in which rushing around prevails over any reflection, to the point where, in the United States most notably, the popularity of the 'express marriage' clearly signals that future weddings will privilege the voyage over the 'wedding ceremony': the accelerated nomadism of the *drive-in marriage* will soon be outdone by a *virtual marriage* along the lines of what happened in 1995 at the Salon de l'Institut National de l'Audiovisuel in Monte Carlo, where telespouses exchanged their vows, decked out in video headgear and DataSuits.

From now on, distancing prevails over nuptial abduction; as, with teleconferencing, what counts above all is separation, the putting asunder of face-to-face parties; touch, physical contact between partners, being no longer the go so much as the rejection of the other person.

Hence the development of *sex tourism* and the setting up, here too, of worldwide child prostitution networks, as in Thailand, where this brand of *sexual diversion* represents more than 80 per cent of national revenue.

A bit like extreme mountaineering, where scaling a summit now counts less than how fast you can race across the mountain on a trail bike, sexual practices are preparing to **diverge**.

Like a reactor that can no longer keep up its production of nuclear energy and gears up to explode, *the couple that was the driving force* of history is entering divergence mode and gearing up to vanish into the ether. So much so that mutual repulsion is already winning out over attraction, over sexual seduction.

So, it is easy to see why there is such a sharp rise in *sexual harassment* complaints in the United States, why more and more women are bringing 'legal proceedings on the basis of alleged intentions' at the precise moment when the vogue in serial divorces has given way to a vogue in the series decay of the generator couple.

Despite appearances, this has nothing to do with morals or the permissive nature of postmodern society, since what we have here is chiefly a technological and anthropological phenomenon of unknown magnitude.

Potentially to be able to substitute a discrete *media-generated* disconnection for the immediate connection of bodies thanks to cybersex's bag of tricks is to trigger a process of *physiological and demographic disintegration* without precedent in history.

Far from reproducing the usual dichotomoy between the pleasure of the senses – the art for art's sake of the sex act – and the act of the flesh intended to engender family descendants, the teletechnologies of remote love are inaugurating not only a furtive form of *remote birth control*, but also the beginnings of a *hyperdivorce* that will eventually endanger the future of human begetting.

Leonardo Sciascia warned: 'When you lose sight of the facts anything can happen.' If the *virtual pleasure* of sexual telepresence were eventually to outstrip the *real pleasure* of embodied love, as is probable, soon the only societies left to ensure the continuation of the human race will be those that are underdeveloped and, worse, 'media'-deprived.

After having laid off callgirls, hot on the heels of 'streetwalkers', the cybernetics of future sex hotlines will shortly make redundant the male and female of a totally disqualified human race, to the advantage of the sex machines of media masturbation.

* * *

'The individual of the scientific age is losing his capacity to experience himself as a *centre of energy*,' observed Paul Valéry, applying his intuition to a little-explored area, that of the animate, of the movement that drives the living being. Indeed, the movement of living organisms remains an enigma: the enigma of life itself. 'Batting your eyelids, contracting your muscles or picking up speed if you're a runner all seem to emanate spontaneously *from within*, unlike the motion of a truck, a plane or a rocket, where the driving force comes from the sudden expansion of gas at high temperature; unlike, also, the motion of a sailing boat, of waves or even trees stirring in the wind, since movement here is imposed by external elements.'[3]

As sources of energy, vital organisms accordingly behave like 'biomolecular' complexes transforming light or chemical energy into whatever is necessary to life: motion, heat or inner equilibrium. But this *metabolic* transformation was until now tangible, psychologically speaking, the egocentration of living persons being identified not only with their health, but with their 'form', their being in top form in the morning, for instance, when the nerve impulses wake up and *wake us up*.

How do we interpret admission of defeat by someone like Valéry here? This loss that we anxiously sense within ourselves and around us, with the spread of passivity? Is it premature ageing due to stress, to living at a pace that overloads our reflexes and diminishes *proprioceptive* reflexion? Most likely. But there is another explanation, an *exteroceptive* one that concerns the different ways of driving the vehicles that convey us and aid us more and more frequently in our travels, our excursions.

Again, as I pointed out in an earlier work, it is revealing to consider the historic evolution of the various 'drivers' cabins'.[4] In the recent past, for instance, one drove in the open air, in contact with the atmosphere, listening to the sound of the engine and the wind, and feeling the cell of the machine vibrate; but today excessive speed has contributed to the driver's being gradually shut away, initially behind the screen of his goggles, then behind the windscreen and finally, *right inside the sedan.*

Pioneers drove 'by instinct'; this gave way to driving 'by instrument' and then to 'automatic' steering, to say nothing of the remote-control piloting which an unbelievable assortment of machines have these days.

How can we fail to see that the love relationships will suffer exactly the same fate, with the cybernetic steering of disunited lovers? The remote piloting of sensations and so of physical enjoyment will one day soon echo the loss of contact with the body of that voluptuous 'speed machine' that envelops the driver so closely that an expert, Ayrton Senna, once claimed he not only slipped into his flameproof Formula One driver's bodysuit, *but that he also literally put on his racing car.*

With the body's loss of a sense of its own energy, what is being played out, in a word, is a whole new episode in the history of prosthetics which is a history of debilitation, to put it mildly. In the view of Leroi-Gourhan for one, tools or instruments of any kind were supposed to extend man's organs, as with the fist improved by the hammer, the hand by pliers or tongs, and so on. This is not too hard to swallow in relation to *mechanics*, but it loses all credibility when we move from the notion of *mass* to the notion of *energy* (in particular, electrical energy) and, particularly, to the notion of *information* as the third dimension of matter. Indeed, when *mechanical relays* yield to *electrical relays* the break becomes obvious: the body gets disconnected so completely that the electromagnetic impulses of the new *remote control* end, which channel surfing, for instance, in the behavioural inertia of the individual; the law of least action finally winds up in cybersexuality, pulling the plug on the animate being of the Lover.

With 'biomechanical' *extension* on the one hand and 'energy' ablation on the other, the individual of the technoscientific age effectively loses the capacity to *experience himself* as a centre of energy; he becomes useless and will eventually become totally superfluous when faced with the *automation* of his productive and perceptual functions.

'Only a new way of getting pleasure can save us,' declares one of cyberculture's advertising slogans.

In a very short poem on acceleration, Saint-Pol Roux put this desire well, speaking of transport:

Going faster is playing with death.
Going even faster is getting off on death.[5]

This hits the nail on the head as far as the capabilities of instantaneous transmission go.

With zoophilia now bowing out before the nascent technophilia of long-distance love, so begins 'the game of love and chance', a game of pathological inertia bound up with the triumph of comfort and emotional self-sufficiency.

'For whoever has understood that he is mortal, the pangs of death begin,' observed Arthur Schnitzler. To get off, if not on death itself, then at least on the death throes of its virtual presence, on a gradual paralysis of one's faculties, is indeed the as-yet unavowed stake of 'teleoperations', in which divided lovers are no longer there together except via their respective remote controls, the ghost of the emission-reception of an energy signal now replacing orgasm. Games of reciprocal electrocution of which laboratory rats once had a little foretaste before going under the knife.

By way of comparison, let us look at another kind of death rattle of presence in the world: Alzheimer's disease, the senile dementia that affects the tangible reality of the subject.

Cut off from a body that has become independent from his mind, *the victim is not there for anyone, not even for himself.*

Unconscious, subject to irreversible memory lapses and to spatial and temporal disorientation, he *ceases to exist in the here and now*, only occasionally to wake up completely out of sync with his environment, no matter how hard nursing staff may try to offer a few spatiotemporal pointers in the patient's brief periods of alertness to force him, if only for a moment, to maintain some connection with his body, some relationship with those around him.

At the precise moment when reality is not what it was, the victim escapes to a world of his own in a pathological virtuality not dissimilar to the *cyberpathology* of divided lovers, skilled players of an interactive game that keeps them apart, in the middle of a virtual space that no one but they will ever know. *Cybernauts* of a precocious dementia, that enables each one of us to plug into any network whatsoever where *sexual harassment* is not only tolerated, but actively encouraged (by subscription), 'telesexual' decentralization cleverly completing that of the electronic workplace.

*   *   *

Sex no longer exists; it has been replaced by fear.

Fear of the other, of the dissimilar, has won out over sexual attraction. After the struggle against the gravity of weighty bodies and all the research done on techniques of levitation and weightlessness, there begins a similar war on that universal attraction that enables the species to survive: genetic engineering, artificial fertilization and so on are all permutations of the same assault on the living being.

'If the act of procreation were neither the outcome of a desire nor accompanied by feelings of pleasure, *but a matter to be decided on the basis of purely rational considerations, is it likely the human race would still exist?'* asks Schopenhauer in his essay on the metaphysics of love.[6]

A century later, cybernetic research into sexual hijacking once again poses the question of knowing where this separation of bodies, this *diastase* of the living, will land us.

After the various 'unnatural' *perversions*, new alternative practices of love are emerging: complex *diversions* these, no longer 'animal' and zoophile, but 'mechanical' and blatantly technophile.

But what really lurks behind this panic-stricken withdrawal, this retreat, before the act of the flesh? Fear of catching AIDS or other fears, other, disavowable terrors?

Mysteriously, the science of machines exiles us both from the geophysical world and from the physical body of another who always contradicts my ego and whose vital necessity is a mere shadow of what it once was in the age when the reign of the animal in all its energetic power still dominated the *synthetic*, or rather *surrogate, energies* that have since carried the day.

Defeat of the facts before the proliferation of information, itself *synthesized* to an incredible degree by mass communication tools, in which the image is already more important than the thing which it is never anything more than an 'image' of. But also – and this is what matters to us here – *defeat of the fact of making love*, here and now, to the benefit of a mechanical medium in which 'distance' once more becomes *distentio*, distension and dissension between partners, the game of love and chance becoming a vulgar *parlour game*, a sort of virtual casino, not unlike the stock exchange where, on those celebrated *derivatives markets*, traders and other golden boys amuse themselves breaking the bank the whole year long.

Here is Schopenhauer again on the subject of sexual interest – forgetting financial interest for the moment – apropos the coming cybernetic monopolization of sensual pleasure: 'This interest, which is the source of all commerce in love, from the most passing fancy to the most serious passion, remains for each of us the truly great affair, the one whose success or failure touches us most keenly, from which it derives the name, par excellence, of "love affair".'[7]

Imagine for a moment that the oldest profession in the world were to become the biggest 'multinational' there is; better still, that the consumer society, looking beyond the products currently available at the supermarket, were shortly to turn into a telesexual consumer society. The multimedia world would no longer just be the casino so loudly decried by economists but an actual brothel, a *cosmic brothel*, the startling commercial success of the sex hotline repeating itself ad infinitum thanks to the prowess of interactive telecommunications.

But another aspect of the emergence of sexual diversion becomes clear, reinforced as it is by the maniacal individualization that, with the demographic crisis, threatens our society. As we all know from experience of our own relative lack of philanthropy: '*The intensity of love is tied to a very obstinate selectivity.*'[8] So conditions of life in the world-city, with the decline in the family as a unit, will further accelerate the self-sufficiency of the hardened celibate, thereby bolstering the quest for intensity, 'extreme sports' more and more frequently finding their equivalent in the search for high-risk sexual experiences.

Indeed, if the existence of the social body patently comes before the existence of the animal body that it generates, and if 'being per se resides in the species more than in the individual', contemporary individuation menaces the persistence of being at every turn.[9]

'Well, what other subject could be of greater interest than that which touches on the good or the bad of the species? *For the individual is to the species what the surface of the body is to the body itself.*'[10]

Surface still, not so long ago, with the incomparable depth of the skin (Valéry); **interface** today, thanks to the performance of telecommunication between bodies **indivi** which achieves the paradox of a **totalitarian individualism** by enabling not only 'remote union' (teleconferencing), but also the telesexual union of genital sensations; **hyperdivorce** for a humanity united in its very disunity, whereby *interactivity* produces a disintegration of bodies analogous to the disintegration of the elementary particles of matter caused by *radioactivity*.

It is hard to resist comparing Schopenhauer to Heidegger here. According to Heidegger, technology *really* accomplishes metaphysics; but *cybernetics* will *virtually* achieve the 'metaphysics of love' – to the detriment of the species and its sexual reproduction.

'**Cyberfeminism** participates in the development of a feminist consciousness and emphasizes the importance of the multimedia in perception of the body.'[11] With these words a new group begins its manifesto. Taking up the terms of an article that appeared in *Socialist Review* ten years ago, the women's collective continues: 'Communication technologies and biotechnologies *are important tools that enable us to reinvent our bodies* . . . The emergence of post-industrial culture is going to entail a profound change in human societies. *Similarly, the sensory and organic architecture of the human body, sexual and cultural identities, indeed our modes of thinking, and the place each of us occupies will be modified.'*

Further extending this statement of the obvious political and cultural importance of **cyberspace** in moral liberation, the author finally poses the key question of control: '*Who will in future generate the codes and the specifications by which bodies will be represented in cyberspace where everything exists as metaphor?* This already depends on the manner in which cybernauts choose to engage with the virtual body.'

Cyberfeminism then weighs in with the big question of political responsibility in the construction of such a body, 'a truly revolutionary subject': 'What will happen to the social relationships of sexuality, the body's sexual modes of communicating, desire and sexual difference in the age of the coded metaphor? *Control of interpretation of the body's boundaries is a truly feminist issue.*'

As one can readily appreciate, at a time when the boundaries between biology and technology, man and the machine, are being effaced one by one, it is simply high time we took a fresh stand. Hence the final appeal: 'It is urgent that women participate in the construction of cyberspace by developing a **cyberimaginary** capable of becoming a tool of their own self-construction. If it is true that the multimedia can be a formidable instrument of control and subjugation, it is up to us women to turn it into a tool of emancipation.'

Much more than a manifesto of militant feminism, this text already has the ring of a cry of alarm in the face of a mechanical surrogacy that would supplant the carnal attractions of femininity. Despite a whole host of surrogates for sexual organs (vibrators, dildos), simulation has in fact already ceased to be viable since it is itself about to be given a new twist through 'alternative' practices in which the hyperrealism of the virtual body would be to the flesh what drugs are to the mind – a deadly addiction to narcotics heralding what will, in the near future, become the implacable imaginary of **cybersex**.

'**Speed: the coitus of the future**' prophesied, over half a century ago, Saint-Pol Roux, the surrealist specialist in a living cinema capable of engendering a human race full of spectators: '*O camera womb, dare to really give birth!* Flattened images, swell into relief! Make those French letters reek of sex, breathe life into all those hollow windbags.'[12]

Today, it is in the can. Thanks to the force-feedback control glove (DataGlove) and, especially, to the DataSuit, *everything is ruled by lightning*, and the *coup de foudre* of disunited lovers suddenly becomes a *coup de grâce*. From erotic entertainment we then move on to sexual diversion and shortly to a fatal divergence – that of the reactor that sets off nuclear fission.

It's a very thin line between *ecstasy* and *diastase* for, in future, it is at the speed of electromagnetic radiation that cybernetic orgasm will occur.

In effect, if distancing brings (interactive) lovers together to the point where they manage *to love those far-off as they do themselves*, the gap between the wedding and the divorce will have been closed once and for all.

By way of a provisional conclusion, let us review the early ethical reactions to this telematic mutation in sexuality. In an apostolic letter published in 1994, in honour of the International Year of the Family, Pope John Paul II declared: 'Union and procreation cannot be *artificially* separated without altering the intimate truth of the conjugal act itself.'[13]

Far from chiming in as a simple rejection of contraception or the usual repetition of the indissoluble nature of the bonds of marriage, this statement points to another major question: the question of the nature of the separating **artefact**. What *artificial construct* are we in fact talking about when even bodily union is eclipsed by a virtual telesexuality that advocates the *separation of bodies* and no longer just divorce?

What happens not only to the future of holy matrimony, but also to divorce, when they are now literally dissolving, not the *couple*, but *copulation*?

More recently still, at a congress held in Rome in the spring of 1995, experts from the Catholic Church launched an appeal against the all too predictable development of cybernetic love. Denouncing such interactive practices as a 'catastrophe for love', the Roman contingent noted that the sex industry now offers lovers *'an illusory and artificial space, an easy way out of people's inability to deal with each other responsibly'*, and that the best of all possible worlds of the remote consummation of sex with one or more partners is never anything but a denial of human coupling, being no longer merely an accident of marriage, like adultery or divorce, but a denial of the very reality of the 'act of the flesh' and so of true knowledge of the other for, in biblical terms, *to know the other is to love him*.[14]

As we have seen, the 'information revolution' that has today superseded the revolution in industrial manufacturing is not without danger, for the damage done by progress in **interactivity** may well be as harmful in the future as that done by **radioactivity**. The 'computer bomb' previously denounced by Einstein will shortly necessitate a new type of *deterrence*: no longer military and nuclear, as it had to be when the major danger was the 'atomic bomb', but this time political and societal. Unless social disintegration has already entered an irreversible phase, with the decline in the nuclear family and the boom in the population unit of the **single-parent**.

Notes

1. 'I like having the kids, but I don't want them on my hands', an ad for the *Nouvelles Frontières* travel agency chain.

2. In ancient China, being carted off in the bridal wagon was an essential part of the wedding ceremony.

3. Dan Urry (1995), 'Les Machines à protéine', in *Pour la Science*, February.

4. Paul Virilio (1984), 'La Conduite intérieure', in *L'Horizon Négatif*, Paris.

5. Saint-Pol Roux (1973), *Vitesse*, Paris.

6. Schopenhauer (1970), 'On the suffering of the world', in *Essays and Aphorisms*, trans. R. J. Hollingdale, London, pp. 47–8.

7. Schopenhauer (1913), 'On the suffering of the world' (untranslated parts of chapter 7 of *Parerga und Paralipomena*, Munich).

8. Ibid.

9. Ibid.

10. Ibid.

11. 'En attendant', in *Lettre d'Information de la Maison de Toutes les Chimères*, no. 3, December 1994.

12. Saint-Pol Roux (1972), *Cinéma Vivant*, Paris.

13. *Le Monde*, 23 February 1994.

14. P. Georges (1995), 'Le Cybersexe à l'index', in *Le Monde*, 15 March.

CHAPTER FIFTEEN

Delirious New York

The architecture profession in the 1990s spawned a number of international celebrity architects who also did 'theory', including the Dutch master Rem Koolhaas. The 1993 essay by Paul Virilio reprinted here has the same title as Koolhaas' well-known book about the architecture of the iconic American city published later in the 1990s. In 1996 Editions Galilée in Paris published *Un Paysage d'Evénements*, a collection of a series of pieces by Virilio on the 'events' of the previous twelve years. The idea, Virilio told Lotringer in 1997, was that the book was a 'countdown'. Essentially, Virilio was turning the clock back on the 'mediated blitzes' (the Berlin wall, the Gulf War, the implosion of the Soviet Union) from 1984 to 1996. The novelty of the order of the book was it started, after a brief 'calling card' introduction, with a short essay written on 15 May 1996 then 'we trace things backwards '96, '95, back to '84' so that 'you get a sense of the modification of history' collapsing 'twelve years in which everything happened'. It was, for Virilio, a 'travelogue in time' and an 'impressionistic work'. The dates of the composition of the original French language short essays were attached at the end of each piece, going all the way back to 15 November 1984. In 2000 Massachusetts Institute of Technology Press published an English translation by Julie Rose of a selection of most, but not all, of the original book's essays in their 'Writing Architecture' series, with a telling introduction by fellow guru from the French architectural milieu Bernard Tschumi. Tschumi, along with superstar architect Daniel Libeskind, had originally collaborated with Paul Virilio and Claude Parent on the thirtieth anniversary edition of *Architecture Principe* in 1996. 'New York Délire' was originally composed on 30 March 1993 and, as can be seen here, consisted of Virilio's account of the first World Trade Center bombing in New York on 2 February 1993.

'Delirious New York', in *A Landscape of Events*, trans. Julie Rose, Cambridge, MA: MIT Press, 2000.

The attack on the World Trade Center is the first of the post-Cold War. No matter who is responsible, it ushers in a new era of terrorism having nothing in common with the explosions that regularly rock Ireland or England.

Indeed, the outstanding feature of the attack is that it was seriously intended to bring down the World Trade Center building; in other words, to bring about the deaths of tens of thousands of innocent people. In the manner of a massive aerial bombardment, this single bomb, made of several hundred kilos of explosives placed at the building's very foundations, could have caused the collapse of a tower 400 metres high. So it is not a matter of a simple remake of the film *Towering Inferno*, as the image-conscious media like to keep saying, but much more of a strategic event confirming for us all *the change in the military order of this fin-de-siècle*.

As the bombs of Hiroshima and Nagasaki, in their day, signalled a new era for war, the explosive van in New York illustrates the mutation of terrorism.

Inaugurated by the collapse of the Berlin Wall and even more by the Gulf War, the end of the age of nuclear deterrence is today confirmed by the civil war in the former Yugoslavia but also by this luckily abortive attempt to bring down the New York tower.

Driven to a frightening escalation by the uncertainties of American foreign policy, and especially by the question mark hanging over young President Clinton's capacity to implement it – will he turn out to be a Kennedy or a Carter? – the enemies of Western policies are putting the adversary to the test! Though we too often forget, military intervention has not hung back waiting for the recent resolutions of the UN Security Council, with their 'humanitarian' dimension. The gunboat diplomacy of colonialism has long since been thoroughly revived by terrorist action, the offensive intervention of commandos more or less controlled by certain states as well as the fledgling power of narco-capitalism.

With the New York bomb, we thus find ourselves faced with

the latest escalation in the kind of military-political action that is based simultaneously on a limited number of actors and guaranteed media coverage. It has reached the point where soon, if we don't look out, a single man may well be able to bring about disasters that were once, not long ago, the province of a naval or air force squadron.

Indeed, for some time the miniaturization of charges and advances in the chemistry of detonation have been promoting a previously unimaginable equation: One man = Total war.

At the very moment that the United Nations is hoping to reestablish an international tribunal to try the authors of war crimes, it is equally urgent to severely punish terrorist practices, no matter what their source; otherwise we will look on, powerless, as this type of 'economical' operation suddenly proliferates, capable as it is of inflicting incredible damage not only on the innocent victims but also, and especially, on democracy.

After the age of the *balance of terror*, which lasted some forty years, the *age of imbalance* is upon us. The historic attack on the World Trade Center marks its beginning. A veritable big bang, this criminal act cannot continue to be downplayed for fear of causing panic for the inhabitants of the great metropolises. Indeed, there is no point in waiting for the future 'nuclear terrorism' to begin, if the states responsible or those more or less controllable organizations are already daring to take such action: trying to bring down one of the tallest buildings in the world to express their differences or their political opposition, regardless of whether they kill 20,000 or 30,000 people in the process. It is urgent that we protect ourselves effectively at the very moment that the American media are set to launch the Military Channel, which will broadcast documentaries and serials about war, weapons, and explosives twenty-four hours a day!

After New York on 2 February, it was Bombay on 13 March and Calcutta four days later, where new charges were exploded with the intention of destroying the stock exchange of India's economic capital and three buildings in the commercial district of Bow Bazaar, not far from the centre of the country's former colonial capital.

If we add to this the IRA's recent attack on the City of London, we find ourselves faced with a large-scale offensive from the proponents of terror. Even if there are clearly different causes and objectives involved, affecting regions with no apparent connection, no one can deny the catalogue of disasters that are today striking the world's great strategic centres.

In the United States, the World Trade Center is, as we know, an economic nerve centre; the same goes for the Bombay Stock Exchange or the City of London, and the Bow Bazaar of Calcutta is likewise an important business mecca in India.

Three hundred dead in Bombay and close to 1,000 seriously injured, fifty dead in Calcutta and close to 100 injured . . . Even though there were no more than five dead and ten seriously injured in New York, the terrorist dimension of such bomb attacks no longer has anything in common with the political petty crime of recent years. The perpetrators are determined not merely to settle the argument with guns now, but to try to devastate the major cities of the world marketplace.

We now find ourselves faced with a model of 'organized terrorism', and just as we speak of organized crime as opposed to classic petty crime in matters of public safety, we must get used to distinguishing between the 'petty terrorism' of the age of nuclear deterrence and this terrorism that, with the end of the Cold War, inaugurates the age of nuclear proliferation.

Yet we need to review the recent revolution in weapons systems to interpret a mutation that is qualitative as well as quantitative. From the beginning of the 1990s and particularly with the war in the Persian Gulf, we have seen the strategic emergence of 'communications weapons' that have superseded the traditional supremacy of 'weapons of destruction' and 'weapons of obstruction' – in other words, the duel of arms and armour.

After the three military fronts of land, sea, and air, we are seeing the gradual build-up of a fourth front: that of the power of information.

Let's not forget that international terrorism is inseparable from this *media front* and that terrorist attacks make sense and have political value only because of the televised publicity they invariably have at their disposal. With the telegenic quality of such atrocities constantly reinforcing their evocative power, certain countries, such as the former Soviet Union and Italy, have even gone as far as placing a blanket ban on media coverage of the worst terrorist atrocities (along with accidents).

If the miniaturization of destructive power can now allow a single man or a small commando unit to inflict damage similar to that of a broad-based military operation, it goes without saying that the mass war of the armies of yore risks being supplanted by some mass killer using the impact of the mass media to exert maximum pressure on international public opinion.

What is remarkable here is that the sudden proliferation of the 'molecular' terror of traditional explosives – in anticipation of the proliferation of 'nuclear' terror – is accompanied by a growing impoverishment of war. We are going back to the conflicts of the fifteenth century, to the *condottieri* and the great bands of brigands that once plundered the European countryside in the days of private wars . . . In the end, you don't need much money if you have enough charisma, religious or otherwise, to buy a band of paramilitary assassins.

This is what we see happening today, as much in the Balkans as in Medellín or Burma, within the golden triangle of drugs – not to mention the various mafias in Russia and elsewhere.

Note by way of provisional conclusion that the attack on the World Trade Center is testimony to the clever combination of a strong symbolic dimension and an urban demolition capability involving only a small number of individuals who used a delivery van to deliver terror. In the days of cruise missiles and the most sophisticated nuclear weapons carriers, you have to admit that this is a striking example of political economy!

30 March 1993

CHAPTER SIXTEEN

The Information Bomb

By the late 1990s Editions Galilée's 'Collection L'Espace Critique' series, run by Paul Virilio since the mid-1970s, was moving into over-drive, at least as far as the publication of original French language work by Virilio himself was concerned. In 1998 the cool cream 'hard' backs of Galilée (red titles, black author names) boasted another Virilio 'logic bomb' to go with his many others in the series, all of which sat so well with the best of the back catalogue by Jean Baudrillard, Félix Guattari, Georges Perec and Alain Joxe. The list 'dans la même collection' at the back of each book in the series was always a tribute to Virilio's quiet 'editorial' influence on the French intellectual scene for three decades. It also provided a convenient vehicle for most of his own writings. This latest work was entitled, simultaneously acknowledging Albert Einstein's influence on Virilio, *La Bombe Informatique*. After the Second World War, Einstein had conceptualized three stages of future social development: the atomic bomb, the computer or information bomb, and the population or genetic bomb. One key to the oeuvre of Paul Virilio is the fact that he does not stray too far from this schema, and in this particular work the title is explicitly Einsteinian. Much of *La Bombe Informatique* was made up of overtly journalistic pieces written by Virilio in the European media during 1996, 1997 and 1998. German, Swiss and Austrian newspapers were the source of several of the essays collected in the book. Virilio's status as a European public intellectual was being consistently confirmed in the 1990s and a host of often very brief interviews with him appeared in Europe at this time. Whereas his friend Jean Baudrillard, for instance, had been lecturing widely on the international circuit, especially in the United States, since the 1980s, Virilio rarely travelled outside his home city. In 2000 Verso in London and New York published an English translation, by Chris Turner, of *La Bombe* as *The Information Bomb*. The extract reprinted here is the last of fourteen short chapters in the book.

The Information Bomb, trans. Chris Turner, London: Verso, 2000.

With the end of the twentieth century, it is not merely the second millennium which is reaching its close. The Earth too, the planet of the living, is being closed off.

Globalization is not so much, then, the *accomplishment* of the acceleration of history as the *completion*, the closure, of the field of possibilities of the terrestrial horizon.

The Earth is now double-locked by the endless round of satellites and we are running up against the invisible outer wall of habitable space, in the same way as we bump up against the envelope, the firm flesh, of a liveable body. As mere men and women, mere terrestrials, the world for us today is a dead-end and claustrophobia an agonizing threat. Our metaphysical hopes have wasted away and our desires for physical emancipation are similarly withered.

The Earth of the great multiplication of the species is becoming, then, the colony, the camp of the great ordeal. Babel is returning – as cosmic ghetto, city and world all in one – and perhaps this time it is indestructible.

Less than 1,000 days before the end of a pitiless century, a series of facts, of events of all kinds, alerts us to an untimely emergence of limits, the end of a geophysical horizon which had till then set the tone of history.

Between the astrophysical suicide of the Heaven's Gate sect and the Assumption of Princess Diana, we had the announcement, the official annunciation of the genetic bomb, the unprecedented possibility of cloning human beings on the basis of a computer read-out of the map of the human genome.

Since then, thanks to the coupling of the life and information sciences, the outlines of a **cybernetic eugenicism** have emerged, a eugenicism which owes nothing to the politics of nations – as was still the case in the laboratories of the death camps – but everything, absolutely everything, to science – an economic techno-science in which the single market demands the commercialization of the whole of living matter, the privatization of the genetic heritage of humanity. Besides this, the proliferation of atomic weapons, freshly boosted by India, Pakistan and probably other destabilized countries on the Asian continent, is prompting the United States – the last great world power – to accelerate its famous 'revolution in military affairs' by developing that emergent strategy known as 'information war', which consists in using electronics as a hegemonic technology: a role it now takes over from nuclear physics.

The atom bomb can then be merely a last guarantee, provided of course that the information bomb effectively proves its credentials as the new absolute weapons system.

It is in this context of financial instability and military uncertainty, in which it is impossible to differentiate between information and disinformation, that the question of the **integral accident** arises once again and that we learn, at the Birmingham summit of May 1998, that the Central Intelligence Agency not only takes seriously the possibility of a 'widespread computer catastrophe' in the year 2000, but that it has scheduled this hypothetical event into its calendar, indicating on a state-by-state basis how far individual nations still have to go to forearm themselves against it.[1]

Similarly, the United States Senate announced the creation of a committee to assess this potential electronic disaster and the Bank of International Settlements in New York followed suit shortly afterwards, setting up a highlevel committee to attempt to forestall a **computer crash** in which the damage caused by the serial downturns in the Asian economies might produce global meltdown.

As the first great global manoeuvre in 'Information Warfare',[2] what we see here is the launch of a new logistics, that of the cybernetic control of knowledge: politico-economic knowledge, in which the single market affords a glimpse of its military and strategic dimension in terms of 'information transfer'. To the point where the *systemic risk* of a chain reaction of the bankruptcy of the financial markets (for so long masked during the

promotional launch of the internet) is now officially acknowledged, showing that this *major risk* can also be used to exert pressure on those nations which are reluctant to give in to free-trade
blackmail.[3]

As I pointed out some considerable time ago, if *interactivity* is
to information what *radioactivity* is to energy, then we are con-
fronted with the fearsome emergence of the 'Accident to end all
accidents', an accident which is no longer *local* and precisely sit-
uated, but *global* and generalized. We are faced, in other words,
with a phenomenon which may possibly occur everywhere
simultaneously.

But what we might add today is that this *global systemic risk* is
precisely what makes for the strategic supremacy of the future
'weapons systems' of the infowar, that electro-economic war
declared on the world by the United States and that, far more
than the viruses and other 'logical bombs' hidden away by
hackers in the software of our computers, this **integral accident**
is the true detonator of the **information bomb**, and hence of its
future power of deterrence over the political autonomy of
nations.

As the ultimate exemplar of monopoly, the **cyberworld** is thus
never anything else but the hypertrophied form of a cybernetic
colonialism, with the interconnectedness of the internet prefiguring the imminent launch of the **cyberbomb** – the future information superhighways – and, subsequently, the establishment,
still under the aegis of the United States, not just of an expanded
NATO but also of *new all-out defences* on the Cold War model,
with cyberglaciation here supplanting nuclear deterrence.

On 12 May 1998, again at the meeting of heads of state in
Birmingham, the American president, in his report on 'the strategy for controlling cybernetic crime', stressed the urgent need to
establish legislation against the **cybercrime** of mafias using
remote technologies and also against the risks involved in the
emergence of 'digital money', 'e-cash', which too easily evades
any economic control. 'Cybercriminals can use computers to raid
our banks . . . extort money by threats to unleash computer
viruses,' declared Bill Clinton,[4] explaining to the heads of state
present that the United States was in the front line of the battle

against this, but that 'international crime requires an international response. America is prepared to act alone when it must, *but no nation can control cybercrime by itself any more.'*[5]

It is hard to believe one's ears. The president of the state responsible for the greatest economic deregulation in history still seeks to pose as the first person daring to shout 'fire!' so as to lead a crusade against a chaos he himself has organized, together with his vice-president, prime mover in the creation of the future information superhighways.

The atom bomb, the information bomb and the demographic bomb – these three historical deflagrations evoked by Albert Einstein in the early 1960s are now on the agenda for the next millennium. The first is there, with the dangers of nuclear weapons becoming generally commonplace, as heralded in the Indian and Pakistani nuclear tests. And the second is also present, with the threat of cybernetic control of the politics of states, under the indirect threat of a *generalized accident*, as we have seen above.

As for the third, the demographic bomb, it is clear that if the use of computers is indispensable in the development of atomic weapons, it is equally indispensable in the decipherment of the genetic code and hence in the research aimed at drawing up *a physical map of the human genome*, thus opening up a new eugenicism promoting not the *natural* but the *artificial* selection of the human species.[6]

And given the considerable growth in the demography of our planet in the twenty-first century, are we not right to suspect that experiments on the *industrialization of living matter* will not be content merely to treat patients and assist infertile couples to have children, but will soon lead back to that old folly of the 'new man'? That is to say, the man who will deserve to survive (the superman), whereas the man without qualities, the primate of the new times, will have to disappear – just as the 'savage' had to disappear in the past to avoid cluttering up a small planet – and give way to the latest model of humanity, the **transhuman**, built on the lines of transgenic crops, which are so much better adapted to their environment than the natural products. That this is indeed the case is confirmed by the recent declarations of Professor Richard Seed on his attempt to achieve human cloning, or the statements of those who openly advocate the production of *living mutants*, which are likely to hasten the coming, after the extra-terrestrial, of the extra-human, another name for the super-human race which still looms large in our memories.

And is the 'human genome project', which has now been running for ten years and which is financed to the tune of $3 billion by the Department of Energy and the National Institute of Health for the purpose of deciphering DNA, anything other than a race at last to acquire the *data of life*, just as, in another age, the United States aimed for the moon by financing NASA?

It is always a race! Has not the geneticist Graig Venter just set up a private company with the aim of deciphering, in a project parallel to the public one, the whole of the genetic code *in just three years*, by linking up with a subsidiary of the pharmaceuticals group Perkin Elmer, who are specialists in DNA-sequencing machines, and doing this with an investment of just $200 million?[7]

After Kasparov's symbolic failure against the Deep Blue computer, the summer saga of the automatic Mars Pathfinder probe and the misadventures of the Mir space station, we are seeing the scheduled end of *manned flight* and a questioning of even the usefulness of the future international orbital station. This is the end of an 'extra-terrestrial' adventure for our generation but we have before us, by contrast, the spectacular launch of the 'extra-human' epic, as astrophysics gradually gives way to biophysics.

These are all so many signs of the imminent supplanting of macro-physical *exoticism* by micro-physical *endoticism*. A probable end to the external colonization of the space of distant lands and the dubious dawning of a colonization which will be internal – the colonization of the space-time of living matter, the new frontier of the will to power of the techno-sciences.

'*Homo est clausura mirabilium dei*', wrote Hildegard of Bingen, thus expressing a reality previously masked by the anthropocentrism of origins: man might not be said to be the *centre of the world*, but its closure, the *end of the world*. Significantly, this phrase was uttered by a woman born in the year 1098. It is a phrase which stands opposed to the eugenic myth by throwing a singular light on the origin of nihilism in the *omnipotence of the impotence* of sciences as soon as they reopen the question of the origins of life.

Genetic engineering is fundamentally eugenicist, but only the memory of the Nazi extermination requires it to admit this. Hence the seriousness of the *negationist threat*, not just against the prophetic memory of the death camps but against the principle of the continuity of the living, that 'principle of responsibility' towards the future of humanity.

This is a shamefully 'conservative' principle in the eyes of those who desire nothing so much as *the revolution of the end*, that nihilism of an omnipotent progress which runs through the twentieth century from the *Titanic* to Chernobyl, with an eye always to the coming of the **Survivor**, the messiah so fervently desired by the cult of madness of present times.

In fact, since the end of the Cold War we have been constantly trying to reproduce other ends on this identical pattern: the end of history, the end of representative democracy or, again, the end of the subject, by attempting to create the *double* (the clone) or the *hybrid* (the mutant) thanks to genetic manipulation.

Far from being some kind of achievement, this 'post-industrial' undertaking deploys *the energy of despair* in an effort to escape the conditions favourable to life and thus to arrive at chaos, or, in other words, to regress to the initial conditions which prevailed, as it is believed, before the origins of life.

Transgenic, transhuman – these are all terms which mark the headlong charge forward, in spite of all the evidence, of a *transpolitical* community of scientists solely preoccupied with acrobatic performances. In this they are following the example of those fairground shows mounted in the nineteenth century by the self-styled 'mathemagicians' . . .

Ultimately, this so-called postmodern period is not so much the age in which industrial modernity has been surpassed, as the era of the sudden *industrialization of the end*, the all-out globalization of the havoc wreaked by progress.

To attempt to industrialize living matter by *bio-technological* procedures, as is done in the semi-official project of reproducing the individual in standard form, is to *turn the end into an enterprise*, into a Promethean factory.

In the age of the 'balance of nuclear terror' between East and West, the military-industrial complex had already succeeded in militarizing scientific research to ensure the capability of mutual destruction – the 'MAD' concept. *Genetic* engineering is now taking over from the *atomic* industry to invent *its own* bomb.

Thanks to computers and the advances of bio-technology, the life sciences are able to threaten the species no longer (as in the past) by the radioactive destruction of the human environment, but by clinical insemination, by the control of the sources of life, the origin of the individual.

We can see now that, just as the total war outlined at the end of the First World War was to be actualized during the Second, threatening, between 1939 and 1945, with Hiroshima and Auschwitz, not the *enemy* but the human race, the **global warfare** prefigured today in the great manoeuvres of 'information warfare' will be based on scientific radicalization, threatening – not so much with extermination as with extinction – not a particular population or even the human race (as the thermo-nuclear bomb might), but the very principle of all individuated life, the *genetic* and *information* bombs now forming a single 'weapons system'.

Moreover, if information is indeed *the third dimension* of matter, after mass and energy, each historical conflict has in its time shown up the mastery of these elements. *Mass war*: from the great ancient invasions to the organization of the firepower of armies during the recent European wars. *Energy war*: with the invention of gunpowder and, most significantly, of atomic weapons, with the 'advanced' or high-energy laser still to come. And lastly, tomorrow, *the information war*, which will make general what espionage and police surveillance inaugurated long ago, though they were unable to draw, as we are today, on the limit-acceleration of 'global information'.

'He who knows everything fears nothing,' declared Joseph Goebbels, the head of the Propagandastaffel. In fact, here as elsewhere, the question is not so much one of fearing as of *spreading fear* by the permanent over-exposure of life, of all lives, to 'all-out' control, which is a *fait accompli* – or almost – thanks to computer technology. But let us go back for a moment to the third dimension of organized matter: whether it be speed of acquisition, transmission or computation, *information is inseparable from its acceleration in energy terms* – slowed-up information being no longer even worthy of that name, but mere background noise.

As we may recall, a journalist at the time of the creation of CNN offered the thought: 'Slow news, no news?'

In fact the limit-speed of the waves which convey messages and images *is the information itself*, irrespective of its content, to the point where Marshall McLuhan's famous formula has to be corrected: 'it is not the *medium* which is the message, but merely *the velocity* of the medium'. An ultimate and absolutely final velocity, which has just telescoped the 'time barrier', while tomorrow the photonic computer will calculate in perfect synchronism with the speed of light, which today promotes instantaneous telecommunications.

The 'information war' will soon be based, then, on *global interactivity*, just as the war of atomic energy was based on *local radioactivity* – and this will be so to the point that it will be entirely impossible to distinguish a deliberate action from an involuntary reaction or an 'accident'; or to distinguish an attack from a mere technical breakdown, as was already the case on 19 May 1998 (synchronizing almost perfectly with the Birmingham summit) when the Galaxy IV telecommunications satellite suddenly interrupted the messages of some 40 million American pager devotees after the device's on-board computer had slightly shifted the satellite's position. *An unforeseen accident or a full-scale test for infowar?*

It is impossible to be certain, but the affair immediately triggered a debate on the vulnerability of the USA to breakdowns in a technology essential to the life of the country.[8]

As one might imagine, the internet, the direct descendant of Arpanet, helped to keep certain American public services up and running, such as the NPR radio channel which resorted to the Net to re-establish the link with some of its 600 local stations.

We should not forget that the cybernetic system of the web was set in place more than twenty years ago to counter the electromagnetic effects of an atomic explosion at altitude and thus to forestall a generalized accident affecting strategic telecommunications.

If war has always been the invention of new types of destruction, the promotion of a series of deliberately provoked accidents (the 'war machine' is only ever the inversion of the productive machine), with the infowar which is currently in preparation the very notion of 'accident' is taken to extremes, with the extraordinary possibility of a *generalized accident* which, like a cluster bomb, would embrace a very great range of accidents of all kinds.

Not a local accident, as in the past, but a global one, capable of halting the life of a continent, if not indeed of several at once, as with the threat to the operation of our computers on the eve of the year 2000.

In the field of information warfare, everything is, then, hypothetical; and just as information and disinformation have become indistinguishable from each other, so have attacks and mere accidents . . . And yet the message here is not *scrambled*, as was still the case with the counter-measures in electronic warfare; it has become *cybernetic*. That is to say, the 'information' is not so much explicit content as the rapidity of its feedback.

Interactivity, immediacy, ubiquity – this is the true message of transmission and reception *in real time*.

Digital messages and images matter less than their instantaneous delivery; the 'shock effect' always wins out over the consideration of the informational content. Hence the indistinguishable and therefore unpredictable character of the offensive act and the technical breakdown.

The indeterminacy principle then spreads from the quantum world to that of a computerized information strategy which is independent – or almost independent – of the conditions of the geophysical milieu where its effects are nonetheless felt.

Thanks to the patient establishment of an interactivity extended to the whole of our planet, 'information warfare' is preparing the first world war of time or, more precisely, *the first war of world time*, of that 'real time' of exchanges between the interconnected networks.

We can easily see, then, that the current globalization of the market also has three dimensions to it: *geophysical*, *techno-scientific* and *ideological*. Hence the inevitable connection to be made between the United States' resolve to aim for global free trade by the period 2010–20[9] and the preparations for an information war.

It is, in fact, impossible clearly to distinguish *economic* war from *information* war, since each involves the same hegemonic ambition of making commercial and military exchanges interactive.[10]

Hence the repeated efforts of the World Trade Organization (WTO) to deregulate the various different national sovereignties with the MAI, the Multilateral Agreement on Investment, or, alternatively, with European Commissioner Leon Brittan's New Transatlantic Market.

One would in the end understand nothing of the *systematic* deregulation of the market economy if one did not connect it with the *systemic* deregulation of strategic information.

To render all exchanges **cybernetic**, whether they be peaceful or belligerent, is the discreet aim of the contemporary innovations of the end of this millennium. But here the very last 'fortress' is no longer the Europe of the EEC so much as the living human being – that isolated 'human planet', which has at all costs to be invaded or captured through the industralization of living matter.

Let us sum up: yesterday's was a *totalitarian war*, in which the dominant elements were quantity, mass and the power of the atomic bomb. Tomorrow's war will be *globalitarian*, in which, by virtue of the information bomb, the qualitative will be of greater importance than geophysical scale or population size.

Not 'clean war' *with zero deaths*, but 'pure war' *with zero births* for certain species which have disappeared from the **bio**-diversity of living matter.[11] The warfare of tomorow – and here it will be comparable with the 'desk murders' of yesteryear – will not be so much an affair of desks as of laboratories – of laboratories with their doors flung wide to the radiant future of *transgenic* species, supposedly better adapted to the pollution of a small planet held in suspension in the ether of telecommunications.

Notes

1. Micel Alberganti (1998), 'Un problème majeur pour la commauté internationale', *Le Monde*, 21 May.

2. In English in the original (Tr.).
3. As with the Multilateral Agreement on Investment and the New Transatlantic Market.
4. Aurélien Daudet (1998), 'Les chefs d'Etat contre le cyber-crime', *Le Figaro*, 16–17 May. The full text of this part of the speech, as published by the White House, reads: 'As Agent Riley's remarks suggest, cybercriminals can use computers to raid our banks, run up charges on our credit cards, extort money by threats to unleash computer viruses' (Tr.).
5. Ibid. The text of the speech as released by the White House refers simply to 'crime' here, not to 'cybercrime' as in *Le Figaro*'s report. The italics are Paul Virilio's (Tr.).
6. While Darwin, in *The Origin of Species*, had advanced the principle of the natural selection of the individuals fittest to survive, in 1860 his cousin, Francis Galton, proposed the principle of artificial selection or, in other words, a voluntary policy of the elimination of the least fit, thus institutionaliz-ing the struggle against the alleged degeneracy of the human species.
7. Fabrice Nodé Langlois (1998), '"Coup d'accélérateur" dans la course aux gènes', *Le Figaro*, 16–17 May.
8. 'Un satellite qui dévie et c'est l'Amérique qui déraille', *Libération*, 22 May 1998.
9. Martine Laronche (1998), 'Quelles limites au libre-échange?', *Le Monde*, 26 May.
10. On the control of flows of commercial imagery by the Pentagon, see the development of the National Imagery and Mapping Agency (NIMA).
11. Catherine Vincent (1998), 'Les Suisses conviés à un choix de société sur les biotechnologies', *Le Monde*, 27 May. For the first time a sovereign people was on 7 June 1998 to vote on the initiative for 'for genetic protection' aimed at reinforcing regulation with regard to transgenic manipulation.

CHAPTER SEVENTEEN

Strategy of Deception

Because Paul Virilio was a European-based 'telespectator', as well as an avid reader, he was ideally placed to write about the Kosovo war and the general unfolding of the Balkan atrocities and internecine conflict during the 1990s. His next book was published hot on the heels of the others, again by Editions Galilée, as *Stratégie de la Déception*, in 1999 in Paris, and it was intended to situate the Balkans and Kososvo in a regime of 'des problèmes politiques de l'Europe', as the back jacket of the French edition proclaimed. However, it was the role of 'l'OTAN' (NATO), 'celebrating' its fiftieth anniversary in the war in Yugoslavia, which took centre stage. The book consisted of four chapters, three of them written in April, May and June 1999 as articles for newspapers like the *Frankfurter Allgemeine Zeitung* in Germany and subsequently reprinted to form the bulk of this short contemporary treatise on Kosovo and end-of-the-century war. The fourth chapter was written afterwards as a kind of conclusion to the first three. Verso in New York and London published an English translation of all chapters by Chris Turner as *Strategy of Deception* in 2000. Turner's slight translator's preface is a delight, as he points out that 'la déception' in French normally means 'disappointment' but that Virilio is also using the term in the military sense of 'deflection' of missiles in a conflict from their intended course to another, less harmful destination. An English newspaper review of the book misleadingly saw it as a potentially lethal mix of Chomsky, Baudrillard and Foucault, but in fact, in the chronological order of the texts collected in this reader, it appears as an accessible and reasoned argument by an increasingly familiar Paul Virilio, growing into the role of a singular public intellectual accustomed to intervening in the everyday politics of international affairs as the new millennium dawned. The extract reprinted here was the fourth chapter of the original book, composed in July 1999.

Strategy of Deception, trans. Chris Turner, London: Verso, 2000.

Nothing is still a programme.
Even nihilism is a dogma
(Cioran)

In June 1999, the United Nations Food and Agriculture Organization (FAO) reported that thirty countries – sixteen of them in Africa – were suffering serious food shortages. One of the countries on that list was . . . Yugoslavia. *The desert is spreading*, they say. Yet it is not the desert that is spreading over the planet, but the *urban wasteland* – that place where, without ever mixing, the multitude of ethnic microcosms survive – in the shanty towns, the half-way hostels, the sink estates . . .

Recently, when some young North Africans were asked why they did not want to stay in the Maghreb and preferred to emigrate, they replied, with the simplicity that comes of stating the obvious: '*Because there's nothing here to take!*' They could just as well have said, '*Because it already looks like a desert here!*' The 'deportees' in the 'camps' of our urban wastelands are not, as our ministers go on joyfully repeating, 'savages' or even 'new barbarians'. In reality, they are merely indicating the irresistible emergence of a previously almost unknown level of deprivation and human misery. They are waste-products of a military-industrial, scientific civilization which has applied itself for almost two centuries to depriving individuals of the knowledge and skill accumulated over generations and millennia, before a post-industrial upsurge occurred which now seeks to reject them, on the grounds of definitive uselessness, to *zones of lawlessness* where they are exposed defenceless to the exactions of *kapos* of a new kind.

It is no use, then, speculating on the regional aspects of the

Yugoslav conflict when you understand that it is not the **world-city**, but the great **world urban wasteland** which now extends to the eastern portals of Europe. The great urban wasteland, with its bands of predators – such as the UCK or the Serbian irregulars – whose methods and excesses (kidnapping, extortion, torture, murder, arms and drug trafficking) shade dangerously into those of the mafia families and other 'honourable societies' of Europe, America and Asia.

Indeed, the Allies have learned to their cost in their offensive against the Serbs that the paramilitary groups they had armed were not very interested in *making war*. Indeed, they preferred to *thumb their noses at war, never coming together at any particular point*.[1] On the other hand, as soon as the Albanian refugees began to get back to Kosovo at the end of June, it was clear that the 'open frontier' enabled the leaders and bosses of the mafias from the Kukes and Tropoje regions to gain a foothold in the country. 'There are more and more big cars about on the roads, with tinted windows and Albanian number plates or no number plates at all,' writes a correspondent. 'Two days ago, these men of the shadows and the shady deals reached Mitrovica and Pristina, having first established a base in the Pecs region.[2]

The fluidity of this criminal osmosis largely explains the spread of chaos and ruin in Latin America and Africa where, as Jimmy Carter observed, crossing the continent the traveller is constantly passing through countries that are prey to conflicts which are of interest to no one. And, we might add, to conflicts *which never end*. Balkanization, Sicilianization, endo-colonization are merely the outdated words for this permanent warfare, which is no longer *civil* war, but war *waged against civilians* – this perpetual menace which, sooner or later, causes the emigration, in panic, of (pillaged, ransomed and raped) local populations towards the last lands of Cockaigne where *the rule of law* still exists. This tragic curbing of *popular rights*, which signals the fundamental reversal that is currently occurring on a ruined planet, where *there will soon be nothing left to take*. We need be in no doubt that, more than ever in the twenty-first century, the abandonment of the old *anthropocentrism* will be on the agenda. With the appearance of new forms of bio-political conditioning, in which the *other* will no longer be considered as an *alter ego*, nor even as a potential enemy (with whom reconciliation is always possible), but as the ultimate quarry. Neitzsche had, in his day, predicted the imminent arrival of this new misanthropy – *an anthropophagy which would have no particular ritual*, as he put it. Unless . . . unless the revolutionary innovations of the biotechnologies, by abolishing the last taboos of a degenerate humanism, have not already taken us, without our knowing it, into this new biocracy.

A new aspect which has emerged – ten years after the ideological collapse of the Soviet Union – and which reveals this imminent mutation, is the breakdown we have seen in the Balkans of the *moral front* which previously claimed to justify Western military interventions in the name of the 'defence of the values of the free world'.[3] The discreet abandonment of the old 1940s 'programmes for world peace' explains why being spokesperson for – or, even worse, commentator on – the parade of American technology in the Balkans, was the most hazardous job in the NATO hierarchy:

> In forty days of conflict, three high-ranking officers have already fallen in the information war. None was up to the job: with their confused comments, contradictory explanations and flagrant untruths, they had to be dropped for lack of credibility . . . It is to be hoped that the next one to go over the top in the media war will last out for more than a week.[4]

As a TV reporter on the French channel TF1 was to say, '*They don't know how to handle this business at all.*'

If the *phoney war* in Kosovo was not to become a *dirty war* in the eyes of international opinion, it was urgent, as Pierre-Luc Séguillon observed on 28 May on LCI,[5] that

> Slobodan Milosevic should at last be charged by the International Criminal Tribunal for the former Yugoslavia so as to legitimate the Allies' campaign and a war unleashed by NATO in violation, not only of the UN Charter, but also of the Charter of the Atlantic Alliance – the former authorizing recourse to armed action only to enforce a decision of the Security Council, the latter stipulating that the Alliance is a defensive organization and that its members are committed to settling any dispute in which they might be involved by peaceful means.

In fact, nothing of these ideal dispositions remained when, on 2 June, shortly after Milosevic was charged by prosecutor Louise Arbour, the International Court of Justice at the Hague declared inadmissable the action brought by Serbia requesting a halt to the Allied bombing.[6] This rejection on the part of the oldest court of law of the United Nations received virtually no coverage in the Western media.

Extraordinarily, the 'justice of nations' discreetly retreated behind the International Criminal Tribunal for the Former Yugoslavia (ICTY), that makeshift judicial structure, which was called upon to provide an illegal war with a hasty legitimacy, but which had every need to legitimate its own existence, as indeed was underscored by Jean-Jacques Heintz on 7 June 1999 during a conference organized by the Nantes law faculty. This French law officer, clerk to the ICTY, declared in effect that the body was a 'judicial laboratory' *which, in order to justify its existence*, had at first tried to pick up 'a few little cases' and was not, indeed, empowered to call suspects before it.

Yet, on that very day, we learned that two Bosnian Serbs, charged by this 'court of experimental justice', had been arrested by British KFOR soldiers at Prijedor in the north-west of Bosnia. This raised to thirty-one (out of sixty-six) the number of those charged with 'minor offences' who had fallen into the hands of a police that was both military and anational, as NATO confirmed on 18 June when it issued a mandate to the forces deployed in Kosovo to assist the ICTY's investigators . . . while awaiting the expected arrival of the FBI.

States of emergency, special tribunals – between the countless exactions of the one side and the 'judicial laboratories' of the other, one wonders, with Jack London's Mr Owen, whether, in the near future, there will still be *'such a thing as civil law'* on the planet.[7] As for that 'floating sea of opinions' on which the new international legislation is doing its best to chart a course, the question arises why one type of aggression (the primitive type – Milosevic's) is judged criminal by the ICTY, whereas another (the high-tech type – NATO's) was not even worthy of consideration by an international court of law like that at the Hague? Is this because, since the conflict in the Persian Gulf, American forces have boasted endlessly of the 'surgical precision' of their strikes? One might, as a consequence, suppose that a just war would be one characterized by justness of aim, the high technological level of an attack becoming the warrant of its morality and legality . . . Yet, since the middle of the Serbian affair, NATO lost this presumption of high-tech innocence when it brutally intensified its bombing, thus revealing its desire to do lasting harm to all the civilian populations of the region by the systematic destruction of their habitat.

As a result, opinion began to turn against the Allies, everyone coming to ask late in the day whether this humanitarian war and its high-tech arsenal did not in reality form a kind of Jekyll and Hyde pairing. If we held to the high-tech credo of the good doctor Jekyll, every method of spreading violence to inflict maximum pain on civilian populations should have been excluded as a matter of course from this conflict – such as those *long-term indirect strategies* with which, unfortunately, Mr Hyde is only too familiar, involving the application of economic blockades (Cuba, Libya, Iraq, etc.), which create social, sanitary and institutional paralysis . . . or the support given to powerfully armed paramilitary groups (Joseph Kennedy's Katangans, the Khmer Rouge, the Taliban, the UCK), promoting the spread of the lawless no-go areas of the world's urban wastelands. We can see, then, that all the current legal cavilling is merely a smokescreen – disinformation on an industrial scale – aimed at masking the breakdown of the apparent *equity* which, until the Kosovo affair, seemed to prevail between the great democratic nations. Lawyers *sans frontières*, judges *sans frontières*, an attempt to create an ICT (International Criminal Tribunal) at the Hague, a pale imitation of the ICTs for Yugoslavia and Rwanda, in which three of the world's major nations, two of them permanent members of the Security Council (the USA and China), refuse to participate.

The old international relations will not survive the disappearance of this *impartiality* – this moral justice independent of law – which claimed to undergird the armed actions jointly decided by the allies of the old UN Security Council.

When the edifice of the law *ceases to be a safeguard and becomes a threat*, it is difficult to believe in the discrediting, blatant though it is, of courts which are the legacy of an already long-standing established order. In the Balkans, it was no longer a question of instituting a *just war*, but a *legitimate* or even a legalist war – a war tailored to the interests of the world's last superpower and its absolute supremacy, particularly in the fields of satellite surveillance and information-gathering.

As in the old, statolatrous days of the ancient Romans – whom the Americans have always fervently admired – any activity, head of state or leader seen as threatening by this new unilateral legalism is now to be pursued, deposed, destroyed and punished for the crime of anti-Americanism. McCarthyism in the 1950s gave us an idea of this legalism, before the many bombardments carried out without a mandate in Iraq and elsewhere brought it into even clearer focus. A Livy-style legalism, a new cadastral law, exercized from space by the United States, on the lines of the old centuriation: 'the indelible mark of a seizure of the Earth, where a division is made in order to dominate, this being the basis of the education of the masses.'[8] 'Tremble and obey!' The end of the balance of nuclear terror and the new world supremacy of the United States required the restructuring of the old front of fear.

So, after the fall of the Berlin Wall, we saw the development of a strange 'defence of the human species', popularized in the media by any number of 'TV marathons' and other interactive shows (on social, health and ecological issues). In actual fact, these were intended to prepare people's minds for future large-scale humanitarian manoeuvres of a much less peaceful kind, such as those in Kosovo. Successful manoeuvres, since, on that latter occasion, one clearly saw 'the birth of an immense upsurge of solidarity in favour of the Kosovars, sustained by stars from show-biz, the cinema and finance'.

Here the *missionary* element of the colonial massacre or the *messianic* dimension of the world wars with their mass slaughter are supplanted by the *humanitarian* impulse – overcoming even religious affiliations, since Westerners were going to the aid of Muslim populations who were in principle hostile to them. '*Faith begins with terror*' – the theologian's device is as appropriate now as ever it was, war propaganda being, alongside the *propaganda fide* (the propagation of religious faith from which it derived), one of the oldest forms of marketing.

This is why it was so apposite, at the end of the balance of terror, to replace the shared fear of nuclear firepower – which I have termed the *nuclear faith* – with the administration of multiple intimate and quotidian terrors. Alongside an increasingly active *terrorisme ordinaire*, the public has thus been treated, during this last decade of the century, to the repellent advertising of the Benetton kind, or the lavish shows staged to combat AIDS or cancer, with the incurably disabled and the terminally ill being paraded before the cameras. *'Prevention is cure!'* Veiled threats, creeping eugenicism, secret terrors, causes of defiance, disgust and mutual hatreds. All this leading up to those high-frequency adverts depicting the misery of the unfortunate Kosovars, decidedly involuntary bearers of a subliminal message of the same order: 'See, none of us was safe. Women, children, the old, the rich, the poor – we all fled after losing everything. You have to prepare yourselves. If you're not careful, *it will be your turn tomorrow!'*

Without a doubt, the unprecedented exercise of the new right of intervention in the internal affairs of a sovereign nation would not have been accepted by public opinion were it not for this long psychological preparation, *this total cinema* born during the Cold War with the de-neutralization of the East–West media and, in March 1983, the signature by the actor-president Ronald Reagan of *National Security Decision – Directive 75*, the first draft of 'Project Democracy', calling for an increased American propaganda effort to accompany the measures of economic repression and military effort of the USA – a manna distributed mainly in *central and eastern Europe* to support the activities of minorities and free trade unions inside the nations of the Eastern bloc.

When, in April 1999, at the beginning of the Kosovo affair, Tony Blair declared that, in this conflict, the defence of the 'new values' should supplant the defence of the historical frontiers of nations, he was repeating word for word the terms of Reagan's old *Directive 75*. In May 1999, Theodoros Pangalos, the Greek minister of foreign affairs, observed of this *topological upheaval* of nations resolved upon by Washington, 'We're in the Balkans here. And if we change one of the frontiers today, nobody can say what they will be tomorrow.' Speaking from long experience, the

Greek minister knew that this was not a one-off operation that had been illegally unleashed in Kosovo, but a long process of the geographical decomposition of nations in Europe and throughout the world.

To the question posed so many times during the conflict, 'What does the United States want in the Balkans?', we should today substitute this other question: 'What did NATO want in the Balkans?' A large number of Americans who were hostile to the military action were content to believe, like former President Carter, that, if it was to retain its credibility, NATO could not change *what had already been done*! In other words, everyone was more or less aware of being *faced with a fait accompli*.

The time has come, then, it would seem, to call things by their names and to cleave strictly to the operational reality of the event: what we have witnessed in Kosovo has been *a globalist putsch*. That is to say, a seizure of power by an anational armed group (NATO), evading the political control of the democratic nations (the UN) – evading the prudence of their diplomacy and their specific jurisdictions. It then becomes easier to understand the extent to which this *purely revolutionary* state of affairs necessitated the *mass-consumption version* of the events we have had served up to us with the aim of obtaining a popular consensus. After the humanitarian stratagem, which was beginning to wear a little thin, came the judgement *'pour l'exemple'* of a serving head of state – a kind of Western-style *fatwa* affording the twofold advantage of convincing public opinion that the allied military intervention was justified and serving as a salutary warning to any head of government who might not subscribe to the mysterious *new values* dictated by the ICT.

Adherence to the military–humanitarian dimension replaced the military–liberatory, before being itself supplanted by the noble figure of the armed dispenser of justice. With providence playing its part here, it was announced during the first week in July that British KFOR troops had discovered Serb documents in Pristina proving 'the meticulous planning of ethnic cleansing by the Belgrade leaders'. To intensify the effect of this opportune discovery and give it full media value, a secret document was at the same time removed from the safe of a small library near Los

Angeles where it had lain for fifty-four years. That document was, we are told, the original of the Nuremberg Laws, a text, signed in Hitler's hand on the eve of the Nazi rallies of 1935, in which the 'final solution' already lay encoded.

In this connection, a journalist wrote: 'Dictators have always felt the need to give a semblance of legitimacy to their darkest schemes.'[9] As if it were not essentially the role of such 'revelations' to justify NATO's putsch and the succession of internal and external *coups d'état* which the old national entities can henceforth expect to suffer.

Similarly, the Albanian tragedy retrospectively casts light on the apparently nonsensical triggering of the Clinton/Lewinsky affair, which may now appear to have been a preparation of world opinion for the new military revolution. In 1998, the obscene attacks of Kenneth Starr and the worldwide broadcasting of Clinton's confessions made the president a global laughing-stock, but above all it made him *the plaything of the Pentagon*. It was also necessary, then, that in 1999 this adulterous president, former draft-dodger and defender of gays, who was held in contempt by a purportedly puritanical American army, should not be put out of office. At the time when the Kosovo conflict came about, President Clinton's poll rating was lower than it had ever been before, with many of his compatriots beginning to understand that the political power he was supposed to defend had, thanks to him, not only been made a laughing-stock, but also despoiled, and that the affair in the Balkans was perhaps *the beginning of the end* for the democratic model.

'*That which precedes the event is not necessarily its cause,*' claims the wisdom of the ancients. The century which is coming to a close has most often proved the opposite and no one can really claim to be safe from military–industrial and scientific determinism and determination – safe from that race to *the absolute essence of war* which, even in his day, Clausewitz imagined – war conceived as a 'whole, which must have one final determinate object, in which all particular objects must become absorbed'.[10] A race towards a global, universal state, deriving directly from the nuclear status quo, as outlined by the physicist Werner Heisenberg in *Physics and Philosophy* or, a little later, by Ernst Jünger.[11]

In this totalitarian dramaturgy, must we regard every item of information, every event as one of the 'particular objects' intended to be absorbed in this 'whole'? Eight weeks into the NATO bombing, the satellite broadcasting of Serb television (RTS) was to be interrupted, thereby effectively violating the principle of non-discrimination, which had until then been upheld by EUTELSAT, and once again flouting UN Security Council resolutions.

At the same time, an American State Department spokesperson formally denied rumours that the US was imminently to cut off internet connections between Yugoslavia and the rest of the world. Unlike the local, conventional television service, the **World Wide Web**, promoted in a multi-million dollar campaign at the end of the Gulf War, logically has its place in the Balkan conflict.

The internet is of military origin and has military purposes. In the field of information it plays more or less the same role as the *jamming* of enemy broadcasts in earlier world conflicts. As Negroponte has rightly remarked, with the 'liberation of information' on the web, what is most lacking is *meaning* or, in other words, a *context* into which internet users could put the facts and hence distinguish **truth** from **falsehood**. On the web, where, as everyone knows, the terrorist temptation is constant and where the depredations of hackers are committed with impunity in a strange state of legal indeterminancy, the difference between (true) information and (false) deception fades a little more each day. In entering the looking-glass worlds of television and home computers, we are in the end left in the position of Kinglake's old 'English solidiery'. As they saw it,

> insofar as the battlefield presented itself to the bare eyesight of men, it had no entirety, no length, no breadth, no depth, no size, no shape and was made up of nothing . . . In such conditions, each separate gathering . . . went on fighting its own little battle in happy and advantageous ignorance of the general state of the action; nay, even very often in ignorance of the fact that any great conflict was raging.

As Albert Camus asserted: '*When we are all guilty, that will be true democracy.*' All guilty, all volunteers in the great interactive manouevres of information warfare and, above all, ignorant of the fact that any great conflict is raging.

'For the first time, there is no longer any difference between domestic and foreign policy,' declared President Clinton last year. In the context of the metapolitical undertaking which is aimed at transforming the planet into a single urban wasteland, every sign of the criminal law being diverted to new, anational tasks necessarily assumes its full meaning.

Like the creation in recent years of these curious 'ethics committees' that are supposed to convince public opinion of the harmlessness of the experimental sciences which have today largely been diverted from their proper purposes. Made up haphazardly from technical and scientific experts, a few rare 'moral' personalities and, most recently, representatives of the big corporations, the recommendations of these makeshift institutions have, as we know, long been rendered ridiculous by the research institutes and major companies of the world's most industrialized (G8) countries switching over within a few years first from chemicals to pharmaceuticals, then on to biotechnologies – those same eight countries which – once again substituting themselves for the UN! – concocted the peace plan presented to Milosevic.

Similarly, when our new 'judicial laboratories' claim to legitimate their existence by reference to an ethic drawn from the great Nuremberg trials (25 November 1945–October 1946), the comparison seems particularly inappropriate. To appreciate this, one has simply to recall that during that unprecedented trial, in which twenty-four members of the Nazi party and eight organizations from Hitler's Germany were judged by an international military tribunal, the charges related to war crimes and, most importantly, to **conspiracy against humanity**. This was a remarkably precise charge, since it indicated that, above and beyond the blatant massacres on the battlefields and the devastation of the bombed cities, crimes of a new kind had been conceived and committed in the secrecy of the deportation camps of total war – and that they were committed, let it be noted, by way of the reform of a German judicial system which was already in decay. This was *the 'terrible secret'*[12] – the secret of the 'biological' disappearance of millions of men, women and children; millions of civilians who believed they were still protected by the rule of law, being unaware that it was no longer in force.

And with it went a new 'science of man' in which not only the nominal identity of individuals was denied, but their *anthropological identity*, their belonging to 'humanity', the living body of the human being becoming an object of experimentation and a *raw material* in a period of extreme shortages. But was not the peaceable, bureaucratic planning of the 'final solution', which Hannah Arendt discovered during the Adolf Eichmann trial, that of the *new anthropophagy* announced sixty years earlier by Nietzsche?

On 29 June 1999, a file bearing red swastika seals went on display at the Skirball Cultural Center in Los Angeles. This was said to be the original of the Nuremberg Laws, introducing, among other things, the code of discrimination against the Jews. The document, we are told, had been recovered by General Patton in April 1945 from the coffers of a little Bavarian town near Nuremberg. During the advance of the American Third Army in Europe, the general had been a witness: *everything contained in germ in that file had become reality*. When he returned to the United States, Patton had consequently entrusted the document to friends, the Huttingtons, the owners of a small library and gallery not far from Los Angeles, recommending that they lock it up in their safe and keep it hidden there. Subsequently, the various trustees of the library complied with the general's orders and the 'terrible secret' was thus scrupulously kept for more than half a century.

At precisely the point where *experimental tribunals* were being set up with the aim of redefining new 'human rights' on the planet, the opening of this Pandora's box – in which not even Hope remained – puts one in mind of the reactivation of a dangerous substance . . .

At a time when plans are being hatched for the 'industrialization of living matter' and a new eugenics is secretly being elaborated, this time promoting not the natural, but the artificial, selection of the human race.

And when, right in the middle of the resolution of a 'humanitarian conflict', we can already see the first fruits of the postwar period on the front pages of our newspapers,[13] with the ravings of the gurus of historical anthropophagy, announcing that, thanks to 'the open-ended character of modern natural science', biotechnology will provide us with the tools which will

allow us to accomplish what social engineers of the past failed to do. *At that point, we will have definitively finished human history because we will have abolished human beings as such. And then a new post-human history will begin.*[14]

Notes

1. On the dangers of 'people's wars', see Clausewitz (1976), Princeton, NJ: Princeton University Press.
2. *Le Journal du Dimanche*, 27 June 1999.
3. On 6 January 1941, President Roosevelt delivered his famous State of the Union message on the 'Four Freedoms'. From being initially a blueprint for a social system, that text became a war aim, being subsequently embodied in the Atlantic Charter of 14 August 1941.
4. *Le Figaro*, 7 May 1999.
5. La Chaîne de l'Information [Tr.].
6. On Thursday, 10 June, the very day hostilities ended in Yugoslavia, prosecutor Louise Arbour resigned from the International Criminal Tribunal to take up an important post in the legal hierachy of her country. This Canadian law officer is the first to have laid charges against a serving foreign head of state.
7. Jack London, *The Iron Heel* (chapter 8: 'The Machine Breakers').
8. Colonel Barrader (1949), *Fossatum Africae*, Paris: Editions Arts et Métiers Graphiques.
9. *Le Journal du Dimanche*, 4 July 1999.
10. *On War*, book V, ch. II, 'Absolute and Real War'.
11. Werner Heisenberg (1962), *Physics and Philosophy*, New York: Harper and Row (first German edition 1958); Ernst Jünger (1960), *Der Weltstaat*.
12. The title of a work on the holocaust by the historian Walter Laqueur [Tr.].

13. The newspaper in question was *Le Monde des Débats*, no. 5, July–August 1999. Fukuyama's article is printed there in translation, together with 'replies' by Alain Touraine, Immanuel Wallerstein and Joseph S. Nye [Tr.].

14. Francis Fukuyama (1999), 'Second thoughts. The last man in a bottle', *The National Interest*, no. 56, summer, p. 33. Continuing his work of ten years earlier on the 'end of history', Fukuyama, far from admitting the absurdity of his theory, is now prophesying the 'end of humanity'.

CHAPTER EIGHTEEN

Silence on Trial

Editions Galilée's next foray into what was becoming the yearly Paul Virilio publishing round turned out to be *La Procédure Silence* in 2000. The title comes from a phrase used in *Stratégie de la Déception* which Virilio lifts directly from NATO generals who use it to mean a 'process whereby they give the green light by implicit consensus' which would otherwise take too long to achieve and undermine the 'speed which is the essence of war'. Continuum in New York and London published an English translation by Julie Rose with the completely different title of *Art and Fear* in 2003. 'La Procedure Silence' was also the title of the second part of the original French-language book. In the English version it is translated as 'Silence on Trial'. The extract reprinted here is a part of that section of the book. The first part of the French-language edition was called '*Un Art Impitoyable*' or in English 'A Pitiless Art'. Julie Rose's translator's preface to the English edition notes that she used 'pitiful' and 'pitiless' throughout the text of the book, as indeed Virilio does in the original. But she argues that being full of pity and without pity as a binary opposition is crucial to Virilio's argument, and that 'pitiful' as a positive human attribute and also as a 'pathetic' state to be condemned (as in 'this pitiless century, the twentieth' the quotation from Albert Camus with which Virilio begins the book) is in constant deconstructive play throughout. John Armitage, a British academic who has done much to amplify Paul Virilio's international profile since the late 1990s, contributes an explanatory introduction, also entitled 'Art and Fear', to the English edition, where he points to Virilio as contemporary critic of the art of technology as being in danger of being overcritical, leaving him talking and writing only to himself. The jacket blurb for the French-language edition of *Art and Fear* screamed 'L'art contemporain est en crise' but Virilio's book is as much aimed at the genetic engineering projects of the twenty-first century as the art movements of the twentieth.

'Silence on Trial', from *Art and Fear*, trans. Julie Rose, London: Continuum, 2003.

'Remaining silent, now there's a lesson for you! What more immediate notion of duration?', Paul Valéry noted in 1938, shortly before the tragedy of the camps, the silence of the lambs . . .

To speak or to remain silent: are they to sonority what *to show or to hide* are to visibility? What prosecution of meaning is thus hidden behind the prosecution of sound? Has remaining silent now become a discreet form of assent, of connivance, in the age of the sonorization of images and all audiovisual icons? Have vocal machines' powers of enunciation gone as far as the denunciation of silence, of a silence that has turned into MUTISM?

It might be appropriate at this juncture to remember Joseph Beuys whose work, *Silence*, parallels, not so say echoes, Edvard Munch's 1883 painting, *The Scream*. Think of the systematic use of felt in Beuys' London installations of 1985 with the gallery spaces wadded like so many SOUNDPROOF ROOMS, precisely at a time when the deafening explosion of the AUDIOVISUAL was to occur – along with what is now conveniently labelled the crisis in modern art or, more exactly, *the contemporary art of the crisis of meaning*, that NONSENSE Sartre and Camus were on about.

To better understand such a heretical point of view about the programmed demise of the VOICES OF SILENCE, think of the perverse implications of the *colouration of films* originally shot in BLACK AND WHITE, to cite one example, or the use of monochromatic film in photographing accidents, oil spills. The lack of colour in a film segment or snapshot is seen as the tell-tale sign of a DEFECT, a handicap, the loss of colour of the rising tide under the effects of maritime pollution . . .

Whereas in the past, engraving enriched a painting's hues with its velvety blacks and the rainbow array of its greys, BLACK – and

WHITE – are now no more than traces of a degradation, some premature ruin.

Just like a yellowed photograph of the deceased mounted on their tomb, the MONOCHROMATIC segment merely signals the obscurantism of a bygone era, the dwindling of a heroic age in which the VISION MACHINE had yet to reveal the PANCHROMATIC riches of Technicolor . . . gaudy, brash AGFACOLOR[1] overprivileging hot colours to the detriment of cold. But surely we can say the same thing about the sonorization of what were once *silent films*.

Nowadays everything that remains silent is deemed *to consent*, to accept without a word of protest the background noise of audio-visual immoderation – that is, of the 'optically correct'. But what happens as a result to the SILENCE OF THE VISIBLE under the reign of the AUDIO-VISIBLE epitomized by *television*, wildly overrated as television is? How can we apply the lesson of Paul Valéry's aphorism in considering the question, not of the *silence of art* so dear to André Malraux, but of the DEAFNESS of the contemporary arts in the age of the multimedia?

Silence no longer has a voice. It LOST ITS VOICE half a century ago. But this mutism has now come to a head . . . The voices of silence have been silenced; what is now regarded as obscene is not so much the image as the sound – or, rather, the lack of sound.

What happens to the WORLD OF SILENCE once the first SON ET LUMIÉRE productions are staged, again under the aegis of Malraux, invading as they do the monumental spaces of the Mediterranean? The 'son et lumière' phenomenon has been followed most recently by the craze in museums as venues for live shows, though you would be hard-pressed to beat the calamitous NIGHT OF THE MILLENNIUM, when the mists of the Nile Valley suddenly broke up a Jean-Michel Jarre concert. After the deafening felt of Beuy's London installation, PLIGHT, they managed to bring SMOG to the foot of the pyramids.

'I don't want to avoid telling a story, but I want very, very much to do the thing Valéry said – to give the sensation without the boredom of its conveyance.' These words of Francis Bacon's, taken from David Sylvester's interviews with the artist and quoted as a lead-in for the 'Modern Starts' exhibition at the

Museum of Modern Art in New York, 1999, beautifully sum up the current dilemma: the less you represent, the more you push the simulacrum of REPRESENTATION!

But what is this 'situation' concealing if not the *contraction of time?* Of this *real time* that effaces all duration, exclusively promoting instead the *present*, the directness of the immediacy of ZERO TIME . . . a contraction of the LIVE and of LIFE, which we see once more at work in the recent appeal of *live shows*, which are to dance and choreography what the video installation already was to Fernand Léger's *Mechanical Ballet*.

All in all, the invention of the CINEMATOGRAPH has radically altered the experience of *exposure time*, the whole regime of temporality of the visual arts. In the nineteenth century, the aesthetics of CINEMATIC disappearance promptly supplanted the multimillennial aesthetics of the appearance of the STATIC.

Once the photogram hit the scene, it was solely a matter of mechanically or electrically producing some kind of *reality effect* to get people to forget the lack of any subject as the film rolled past.

Yet one crucial aspect of this mutation of the seventh art has been too long ignored and that is the arrival of the TALKIES. From the end of the 1920s onwards, the idea of accepting the absence of words or phrases, of some kind of dialogue, became unthinkable.[2] The so-called *listening comfort* of darkened cinema halls required that HEARING and VISION be *synchronized*. Much later, at the end of the century, ACTION and REACTION similarly would be put into instant *interaction* thanks to the feats of 'tele-action', this time, and not just radiophonic 'tele-listening' or 'tele-vision'.

Curiously, it is in the era of the Great Depression that followed the Wall Street Crash of 1929 that SILENCE WAS PUT ON TRIAL – in Europe as in the United States. From that moment, WHOEVER SAYS NOTHING IS DEEMED TO CONSENT. No silence can express disapproval or resistance but only consent. The silence of the image is not only ANIMATED by the motorization of film segments; it is also ENLISTED in the general acquiescence in a TOTAL ART – the seventh art which, they would then claim, contained all the rest.

During the great economic crisis which, in Europe, would end in Nazi TOTALITARIANISM, silence was already no more than a form of abstention. The trend everywhere was towards the *simultaneous* synchronization of image and sound. Whence the major political role played at the time by cinematic NEWSREELS, notably those produced by Fox-Movietone in the United States and by UFA in Germany, which perfectly prefigured televisual *prime time*.

Alongside booming radiophony and the *live rallies* of Nuremberg and elsewhere, the talkies would become one of the instruments of choice of the fledgling totalitarianisms. For Mussolini, *the camera was the most powerful weapon there was*; for Stalin, at the same moment in time, *the cinema was the most effective of tools for stirring up the masses*.

No *AGITPROP* or *PROPAGANDA STAEFFEL* without the *consensual power of the talkies*. Once you have the talkies up and running, you can get walls, any old animated image whatever to talk. The *dead* too, though, and *all who remain silent*. And not just people or beings, either, but things to boot!

'*The screen answers your every whim, in advance,*' as Orwell put it. Yet though the walls may well talk, frescos no longer can. The seventh art thus becomes a VENTRILOQUIST ART delivering its own oracles. Like the Pythian prophetess, the image speaks; but, more specifically, it *answers* the silence of the anguished masses who have lost their tongues. As a certain poet put it, '*Cinema never has been SILENT, only DEAF*'.

Those days are long gone. No one is waiting any more for the REVOLUTION, only for the ACCIDENT, the breakdown, that will reduce this unbearable chatter to silence.

In olden days a pianist used to punctuate segments of old burlesque movies; now the reality of scenes of everyday life needs to be subtitled in similar vein, the AUDIOVISUAL aiming to put paid to the *silence of vision* in its entirety.

All you have to do is dump your mobile phone and grab your infra-red helmet. Then you are ready to go wandering around those museums where the *soundtrack* amply makes up for the *image track* of the picture-rail.

Does art mean listening or looking, for the art lover? Has

contemplation of painting become a reflex action and possibly a CYBERNETIC one at that?

Victim of the *prosecution of silence*, contemporary art long ago made a bid for *divergence* – in other words, to practise a CONCEPTUAL DIVERSION – before opting for *convergence*.

Surely that is the only way we can interpret the Cubists' newspaper collages or the later, post-1918, collages and photomontages of Raoul Hausmann, say, or his Berlin Dadaist confrère, John Heartfield, not to mention the French Dadaists and Surrealists, among others.

In a decidedly *fin-de-siècle* world, where the automobile questions its driver about the functioning of the handbrake or whether the seatbelt is buckled, where the refrigerator is gearing itself up to place the order at the supermarket, where your computer greets you of a morning with a hearty 'hello', surely we have to ask ourselves whether the silence of art can be sustained for much longer.

This goes even for the mobile phone craze that is part and parcel of the same thing, since it is now necessary to *impose silence* – in restaurants and places of worship or concert halls. One day, following the example of the campaign to combat nicotine addiction, it may well be necessary to put up signs of the 'Silence – Hospital' variety at the entrance to museums and exhibition halls to get all those 'communication machines' to shut up and put an end to the all too numerous cultural exercises in SOUND and LIGHT.

Machine for *seeing*, machine for *hearing*, once upon a time; machine for *thinking* very shortly with the boom in all things *digital* and the programmed abandonment of the *analogue*. How will *the silence of the infinite spaces of art* subsist, this silence that seems to terrify the makers of motors of any kind, from the logical inference motor of the computer to the research engine of the network of networks? All these questions that today remain unanswered make ENIGMAS of contemporary ethics and aesthetics.

With architecture, alas, the jig is already up. Architectonics has become an *audiovisual art*, the only question now being whether it will shortly go on to become a VIRTUAL ART. For sculpture, ever since Jean Tinguely and his 'Bachelor Machines', this has been merely a risk to be run. As for painting and the graphic arts, from the moment VIDEO ART hit the scene with the notion of the installation, it has been impossible to mention CONCEPTUAL ART without picking up the background noise of the mass media behind the words and objects of the art market.

Like TINNITUS, where a ringing in the ears perceived in the absence of external noise soon becomes unbearable, contemporary art's *prosecution of silence* is in the process of lastingly polluting our representations.

Having digested the critical impact of Marcel Duchamp's retinal art, let's hear what French critic, Patrick Vauday, had to say a little more recently:

> The passage from image to photography and then to cinema and, more recently still, to video and digital computer graphics, has surely had the effect of rendering painting magnificently *célibataire*. Painting has finally been released from the image-making function that till then more or less concealed its true essence. Notwithstanding the 'new' figurative art, it is not too far-fetched to see in the modern avatar of painting, a *mise à nu* of its essence that is resolutely ICON-OCLASTIC.[3]

At those words, you could be forgiven for fearing that the waxing twenty-first century were about to reproduce the first years of the twentieth, albeit unwittingly!

Under the guise of 'new technologies', surely what is really at work here is the actual CLONING, over and over, of some SUPER, no, HYPER-ABSTRACTION that will be to virtual reality what HYPER-REALISM was to the photographic shot. This is happening at a time when someone like Kouichirou Eto, for instance, is gearing up to launch SOUND CREATURES on the internet along with his own meta-musical ambient music!

What this means is a style of painting not only *without figures* but also *without images*, a *music of the spheres without sound*, presenting the symptoms of a *blinding* that would be the exact counterpart to the *silence of the lambs*. Speaking of the painter Turner, certain nineteenth-century aesthetes such as Hazlitt denounced the advent of *'pictures of nothing, and very like'*.[4] You can bet that soon, thanks to digital technology, *electro-acoustic* music will generate new forms of visual art. *Electro-optic* computer graphics will similarly erase the demarcation lines between the different art forms.

Once again, we will speak of a TOTAL ART – one no longer indebted to the cinematograph, that art which supposedly contained all the rest. Thanks to electronics, we will invent a GLOBAL ART, a 'single art', like the thinking that subtends the new information and communications technologies.

To take an example, think of the influence of Wagner on Kandinsky in 1910, when the very first ABSTRACT canvases emerged; or think of the influence of Kurt Schwitters whose *Ursonate* was composed of oral sounds . . . Then, of course, there is the influence of JAZZ on works like the 'Broadway Boogie Woogie' of New York-based Mondrian, an artist who would not have a telephone in the house during the years 1940–2. Unlike Moholy-Nagy, who was already making TELE-PAINTINGS twenty years earlier using the crank phone to issue instructions at a distance to a sign painter . . . and inventing pictorial INTER-ACTIVITY in the process.

All this interaction between SOUND, LIGHT and IMAGE, far from creating a 'new art' or a *new reality* – to borrow the name of the 1950 Paris salon dedicated to French painter Herbin's geometric abstraction – only destroys the nature of art, promoting instead its communication.

Moreover, someone like Andy Warhol makes no sense as an artist in the Duchamp mould unless we understand the dynamic role played not only by sign painting, but more especially by advertising, that last ACADEMICISM that has gradually invaded the temples of *official art* without anyone's batting an eyelid. So little offence has it given, in fact, that where 'Campbell's Soup' not so long ago turned into a *painting*, today Picasso has become a *car*.

Last autumn, the BBC began broadcasting recordings of murmurs and conversation noises destined for the offices at the big end of town where employees complain about the reigning deathly silence.

'We're trying to get a background of ambient sound,' explains a spokesman for the British station. 'These offices are so quiet that the slightest noise, such as the phone ringing, disturbs people's concentration which, of course, can lead to stuff-ups.'[5]

Following the muzak that is piped through shops and super-markets, let's hear it for AMBIENT MURMURING, *the voice of the voiceless!* After the promotion of domestic consumerism via the euphoria of radiophony, it is now production that finds itself beefed up with a sound backdrop designed to improve office life . . .

Similarly, over at the Pompidou Centre in Paris, the post-renovation reopening exhibition, which was called '*Le Temps Vite*' – or '*Time, Fast*' – was underscored by a sound piece composed by Heiner Goebbels.

Heralding the coming proliferation of *live shows* in museums, silence has become identified with death . . . Though it is true enough that the dead today dance and sing thanks to the record-ing process: 'Death represents a lot of money, it can even make you a star,' as Andy Warhol famously quipped. Don't they also say that, on the night of New Year's Eve 2000, the 'POST-MORTEM' duo of Bob Marley and his daughter-in-law, Lauren Hill, could be heard all over New York?[6]

On the eve of the new millennium, the aesthetics of disappear-ance was completed by the aesthetics of absence. From that moment, whoever says nothing consents to cede their 'right to remain silent', their freedom to listen, to a *noise-making process* that simulates oral expression or conversation.

But did anyone in the past ever fret about the very particular silence of the VISIBLE, best exemplified by the pictorial or sculptural image? Think of what August Wilhelm Schlegel once wrote about Raphael's *Dresden Madonna*. 'The effect is so imme-diate that no words spring to mind. Besides, what use are words in the face of what offers itself with such luminous obvious-ness?'[7]

Today, when the AUDIO-VISIBLE of the mass media reigns, beamed out twenty-four hours a day, seven days a week, what remains of that *effect of immediacy* of visual representation? *Media presentation* dominates everywhere you turn.

Notes

1. 'A subtractive colour process developed in Germany by Agfa AG for 16 mm film in 1936 and for 35 mm film in 1940. Agfacolor was a tripak colour process, in which three emulsion layers, each sensitive to one of the primary colours, were laid on a single base.' I. Konigsburg (1997), *The Complete Film Dictionary*, second edn, London: Bloomsbury, p. 8.
2. *The Jazz Singer*, the Hollywood film directed by Alan Crosland and starring singer Al Jolson, marks the cinematograph's entry into the age of the TALKIES, on 23 October 1927 – the date of the first public screening.
3. Patrick Vauday, 'Y a-t-il une peinture sans image?', a paper given at a seminar held by the Collège International de Philosophie, Paris, during its 1999–2000 programme.
4. Norbert Lynton (2001), *The Story of Modern Art*, London and New York: Phaidon, p. 14, from ch. I, 'The New Barbarians' (originally published 1980).
5. 'La BBC invente le "Mumure d'ambiance"', *Ouest-France*, 16 October 1999.
6. *Le Figaro*, 4 January 2000.
7. August Wilhelm Schlegel, *Paintings*.

CHAPTER NINETEEN

Ground Zero

The events of 11 September, 2001 were no great shock to Paul Virilio. After all, he had been hired as a consultant after the 1993 World Trade Center bombing and he constantly prefigured such another 'act of total war' executed with 'a minimum of resources' in his writing and interviews in the late 1990s. But the book billed as 'Paul Virilio on September 11' was mostly anything but. Finished in October 2001, *Ce Qui Arrive* was published early in 2002 by Editions Galilée in Paris. A speedy English translation by Chris Turner was put out by Verso in London and New York with a striking, distorted cover image of the citizens of New York escaping the attack on the twin towers. A new title, *Ground Zero*, suggested to English-language buyers of the book that there would be a substantial focus on the 'accident' of 9/11 but only the short section extracted here actually does that. The rush by artists and critics to aestheticize the 'live' televised events of 11 September in New York included not only Karlheinz Stockhausen, who Virilio quotes here, but also the bad boy Brit-artist Damien Hirst, whose oeuvre in the 1990s would not have met with Virilio's unequivocal approval. The back-cover blurb of *Ground Zero* contains the seeds of the idea which preoccupied Virilio post-9/11: 'the anonymity of those who initiated the attack signals, for everyone, the rise of a global covert state – of the *unknown quantity* of a private criminality'. *Ce Qui Arrive*, as a whole, found Virilio revisiting some of the territory of *Art and Fear*, and at times it reads like a collection of out-takes from the 2000 French edition on what John Armitage has called the 'aesthetics of Auschwitz'; here an aside on body art, there a warning about scientific totalitarianism in the 'post-human' future of biological engineering. By now the genetic bomb had become Virilio's obsession.

Ground Zero, trans. Chris Turner, London: Verso, 2002.

The great technological events may change our lives but they will not create a new form of art. They may create a generation of art critics who will tell us, 'This is art!' (Orson Welles)

'The world [is going] to ruin,' warned Karl Kraus, and 'man's feeling of superiority triumphs in the expectation of a spectacle to which only contemporaries are admitted.'[1] Like Stockhausen, the grand old master of electronic music, flying into raptures over the spectacle of the New York attacks which killed 4,000 people in September 2001: 'What we have witnessed is the greatest work of art there has ever been!'[2]

Why not 4 million dead next time? Deterring art from being the manifestation of bodies can lead us a long way – to the era of the atom, of biological fiction, of avatars and televisual terrorism.

And this is indeed the paradox of a 'culture mill' which has, since the nineteenth century, hitched itself to the invention of that *consanguinity of man and instrument* (Gabriele d'Annunzio) that will dictate what is or is not modern or revolutionary.

When Lenin writes that 'Communism is the power of the Soviets plus the electrification of the country', one may go beyond the hackneyed formula to think either of the Italian Futurists announcing the advent of the *'multiple man who gets tangled up in iron and feeds on electricity'*, or of the Islamist suicide hijackers hurtling their planes into the towers of the World Trade Center.

Similarly, the clear-sighted art lover will wonder how Van Gogh (whom Signac called a 'mad phenomenon') and, after him, the originators of Fauvism, would have painted without the illumination of industrial lighting, whether by gas or electricity, rivalling the brilliance of the regal star of the Mediterranean.

What would the Realist or Naturalist schools of the nineteenth century have been without the objective accident of the photographic pose, or the Bauhaus and Moholy-Nagy without the aerialization of human vision and the cinema? Or German Expressionists without the industrial production of corpses by military-scientific progress – with the 'ghosts'[3] that were to invade the radar screens of the Battle of Britain in 1940 yet to come, supplanting as they did all other audiovisual warning systems, and hence all other systems for representing coming dangers.

And one will also wonder about the paradoxical logic of Mies van der Rohe asserting that '**less is more**', and the fanaticism of Adolf Loos judging *ornament a crime against modernity* – half a century before Andy Warhol declared: 'If you want to know about Andy Warhol, just look at the surfaces of my paintings . . . There's nothing behind it', and – talking about himself as though, in principle, he did not exist – 'It's all there. There's nothing missing. I am everything my press album says I am.'

There are many ways of being iconoclastic. You can burn pictures and those who painted them, erase or tamper with the cartouches of monuments, break religious statues or blow up those of political idols, as at the end of the Communist era.

But how is it when the iconoclast is the plastician himself?

After the fall of their traditional patrons (divine-right monarchy, princes, the Church of Rome), artists, in an attempt to survive, to be famous for at least fifteen minutes, had at their disposal neither the panoply of the warrior, the tools of the politician, nor the irrefutability of the scientist.

By contrast with a literature which, by its technical calling, had involved itself at a very early stage in current events, thanks to the talent of its writers of serialized fiction and its journalist-novelists (from Rabelais to Stendhal, Balzac, Dickens, London, Zola and Cendrars), the rest of the culture mill stood aloof, bogged down in an official academic staidness, shamefully conservative.

Yet in 1818, *The Raft of the Medusa*, that great manifesto-painting by Géricault, a man with a liking for the stray news item, penetrated the world of political and judicial affairs to make headlines in the French and Anglo-Saxon press. At the Salon of 1857, in a feverish social context, it would be the turn of Courbet and the *naturalist* scandal. And in 1874, 'Impressionism', invented by a mercenary criticism . . .[4]

Cheered by this entry into the grand manoeuvres of the world of news technologies, many plasticians saw here a practical source of substitute activity and renewal, both in terms of profit and aesthetically.

'Slow news, no news!' The artists of the twentieth century, like the anarchist with his home-made bombs, the revolutionary suicide bomber or the mass killers celebrated by the mass-circulation press, would themselves become wielders of plastic explosives, visual mischief-makers, anarchists of colour, form and sound, before coming to occupy the gutter press's gallery of horrors.

Soon, as René Gimpel was to remark – or, later, Orson Welles – contemporary art could no longer do without the connivance of *those art critics who would 'tell us: "This is art"'* simply because art had become *unrecognizable*.

And, like the statues of the great Buddhas of Bamiyan after the Taliban had gone by, it would be impossible to identify it unless its authenticity were duly certified by some specialist or appraiser.

As when paper money replaced gold at the beginning of the last century, it would now be necessary to check out the market prices to learn that in June 2001, for example, a Picasso was worth more than a Monet, or a Warhol more than a Rembrandt – though this is of little consequence on the *global disappearance market*, where telepresence is supplanting the real presence of the art object, and also of its buyer and seller.

*   *   *

What are we talking about today when we speak of art? This is a question it has become increasingly difficult to answer.

Art is like a currency which must remain in circulation, claimed a perceptive August Wilhelm Schlegel.

But in a world that is resolutely accidental – that is to say, an enemy to its *own substance* – one wonders what bonds of authenticity can still unite the market value of our art objects to their plastic presence and, above all, what can still bind us to them?

If, according to the time-honoured formula, 'art is long and life is short', the uproarious entry of contemporary and 'current' works into the all-powerful news market – where, as we know, merchandise is valueless after twenty-four hours or twenty-four seconds – has destroyed the notion of *durée*, which had until then been involved in the assessment of the object, at the same time as it has destroyed that other tangible quality that was its **rarity** –

the fact that the work is considered unique from its conception or has become so over the centuries.

What, at first glance, distinguishes the true work is, as Rainer Maria Rilke wrote, its 'infinite solitude', the enigmatic attraction of a *uniqueness* which, paradoxically, offers the multitude of its sensory adequations to those who, *in looking at them, produce half the pictures* (Paul Klee), and often more than that – like that nostalgic emperor of China who complained to their creator, Li Ssu-Hsur, about the noise made by the waterfalls he had painted, which were preventing him from sleeping.[5]

The true work of art is not, then, one of those arrangements of mirrors in which the magicians of Ancient Greece claimed to re-create the universe for the naive Athenian onlookers, any more than it is, for the creator or the spectator, a narcissistic reflection or the product of some 'real-time' dramaturgy.

The work of art is not academic; it conforms to no preconceived plan and expresses only *the extreme veneration of receptiveness* or, more trivially, of the extreme vigilance of the living body that sees, hears, intuits, moves, breathes and changes.

'*Life's emotions are basically merely steps,*' confided the great dancer Sylvie Guillem. 'I regard my body as an instrument of discovery . . . You have to astonish yourself each time, to discover yourself.'[6]

Unlike that modern Olympic champion who declared that *his body was his worst enemy*, Sylvie, when she is dancing, makes an ally of hers. 'One day,' she adds, '*I danced without being there*, with *only the memory of my technique*. I have regretted it ever since.

Similarly when, at the beginning of the twentieth century – 'that century of machines', as Picabia called it – Sergei Diaghilev commanded his dancers to 'astonish' him,[7] one might understand him to be saying:

> Don't do it like machines, do it the way you would in real life when you do everything for the first and last time, for if, in real life, time never ends, nothing is repeated either, nothing is exactly banal for us, every moment that arrives is a new moment – the ordinary course of life is the extraordinary, the permanent feature of existence is astonishment.

'You make a choice every second – that is the magic of life!' confided one beautiful actress, alluding to the old philosopher's forgotten remark, or the words of that lover of nonsense, André Isaac: 'I am always on the brink, on the brink of something.'[8]

And I myself have written: '**Here** is no longer, all is **now**.' All the arts – and particularly the arts of re-presentation – were, then, to be fatally damaged, then destroyed, by the constant acceleration of technologies of presentation and reproduction both dromological and dromoscopic which, by reducing the space and time between subject and object to zero, were to eliminate, as a matter of course, not just the concepts of rarity and *durée*, but the *nodal points of the potentiality and the 'becoming' of the work of art* – its phenomenology.[9]

*   *   *

The total eclipse of consciousness of the Trinity Site physicists was, then, culturally avant-garde. It would, in effect, be followed by the eclipse of consciousness on the part of the worldly, joining without too many complaints in the countdown of *the balance of nuclear terror*.

As a continuation of total war by other means, nuclear deterrence marked the end of the distinction between wartime and peacetime, and cleared the way for a *worldwide state of undeclared war* between the Western and Soviet blocs – of which, quite logically, terrorism and gangsterism would be the main beneficiaries.

Similarly, techno-scientific retro-progress having exhausted the interest the inhabitants of the biosphere could still take in their future, it was normal that they should turn away from it to the wasteland of origins. At the beginning of the Cold War, a start was made in the United States on digging trenches in suburban gardens, and storing away in prefabricated shelters all that seemed essential to survive the end of the world in the best of conditions . . .

The authorities in the big cities had even organized a few evacuation exercises in urban centres, but facts had to be faced: in the event of a general nuclear alert, millions of drivers, fleeing together on overcrowded exit routes, would be caught in inextricable traffic jams, and perish before they reached their suburban bunkers.

The inhabitants of the old European bastion, for their part, adapted as best they could to the Welfare State's mutation into a suicidal one.

The reversed perspective of a planetary life entering its terminal phase would give rise to a conservatism of a kind previously almost unknown, a *museomania* which would far exceed the old academy of the Muses, and would merely reveal the dreadful poverty of Western techno-culture.

There would be museums for everything – in a kind of cult of trash or 'unrecognized pop art', the fetishistic infatuation of ageing populations with all that had been rejected, forgotten, outdated, all that had previously been found wearisome or repellent.

At the point when we were condemned to leave for ever, we would set about collecting, in no particular order, the old mechanical toys, the products and sentimental flotsam of a failed modernity.

Arctophiles and philumenists, collectors of breweriana and even dachshundiana – we would give names to all these devotees, and to their collecting passions. And they would have their various museums to go to: museums of photography, nougat, coffee-pots, the cinematograph, Camembert, marriage, posters, peasant and working-class life, railways, household electrical goods . . .

Little by little, the differences between the contemporary living-space and the sites of the archaeological past would fade. Modern Europe would take on a discreetly funereal character.

Lost amid their contemporary suburbs, the historic towns and cities – with their palaces, cathedrals and museums – would become like those dead cities of antiquity, with their tombs and mausoleums, where the weapons, vehicles, treasure, familiar objects and images of the pleasures they had enjoyed would be laid out before the unseeing eyes of the dead.

Before ultimately handing them over to an exotic young crowd, some municipal officials are now proposing to parody the libations and funeral orgies of ancient times there. Like Christophe

Girard of the Paris city authority, who announced to the press in April 2001: 'I want to get away from the usual ways of using cultural sites. A museum doesn't have to be a temple. You can dance in the Louvre in front of the Rembrandts, as they have done at the Rijksmuseum in Amsterdam . . . I have set myself the task of restoring the capital's festive character.'[10]

Yet vast tracts were reduced to no-go areas, refugee camps or conservation areas, nature reserves with their moribund fauna and flora.

The mountains, the coast, disused military or industrial sites, worked-out mines, closed-down blast furnaces, the back-to-back housing and tenements of a disappeared proletariat would be listed as historic monuments.

With techno-culture – as flashback or feedback – continuing on its retreat towards the void of origins, the mass media would soon lead with a story of 'Mayan sculpture and Zulu masks to stand alongside the Mona Lisa'.

The time of *primal arts* was the childhood of art, if not indeed its prenatal state.

A museum would be built for it not far from the Eiffel Tower, and the 'scientific adviser' to the enterprise – at the inauguration of the new galleries of primal arts at the Louvre – would be able to tell us: 'There are no longer any grounds for the old quarrel between the so-called aesthetic and the so-called ethnographic approaches.'

Doubtless because, long before playing host to what were called primal arts, the Louvre was no longer anything but a *miroir des limbes*, a huge ethnographic warehouse living on beyond its own end, as André Malraux had predicted, thanks to a considerable pedagogical/commercial effort directed towards the new mass tourism, and also towards a native population for whom its own culture had become, in a few short decades, as alien as that of distant civilizations which disappeared thousands of years ago.

There was, then, really no basis for the quarrel, since 'those who, in looking at them, do half the work of the pictures' (Paul Klee) and those who, by reading them, do half the work of books (Voltaire) had long been marked out for decimation.

Ethnographic museums – above all, *musées des Invalides*.

Here again, we have kept tally of our accursed artists, of the suicide-artists of modernity – the failures, the suicides, the halt and the lame, the alcoholics, the obsessives, the addicts, the insane or the devotees of mutilation or gratuitous crimes – but we have said nothing about the constant aggravation of the ill-treatment inflicted on an equally accursed public – blinded, deafened, despised and, finally, declared the enemy by *arts of sheer terror*.

Yet, in the middle of the fateful 1930s, the author of *Brave New World*, Aldous Huxley, was already concerned at the decline of a European culture in which the stimulation of the senses was coming to mean the organization of ever more violent orgies (sex/blood/race . . .), with the risk that societies in crisis would be pushed into new massacres. He even took the view that these aesthetic problems justified international conferences as urgent as those called to deal with disarmament or the world economy.[11]

And we may well wonder today what poisoned chalice is being offered to a demeaned public when the decision comes down from on high that no distinction is now to be made between the aesthetic and ethnographic approaches to exhibited works; that the field of immediate consciousness will be treated in the same way as things that are necessarily of the order of an instrumentalized knowledge – disembodied and, indeed, far removed from the body.

A bit like Andy Warhol putting his faith, like so many before him, in the inequality created between artists and spectators by the techniques of the advertisers' *high-speed art* and the global public's predisposition to obey the orders and signals of *operative images* . . .

With *The Mystery of Picasso*, a film made in 1956 by Henri-Georges Clouzot, spectators had already been treated to the unveiling of the genesis of the master's works by the camera.

Readers will remember seeing Picasso behind a great translucent panel where he stood to paint – the panel serving as interface between himself and the lens. As in a children's cartoon, the works that were forming appeared in transparency on this medium, thus giving the viewers the illusion of watching the various phases of their gestation 'live', and ultimately, after the usual rethinking and retouching, of watching these images brought painfully into the world by an exhausted but satisfied creative artist.

Shortly afterwards, taking advantage of the remarkable progress of echographic techniques, obstetricians would provide the mass media with a bulk supply of the successive images of a foetal life which had until then remained invisible to ordinary mortals.

In *Le Monde des Débats* (September 2000), Jean-Pierre Mohen, the director of the Centre de Recherche et de Restauration des Musées de France, regaled us with the following announcement: 'Radiographic and other studies are providing new and original information on what painters have done, *consciously or otherwise.*'

With this final puzzle, the fusion/confusion of arts and techno-sciences could be said to have reached its end – that long decon-struction begun, consciously or otherwise, by artists themselves some 150 years ago!

After the biological parent, the 'creative artist' would, in his turn, be declared suspect, and would have to bow out before the scientist and the infallible 'know-how' of his instruments – before those who now call themselves 'art geneticists' and direct their efforts, using the chemical, physical and electronic arsenals at their disposal, 'to making visible and available to everyone what artists had concealed beneath the surface of their works', whereas before *genetics* (in the sense of the genesis of works of art), 'all we had to go on' in literature, painting and music, they claim, 'was the end result'.[12]

'Once the painting is finished, I have nothing to say,' explained Balthus not so very long ago. But no matter; the scientist will make him speak, will get the information out of him. It is as though, running Clouzot's film backwards, the prenatal sequences of the work were to resurface in succession.

After the Cartesian animal-machine or the man-machine, here is the automatic work of art dreamt of by Hugo or by Dada, art reduced to the criteria of the optimal play of self-adapting machines by 'scientific experts' ignorant of what the cyberneti-cist knows: namely, that the machine can become 'more intelli-gent', but it 'does not learn' and, ultimately, soon ceases to interest or astonish the general public.[13]

It is, perhaps, to soften the blow of this probable disaffection that the new cultural promoters are now trying to substitute the advertising displays of *high-speed art* for techno-scientific explication.

We learn, for example, that a powerful cosmetics multinational rcently formed partnerships with the Palazzo Pitti and the Barberini to co-produce art shows and participate in the 'restoration' of old works of art which will, we are told, be *readapted to current tastes.*

Exhibited in this way, after a clean-up and a makeover, the magisterial works of Tintoretto or Titian will be able to convey to the general public and to the students in the schools 'a delightfully effective advertising message, enabling us to divine the pop potential of the masterworks of past art', as was announced by Antonio Paolucci, the superintendent of the artistic treasures and historical monuments of the city of Florence.

The works of Raphael and Velasquez have suffered the same *post mortem* attentions at the Prado.

And Jean-Pierre Cuzin, head curator of the department of painting at the Louvre, announced to the press that '*the Mona Lisa which, like Marilyn, draws in the crowds*' will soon have its own separate room donated by the Japanese private television channel NTV which, as we know, has already funded in full the 'restoration' of the ceilings of the Sistine Chapel.

'Drawing copies the residue of a vision,' observed Alberto Giacometti. 'It is my belief, whether we are dealing with painting or sculpture, that only the drawing counts. If one more or less mastered drawing, all the rest would be possible . . . *Drawing is the beginning of everything.*'[14]

This undisputed master of the aesthetics of disappearance seemed not to know that, from now on, *no beginning would be guaranteed.*[15] For some fifty years, in fact, drawing has been banished from the walls of art galleries, and now it is painting's turn to be considered the technical vestige of another era.

The museomania of the poor was not, then, to spare the privileged, and this would be another meaning of **big optics**: multinational powers aiming for a monopoly of the market in appearances; capitalists no longer rushing for gold, but for the totality of the world's images.

After Ted Turner of CNN, Bill Gates would get in on the act and declare: 'It's possible, you can never know, that the universe exists only for me. If so, it's sure going well for me, I must admit.'[16]

As consenting victims of contemporary solipsism, the Guggenheims, for their part, are expecting to reign supreme over a **global** museum. Similarly, we were to learn that, in the Berlusconi government's Finance Bill for 2002, the management of museums, archives, libraries and archaeological sites would be handed over in its entirety to the Italian private sector for a five-year rental of 160 milion euros . . .

All this gives an unexpected meaning to a recent text in which an art critic commented on *a new way of consuming art thanks to the internet*, and, secondarily, a new way of ensuring the economic survival of authors who would not really be authors since, as in the way the rights to electronic games are tied up, they would no longer be the exclusive owners of their works.

In keeping with the criteria prevailing in the *electro-optical economy*, this new art could in future be regarded as a 'service to society' and these artists, by being admitted to the status of *researchers*, could be sponsored by multinationals for two or three years with an *obligation to publish* – exactly, we are told, as happens in the scientific world.[17]

Another prominent example of this palace revolution, the Paris School of Political Sciences, has announced that its students will in future be trained in 'the management of cultural enterprises', while the great hall of the Ecole des Hautes Etudes Commerciales at Jouy-en-Josas, traditionally reserved for the end-of-year ball, has been rechristened 'Contemporary Art Space'.

This arrangement, which will involve the staging of two exhibitions a year, will be rounded off with artists in residence – a further indication of the replacement of true art lovers and the old gallery owners by transnational managers.

As wedding presents in these unnatural marriages of a kind that have long been solemnized in the United States – Yale, Austin or Berkeley possessing important contemporary collections – our artists would no doubt be required urgently to provide for their new sponsors their power of terroristic change, their meta-design.

This privatization – or, if you prefer, takeover – of the world's appearances had begun in the nineteenth century when, on the Romantic pretext of saving cathedrals from demolition, medieval art and architecture had been disfigured, adapting them to the *machinistic* taste of the engineers. Today it is the turn of the restorers, makeover artists and scientific experts of all kinds to get their hands on the *biodiversity* of a European art in which the gods assumed a human face, in which the museums were simply the temples of a Graeco-Latin and Judeao-Christian anthropocentrism.[18]

To enter the race of economic globalism is then also, for the *compradores* of the Old World, to throw off the cumbersome burden of their own culture. To be convinced of this, we need only listen once again to Christophe Girard of the Paris city authority announcing that there will be dancing in the Louvre where the Rembrandts hang, and – why not, after that? – in churches kept open at night for the purpose . . .

Apart from obvious economic and strategic considerations, one might also see this as one of the causes of the recent moral abandonment of the state of Israel by its traditional allies and systems of information whose traditional task it is to invent every new enemy, every possible accident or crime.

But let us listen to Joseph Roth observing, on the eve of the first total war in contemporary history: 'In the eyes of the Hitlerian pagans, it is not just the Jews, but the Christians too who are the children of Israel, and it is clear to anyone who has eyes to see that anti-Semitism is a pretext and what we have here is, in reality, an anti-Christianism. During the Third Reich they started with the boycotting of Jewish shops and went on to boycott Christian churches. They spat on the star of David in order to attack the cross.'[19]

Let us also look clear-sightedly at what is currently going on: Jewish and Christian graves profaned by 'calculated satanic acts', corpses desecrated, synagogues and churches set on fire in our suburbs . . . the new routine of a local terrorism, systematically ignored by the mass media.

And the manoeuvres of the French prime minister Lionel Jospin also spring to mind, calling up as he did the president of the European Convention, Roman Herzog, to declare the reference to the religious heritage of Europe in the Charter of Fundamental Rights *'unacceptable'* (European Agency press release, 14 September 2000).

Yet, on the eve of the Christian festival of All Saints, Halloween is celebrated in our schools, with its cortege of ghosts, witches and satanaels[20] . . . some even going so far as to propose the cancellation of the Christmas festival and its seasonal rejoicing in favour of that commercial masquerade of which 'Satan is the only God!'

So, when our cultural spokesmen, such as Jean-Pierre Mohen, announce that they have, in their field, to make *political choices*, we shall understand them to mean *transpolitical choices*.

As we saw in the laborious negotiations of the 1995 GATT round, the conversion to planetary economy required the absolute conformity of all goods *without any cultural exception*.

The **nothing but the Earth**[21] of globalism, showing itself gradually for what it is: a return to sender of the old *colonial slave code* which laid down that *no durable civilization must be allowed to constitute itself in the colonies*.

* * *

'Tomorrow you will all be Negroes!' prophesied James Baldwin, turning American racism round against its perpetrators.[22]

In the early years of the twentieth century, art lovers and gallery owners should have been on their guard against what the Cubists, the Expressionists and the mass media crudely dubbed *'art nègre'* or *'art nègro-africain'*. This was predominantly an *airport art*, a commodity from nowhere and no one, to be consumed by anyone at all.

The *art nègre* art object – and its masks which no longer had any actual faces behind them – was a warning to the artists of a Europe which was then still colonial. It heralded their imminent identification with the artists of *voiceless peoples, who are no longer permitted to be conscious of, and take any pride in, themselves*.[23]

From the 1950s onwards, with the coming of decolonization, we were to discover the transcultural and transpolitical power of the new global markets.

Nuclear power, for example, where it was difficult to distinguish what was commercial (power stations) from what was military (the bomb), despite the risk of the technology spreading to terrorists, which was to be reckoned with even then.

Similarly, the future of the vital markets of energy, information and the biotechnologies was already mapped out: it would accompany the drift towards the wholesale disappearance of *raison d'Etat* and its replacement by a multitude of transnational networks. The politico-economic scandals of the late twentieth century have reminded us once again – democracies die, sooner or later, from the secret duplication of state services.

But what is concealed today behind the cracked façade of our republican constitutions?

The tragic events in New York in September 2001 showed us the alarming situation of an overpowerful state suddenly brought up short against its own consciousness – or, rather, against *its techno-scientific unconsciousness*: in other words, against the Gnosticist faith on which it is founded.

Let us not forget that, since the inopportune pursuit of the Manhattan Project by American physicists,[24] the scientific 'sorcerer's spirit' had found itself virtually released from the authority of its former patrons and, particularly, of their axiomatics – the ideological, social, economic and cultural criteria – on which the authority of the State was founded. And that had led to Hiroshima.

A purified dystopia, a watertight system in which, after the collapse of the old epistemological ambitions, the scientist, stripped of his civilizational attributes, *would work only for the scientist, each discovery grafting itself on the prevoius one and science finding the sources and ends of its existence on its own ground*, like the Jehova of Genesis![25]

This lends another meaning, for example, to the remarks of the Franco-Iranian philosopher Daryush Shayegan, who told a journalist: 'To speak of civilizations as blocs counterposed to one another without interpenetration is an illusion.' He went on to say: '*We are all Westerners.*' And he analysed the subtle relationships between Islamism and an omnipresent Marxism in the Third World in the post-colonial period – relations he referred to as a *Bolshevization of religion*.

In fact, in general pan-Islamic terrorism one can see straight-away Arab (or other) multinationals exploiting the beliefs or hatred of a global subproletariat, a lumpen class produced by decolonization and mass immigration, but one sees also an elite of rich Muslim students, military men and technicians (pilots, programmers, scientists, etc.) who, as is immediately noticeable, resemble in every particular the suicidal members of the American 'Heaven's Gate' cybersect.

To speak, as Daryush Shayegan does, of *the light which comes from the West*, and of *a world which will not be able to escape Progress*, is to fall inadvertently into the biblical company of Lucifer (the Bearer of Light), into the tragic irony of Dürer's **Melancholia**, and to forget that the Judaeo-Christian story of Genesis is *the story of a scientific suicide*.

As I have written elsewhere, in emancipating itself from politics, faith in progress has entered the field of pure strategy – the essence of war – the pure strategy of the nuclear status quo.

Like the illusionism to which it owes a great debt, techno-scientific development has become an **art of the false** in the service of the **art of the lie** – a series of manipulations of appearances, tricks and, in some cases, a tissue of absurdities.[26]

When, during the Cold War, the talk was of the **society of the spectacle**, of politics-as-spectacle or alienation to commercialism, what was mainly at issue was the spectacular revolution of an informational complex moving, over a few decades, from the old totalitarian threats to global threats, from Leninist electrification to the global electronic field.

So, when Bill Joy, at the end of the last century, carried out his informal survey among specialists in the most powerful technologies, he introduced us to a curious melting-pot, running from the inevitable superman to Isaac Asimov's robot cycle, Michelangelo or the paths of Buddhism . . . but, first and foremost, to fiction, mainly through productions made for TV, the aesthetic aberrations of the current techno-science futurologists presenting frequent similarities with **Star Trek** or *Alien*.[27]

We have moved, then, from the realism and the rationalist logic of the printed word, and the Jules Verne-type *novel of scientific prediction*, to the teratological phantasmagorias of science-fiction scenarios aimed at the industrial cinema, before these latter were in their turn eliminated by the telescoping, in the new popular cinema, of special effects, whose instantaneity and interactivity exclude any coherent narrative whatsoever, with the spectator no longer being provided with any kind of verisimilitude, but fed exclusively on the *exhibition of accidents*.

It will also be noticed that once this stage of the *meaninglessness of the visible world* was reached, the (American, Asian and other) *dream factories* rapidly laid off a large number of original authors and screenwriters who were regarded as unproductive. Shortly afterwards, we were to see the failure of 'Sillywood'. After being announced in 1992 as the 'new golden age of entertainment', the marriage between Silicon Valley and Hollywood was to end in failure after a few short months – partly for want of a common strategy, but mainly for want of *content*.

'When nothingness becomes reality, reality in its turn tips over into nothingness,' stated the old strategist.

It will be hard to grasp anything of the various expansionist comments currently being heard around the world if we do not keep firmly in mind the oft-neglected fact that every technology expresses itself in its time as a *new field of force*.

Here as elsewhere, what is troubling about the covert state of transnational terrorism – that unknown quantity – is its growing subordination to a techno-scientific progress which is, itself, unauthored and dependent on the development of its own audiovisual media and platforms.

The scientific imagination ultimately suffers the same fate as 'e-tainment'; it comes to resemble that of those TV viewers who thought the attack on the World Trade Center on September 11 was merely another disaster movie, or that of the Islamist suicide-attackers no doubt dying happy at becoming actors in a global super-production in which *reality would tip over* once and for all *into electronic nothingness*.

Notes

1. Kraus, *In These Great Times*, p. 57.
2. In translating this passage, I have followed contemporary

German newspaper reports of Stockhausen's comments ['*das grösste Kunstwerk, das es je gegeben hat*']. These do, however, seem to represent a somewhat questionable account both of the composer's actual words and of the context [Tr.].

3. In *War and Cinema*, Virilio writes of 'the derealization of a battle in which ghosts played an ever greater role – screen ghosts of enemy pilots served to confirm that they had been shot down, and ghostly radar images, voices and echoes came through on the screens, radios and sonars' (London: Verso, 1989), p. 76 [Tr.].

4. The term was coined by the critic Louis Leroy as a derogatory description of Monet's approach in the painting *Sunrise: Impression* [Tr.].

5. François Cheng (1979), *Vide et Plein. Le Langage Pictural Chinois*, Paris: Le Seuil. One thinks, too, of the open systems of Platonic thought and the expression coined by the Greeks, *kalokagathia*, which refers to the beauty and goodness of a consoling art.

6. Sylvie Guillem (1996), 'Mon corps et moi', *Le Nouvel Observateur*, 3 January. 'Avoid over-dancing,' she says.

7. He also famously asked Cocteau to do the same [Tr.].

8. André Isaac, alias Pierre Dac (1893–1975), the great mid-twentieth-century French humorist and parodist [Tr.].

9. See Paul Virilio (1996), *The Art of the Motor*, trans. Julie Rose, Minneapolis: University of Minnesota Press.

10. 'Green, gay and a specialist in the luxury industries, this is the – unprecedented – profile of the new culture spokesman in the Paris *Mairie*' (interview with Sylvie Santini in *Match*), and 'On peut danser devant les Rembrandt', *Le Journal du Dimanche*, 22 April 2001.

11. 'The orgies of nationalism are not Platonic orgies-for-orgies' sake. They lead to practical results – to the piling up of armaments, to senseless economic competition . . . and ultimately to war.' Huxley (1974), *Beyond the Mexique Bay*, London: Chatto & Windus, p. 85. Huxley went on to advocate new 'emotional cultures' (ibid., p. 86).

12. 'Painting belongs essentially to the field of the senses. This is a fact, and all the knowledge in the world will not prevail

against the experience of a painter's eye,' declared Jean Bazaine in February 1992, prefacing with these remarks the irreplaceable work of *Nuances*, the journal of the Association pour le Respect de L'intégrité du Patrimoine Artistique (ARIPA).

13. 'Orson Welles on TV', *De Visu*, no. 4.

14. From the catalogue of the exhibition to mark Giacometti's centenary, Centre Pompidou, winter 2001.

15. Paul Virilio (1994), *The Aesthetics of Disappearance*, New York: Semiotext(e).

16. Walter Isaacson (1997), 'In search of the real Bill Gates', *Time*, vol. 149, no. 2, 13 January.

17. Michel Nuridsany (2000), 'Internet, la grande rupture', *Le Figaro*, 8 September.

18. Compare also the attitude of the Roman Church in the 'icon-oclast crisis' and at the Second Council of Nicaea (787), where *the legitimacy of images and their worship* was decided, 'the Christ of the Incarnation having built a bridge between the visible and the invisible'.

19. Joseph Roth, *Das journalistische Werk*. Quoted here from the French translation, *Automne à Berlin* (Paris: Editions de la Quinzaine/Louis Vuitton, 2000) p. 231.

20. Satanael is the name given to Lucifer in Manichaean mythol-ogy. In Hans-Jürgen Heinrichs's interview with Cioran, which the author quotes above, Cioran also says: 'I have always found the idea attractive that it wasn't God, but Satan, a little Satan, Satanael, who created the world' [Tr.].

21. This is an allusion to Paul Morand's book *Rien que la Terre* (Paris: Grasset, 1926) [Tr.].

22. In *The Fire Next Time* (London: Penguin Books in association with Michael Joseph, 1964), Baldwin writes: 'The white man's unadmitted – and apparently, to him, unspeakable – private fears and longings are projected on to the Negro. The only way he can be released from the Negro's tyrannical power over him is to consent, in effect, to become black himself' (p. 82). And in his last essay, 'Whose Harlem is this anyway?' he writes: 'The profit motive makes everyone a nigger or a nigger's overseer' [Tr.].

23. Caspar David Friedrich.
24. 'There was a moment in the history of humanity when mankind could have taken a quite other path and no atomic arsenal would ever have seen the light of day. That moment very much depended on the behaviour of a handful of scientists who were, for the most part, left-wing humanists . . . But all of them, without exception, continued their work imperturbably' (Charles Mopsik).
25. Here I have adapted a phrase of Schlegel's.
26. Sun Tsu: 'Strategy is the art of lying.'
27. Joy, 'Why the future doesn't need us'. In that article, Bill Joy informs us of his immediate hopes of participating in a wider discussion with individuals from various different horizons in a cast of mind free both from the fear and from the idolizing of technology.

CHAPTER TWENTY

The Museum of Accidents

The year 2002 saw Paul Virilio's long talked-about 'museum of accidents' come to fruition. Late in the year the exhibition, entitled in French *Ce Qui Arrive*, showcasing what he called 'the accident' with hundreds of photographic, movie, webcam and video installations, opened in the Fondation Cartier pour l'Art Contemporain building in Paris. The exhibition actually ran from 29 November 2002 to 30 March 2003. Virilio conceived the exhibition, helped the curator Leanne Sacramone and wrote the substantial text of the catalogue which stretched to seven sections. Thames and Hudson in London published an English edition in 2003 with an English translation of Virilio's original French words by Chris Turner. The phrase *Unknown Quantity* was chosen as the English-language title. It is, in fact, a partial translation of the title of the seventh section in the catalogue written by Virilio. The section extracted here is the fourth of the seven sections. Thames and Hudson had already published one of Virilio's many collaborations with the Fondation Cartier before, namely *The Desert* which Paul Virilio had produced in the 1990s in France with the collaboration of Sir Wilfred Thesiger, Raymond Depardon and Mounira Khemir. The *Unknown Quantity* catalogue was again a beautiful commodity, highlighting colour and black and white illustrations of exhibits from all over the world which included events like 11 September 2001 and Oklahoma City, 1995, but also 'natural disasters' like earthquakes and air crashes, and the effects of officially controlled implosions of high-rise buildings. Virilio's purpose in *Unknown Quantity* was to underline what he had been teaching those of us willing to listen for some years now: that much media image is a strategy of war and that the modern accident is becoming indistinguishable from attack.

'The Museum of Accidents', from *Unknown Quantity*, trans. Chris Turner, London: Thames and Hudson, 2003.

A society which rashly privileges the present – **real time** – to the detriment of both the past and the future, also privileges **the accident**.

Since, at every moment and most often unexpectedly, everything happens, a civilization that sets immediacy, ubiquity and instantaneity to work brings Accidents and catastrophes on to the scene.

The confirmation of this state of affairs is provided for us by insurance companies, and particularly by the recent **Sigma** study, carried out for the world's second-largest reinsurance company, **Swiss Re**.

This recently published study, which each year lists *man-made* disasters (explosions, fires, terrorism etc.) and *natural* catastrophes (floods, earthquakes, storms etc.), takes into account only those disasters causing losses in excess of 35 million dollars. 'For the first time,' the Swiss analysts observe, 'since the 1990s, a period when damage due to natural catastrophes predominated over man-made damage, *the trend has reversed, with man-made damage standing at 70 per cent.*'[1]

Proof, if proof were needed, that far from promoting quietude, our industrialized societies throughout the twentieth century have essentially developed disquiet and the major risk, and this is so even if we leave out of account the recent proliferation of weapons of mass destruction . . . Hence the urgent need to reverse this trend which *consists in exposing us to the most catastrophic accidents* produced by the techno-scientific spirit, and to establish the opposite approach which would consist in **exposing or exhibiting the accident** as the major enigma of modern Progress.

Although some car companies carry out *more than 400 crash tests annually* in the attempt to improve the safety of their vehicles, this still does not prevent television channels from continually inflicting road-death statistics on us (not to mention the tragedies which see the present repeatedly plunged into mourning). It is certainly high time (alongside the *ecological* approaches that relate to the various ways in which the biosphere is polluted) for the beginnings of an *eschatological* approach to technical progress to emerge – an approach to that **finitude** without which the much-vaunted **globalisation** is in danger of itself becoming a **life-size** catastrophe.

Both a natural and a man-made catastrophe, a *general* catastrophe and not one *specific* to any particular technology or region of the world, which would far exceed the disasters currently covered by the insurance companies – a catastrophe of which the long-term drama of Chernobyl remains emblematic.

So as to avoid in the near future experiencing an **integral accident** on a planetary scale, an accident capable of incorporating a whole host of incidents and disasters in a chain reaction, we should right now build, inhabit and plan a laboratory of cataclysms – *the technical progress accident museum* – so as to avoid the accident of *substances*, revealed by Aristotle, being succeeded by the *knowledge* accident – that major philosophical catastrophe which genetic engineering, coming on the heels of atomic power, bears within it.

Whether we like it or not, globalization is today the fateful mark of a finitude. Paraphrasing Paul Valéry, we might assert without fear of contradiction that 'the time of the finite world is coming to an end' and that there is an urgent need to assert that knowledge marks the finitude of man, just as ecology marks that of his geophysical environment.

*　*　*

At the very moment when some are requesting, in an open letter to the president of the French Republic, that he create a 'Museum of the Twentieth Century' in Paris,[2] it seems appropriate to enquire not only into the historical sequence of the events of that fateful century, but also into the fundamentally catastrophic nature of those events.

If, indeed, 'time is the accident of accidents,'[3] the museums of history are already an anticipation of the time of that *integral accident* which the twentieth century foreshadowed, on the pretext of scientific revolution or ideological liberation.

All museology requires a museography, and the question of the presentation of *the harm done by Progress* has not received any kind of answer; it therefore falls to us, as a primordial element of the project, to provide one. At this point we have to acknowledge that it is not so much in history books or in the press that this particular historical laboratory has been prefigured, as in radio, cinema newsreel and, above all, television.

Since cinema is *time exhibiting itself*, as the sequences succeed each other, so with television, it is the pace of its 'trans-border' ubiquity that disrupts the history in the making before our eyes.

General history has, as a result, experienced a new type of accident, the accident of its perception **at first hand** (*de visu*): a 'cinematic' – and soon to be 'digital' – perception which modifies its meaning, its customary rhythm – the rhythm of almanacs and calendars, or, in other words, that of *the long run* – in favour of the *ultra-short* timescale of that televisual instantaneity which is revolutionizing our view of the world.

'With speed man has invented new types of accident . . . The fate of the motorist has become pure chance,' wrote Gaston Rageot in the 1930s.[4]

What are we to say, today, of *the major accident of audiovisual speed* and hence of the fate of the innumerable hosts of TV viewers?

Other than that, with that speed, it is history which is becoming 'accidental' – through the sudden pile-up of facts, through events which were once successive, but are now simultaneous, cannoning into one another, in spite of the distances and time intervals that used to be required for their interpretation.

Let us imagine, for example, the probable damage that will be done to the authenticity of the testimony of historical actors by the practice of live digital **morphing**.

Speaking of the preponderant influence of film on the conception of contemporary art, Dominique Païni has stated: 'For a long time, the cinema came out of the other arts, now it is the plastic arts which come out of it.'

But in fact it is *the whole of history that comes out of cinematic acceleration*, out of this movement in cinema and television!

Hence the ravages wrought by the circulation of images, this constant concertina-ing, this constant pile-up of dramatic scenes from everyday life on the evening news. And even if the written press has always been more interested in derailed trains than the ones that run on time, it is with the coming of audiovisual media that we have been able to look on, thunderstruck, at the **overexposure of accidents**, of catastrophes of all kinds – not to mention wars.

* * *

Where the broadcasting of horror is concerned, television has, since the end of the last century, been the (live) site of a constant raising of the stakes and, particularly with the increase in **live coverage**, it has provided us with an instantaneous transmission of cataclysms and incidents that have broadly anticipated disaster movies. Moreover, after the standardization of opinion, which began in the nineteenth century, we are now seeing the sudden *synchronization* of emotions.

TV channels' competition for viewers has turned the catastrophic accident into a scoop, if not indeed a fantastic spectacle which all pursue with equal vigour.

When Guy Debord spoke of the 'society of the spectacle', he omitted to mention that this scenarization of life was organized around sexuality and violence; a sexuality which the 1960s claimed to liberate, whereas what was actually happening was a progressive abolition of societal inhibitions, regarded by the Situationists as so many unbearable straitjackets.

As was so well expressed at the time by one of the officials of the Festival du Film Fantastique d'Avoriaz, '*At last death will have replaced sex and the serial killer the Latin lover!*'

Television – a 'museum of horrors' or a 'tunnel of death' – has, then, gradually transformed itself into a kind of *altar of human sacrifice*, using and abusing the terrorist scene and serial massacres; it now plays more on repulsion than on seduction.

From the death twenty years ago – allegedly 'live on air' – of a little Columbian girl being swallowed by mud, to the execution this winter of little Mohammed struck down beside his father, when it comes to making horror banal, any pretext will serve.

By contrast, as we may recall, the mass media in the old Soviet Union never reported accidents or violent incidents. With the exception of natural catastrophes, which it would have been difficult to pass over, the media systematically censored any *deviations from the norm*, allowing only visions of a radiant future to filter through . . . until Chernobyl.

However, when it comes to censorship, liberalism and totalitarianism each had their particular method for stifling the true facts. For the former, the aim was, even then, to **overexpose** the viewer to the incessant repetition of tragedies; the latter, by contrast, opted for **underexposure** and the radical occultation of any singularity.

Two panic reactions, but an identical outcome: *censorship by illumination* – a fateful blinding by the light – for the democratic West, and *censorship by the prohibition of any divergent representation* – the darkness and fog of wilful blindness – for the dogmatic East.

*   *   *

So, just as there is a Richter scale of seismic catastrophes, so there is, surreptitiously, a scale of media catastrophes, the clearest effect of which is to cause, on the one hand, resentment against the perpetrators and, on the other, an effect of exemplarity, which leads, where terrorism is concerned, to the reproduction of the disaster, thanks to its dramaturgical amplification. So much is this the case that to Nietzsche's study of the *birth of tragedy* we need to add the analysis of this **media tragedy**, in which the perfect synchronization of the collective emotion of TV viewers might be said to play the role of the ancient chorus – though no longer on the scale of the theatre at Epidauros, but on the life-size scale of entire continents.

It is clearly here that the **museum of the accident** has its place . . .

The *media scale* of catastrophes and cataclysms that dress the world in mourning is, in fact, so vast that is must necessarily make the amplitude of the perceptual field the first stage of a new understanding – no longer solely that of the *ecology of risks* in the face of environmental pollution, but that of an *ethology of threats* in terms of the mystification of opinion, of a pollution of public emotion.

A pollution that always paves the way for intolerance followed by vengeance. In other words for a barbarism and chaos which quickly overwhelm human societies, as has recently been demonstrated by the massacres and genocides, those fruits of the baneful propaganda of the 'media of hatred'.

After a period of waiting for the *'intergral accident'* to occur, we are seeing the forceps birth of a 'catastrophism' that bears no relation whatever (we really must make no mistake about this) to that of the 'millenarian' obscurantism of yesteryear, but which requires just as much in the way of precautions, in the way of that Pascalian 'subtlety' which our organs of mass information so cruelly lack!

Since one catastrophe may conceal another, *if the major accident is indeed the consequence of the speed of acceleration of the phenomena* engendered by progress, it is certainly time, in these early years of the twenty-first century, to take **what is happening**, what is emerging unexpectedly before our eyes and analyse it wisely. Hence the imperative need now to **exhibit the accident**.

In conclusion, one final example: just recently, astronomers have begun to list and observe the asteroids and meteorites which are heading towards Earth.

These so-called NEAs, **near-earth asteroids** some ten metres in diameter, clearly represent a threat of collision with our planet.

The last impact was the one which took place in 1908 in Siberia, above the Tunguska, which exploded at 8,000 metres and ravaged an area of almost 2,000 square kilometres.

In order to attempt to prevent such a cosmic catastrophe recurring, this time over inhabited areas, a working group has been formed.

With support from the *International Astronomical Union*, this team has invented a scale of risk named the **Torino Scale**, after the city of Turin where this course of action was adopted in 1999. Ranking dangers on a scale from zero to ten, it takes into account the mass, velocity and presumed trajectory of the heavenly body in question.

Five zones are identified by the scientists: the *White Zone*, where there is no chance [*sic*] of the object reaching Earth; the *Green Zone*, where there would be a tiny probability of contact;

the *Yellow Zone*, where impact is, in fact, probable; the *Orange Zone*, where that probability is great and, finally, the *Red Zone*, where catastrophe is certain.[5]

This very first attempt to **exhibit the future accident** – an in no way alarmist illustration of cosmic facts of which our moon bears the marks, not to mention the more than one-kilometre-wide **Meteor Crater** in Arizona which is frequently visited by American tourists – demonstrates the urgent need to follow up the famous 'cabinets of curiosities' of the Renaissance[6] with a twenty-first-century **museum of the accident of the future**.

Notes

1. *Le Monde*, 24 February 2001.
2. Jacques Julliard (2002), 'Chronique', *Le Nouvel Observateur*, 30 January.
3. Aristotle, *Physics*.
4. Gaston Rageot (1928), *L'Homme Standard*, Paris: Plon, a work contemporaneous with Paul Morand's *L'homme pressé* (Paris: Gallimard, 1941).
5. Pierre Barthélémy (2002), 'Les asteroïdes constituent le principal risque naturel pour la Terre', *Le Monde*, 28 June.
6. Patrick Mauriès (2002), *Les Cabinets de Curiosités*, Paris: Gallimard.

Paul Virilio: A Directory
by Steve Redhead

Paul Virilio: Extracts in the Reader (English translation)

Chapter 1

Virilio, Paul and Claude Parent (1997), *Architecture Principe 1966 and 1996*, Besançon: Les Editions de l'Imprimeur, English edition.

Chapter 2

Virilio, Paul and Claude Parent (1997), *Architecture Principe 1966 and 1996*, Besançon: Les Editions de l'Imprimeur, English edition.

Chapter 3

Virilio, Paul and Claude Parent (1996), *The Function of the Oblique: The Architecture of Claude Parent and Paul Virilio 1963–1969*, London: Architectural Association.

Chapter 4

Virilio, Paul (1986), *Speed and Politics: An Essay on Dromology*, New York: Semiotext(e).

Chapter 5

Virilio, Paul (1990), *Popular Defense and Ecological Struggles*, New York: Semiotext(e).

Chapter 6

Virilio, Paul (1991), *The Aesthetics of Disappearance*, New York: Semiotext(e).

Chapter 7

Virilio, Paul (1991), *The Lost Dimension*, New York: Semiotext(e).

Chapter 8

Virilio, Paul (1989), *War and Cinema: The Logistics of Perception*, London: Verso.

Chapter 9

Virilio, Paul, Jean Baudrillard et al. (1989), *Looking Back on the End of the World*, New York: Semiotext(e).

Chapter 10

Virilio, Paul (1994), *The Vision Machine*, London: BFI/ Bloomington: Indiana University Press.

Chapter 11

Virilio, Paul (2000), *Polar Inertia*, London: Sage.

Chapter 12

Virilio, Paul (2002), *Desert Screen: War at the Speed of Light*, London: Continuum.

Chapter 13

Virilio, Paul (1995), *The Art of the Motor*, Minneapolis: University of Minnesota Press.

Chapter 14

Virilio, Paul (1997), *Open Sky*, London: Verso.

Chapter 15

Virilio, Paul (2000), *A Landscape of Events*, Cambridge, MA: MIT Press.

Chapter 16

Virilio, Paul (2000), *The Information Bomb*, London: Verso.

Chapter 17

Virilio, Paul (2000), *Strategy of Deception*, London: Verso.

Chapter 18

Virilio, Paul (2003), *Art and Fear*, London: Continuum.

Chapter 19

Virilio, Paul (2002), *Ground Zero*, London: Verso.

Chapter 20

Virilio, Paul (2003), *Unknown Quantity*, London: Fondation Cartier pour l'Art Contemporain/Thames and Hudson.

Paul Virilio: Extracts in the Reader (Original French Publication)

Chapter 1

Virilio, Paul (1966), 'Bunker Archéologie', *Architecture Principe* no. 7, September/October 1966.

Chapter 2

Virilio, Paul (1966), 'Architecture Cryptique', *Architecture Principe* no. 7, September/October 1966.

Chapter 4

Virilio, Paul (1977), *Vitesse et Politique*, Paris: Editions Galilée.

Chapter 5

Virilio, Paul (1978), *Défense Populaire et Luttes Ecologiques*, Paris: Editions Galilée.

Chapter 6

Virilio, Paul (1980), *Esthétique de la Disparition*, Paris: Balland.

Chapter 7

Virilio, Paul (1984), *L'Espace Critique*, Paris: Christian Bourgeois.

Chapter 8

Virilio, Paul (1984) *Guerre et Cinéma 1: Logistique de la Perception*, Paris: Editions Cahiers du Cinema.

Chapter 9

Virilio, Paul (1990), *L'Inertie Polaire*, Paris: Christian Bourgeois.

Chapter 10

Virilio, Paul (1988), *La Machine de Vision*, Paris: Editions Galilée.

Chapter 11

Virilio, Paul (1990), *L'Inertie Polaire*, Paris: Christian Bourgeois.

Chapter 12

Virilio, Paul (1991), *L'Ecran du Désert*, Paris: Editions Galilée.

Chapter 13

Virilio, Paul (1993), *L'Art du Moteur*, Paris: Editions Galilée.

Chapter 14

Virilio, Paul (1995), *La Vitesse de Libération*, Paris: Editions Galilée.

Chapter 15

Virilio, Paul (1996), *Un Paysage d'Evénements*, Paris: Editions Galilée.

Chapter 16

Virilio, Paul (1998), *La Bombe Informatique*, Paris: Editions Galilée.

Chapter 17

Virilio, Paul (1999), *Stratégie de la Déception*, Paris: Editions Galilée.

Chapter 18

Virilio, Paul (2000), *La Procédure Silence*, Paris: Editions Galilée.

Chapter 19

Virilio, Paul (2002), *Ce Qui Arrive*, Paris: Editions Galilée.

Chapter 20

Virilio, Paul (2002), *Ce Qui Arrive*, Paris: Fondation Cartier pour l'Art Contemporain/Actes Sud.

A Guide to Reading Paul Virilio

The best way to begin to understand and appreciate the work of
Paul Virilio is to read the major texts in the original French.
Failing that, the next best key to understanding Virilio is to read
good English translations of his major texts. The purpose of this
reader is to provide a readily accessible inroad into Virilio's major
texts by collecting together relatively short versions of translations of these relatively short books and articles in the order that
they were originally published in French. In the final analysis, as
with any other major theorist, Virilio deserves to be read in full
before his work is unleashed into the vortex of critical commentary, which often alights on only one short, possibly unrepresen-
tative, period of an author's career. Until recently it has been
difficult to find the entire back catalogue of Virilio's published
work in libraries, bookshops or even online. It has also been prohibitive to access it in English translation since it has been scattered among small, rather expensive books and obscure journals.
The Paul Virilio Reader showcases for the first time Virilio's entire
publishing career in a single volume, complementing the explanatory companion text, Steve Redhead's *Paul Virilio: Theorist for
an Accelerated Culture*.

The secondary way into an understanding of the enigmatic
Paul Virilio is through a series of riveting interviews by the joint
commissioner of Semiotext(e) volumes, Sylvère Lotringer. These
book-length interviews, all published by Semiotext(e) in New
York, were originally conducted in French and then translated,
for publication, into English. Beginning in the first six months of
1982, in various meetings between Lotringer and Virilio in Paris
and New York, the interviews resumed fifteen years later in 1997
in a one-off conversation. Before the end of the century new
interviews were conducted, again in Paris and New York, taking
place initially in November 1999 and running through until May
2001. The momentous events of 11 September 2001 prompted a
further interview in Paris in May 2002. The later interviews from
1997 onwards read like a transcript of a casual meeting of two old
friends musing on the events of the years in between, which is
essentially what they are, Virilio and Lotringer having known

each other for more than twenty years by this time. The 1982 interviews, translated by Mark Polizotti, were published by Semiotext(e) in New York in 1983 under the title *Pure War*. The 1997 interview, translated by Brian O'Keefe, formed a 'Postscript' to the reissued, second edition of *Pure War*, published by Semiotext(e) in New York in 1997. The 1999–2001 interviews were previewed in three separate short publications in obscure American journals: 'After Architecture: A Conversation' in *Grey Room* no. 3, 2001; 'Unmade in USA' in *Made in USA* no. 3, 2001; and 'The Genetic Bomb' in *Pataphysics*, Pyschomilitary issue, 2002. The whole of the 1999–2001 interview sessions, together with the May 2002 interview, all translated by Mike Taormina, comprised the third book in the Virilio/Lotringer interviews series. Taking its title from the May 2002 post-9/11 interview, which appears as an epilogue, *Crepuscular Dawn* also had an excellent introduction by Sylvère Lotringer himself, entitled 'Time Bomb'. It was published by Semiotext(e) in New York and Los Angeles in 2002. Reading the whole of the transcripts of these interviews, spread over twenty years, from start to finish in order, is a fascinating introduction to Virilio, and is highly recommended.

Virilio has been interviewed by people other than Lotringer on many occasions. Some of these interviews are interesting, some are poorly translated from the original German or French, still others only serve to confuse. A good compilation of the more informative interviews Virilio has given to journalists and academics over the years can be found in John Armitage's edited volume for Sage in 2001, entitled *Virilio Live: Selected Interviews*. However, by far the best interview with Virilio, outside of those conversations with Lotringer, is that conducted by French journalist Philippe Petit in 1996 in Paris. The long conversation between Petit and Virilio was published in French in booklength form in Paris in September 1996 by Les Editions Textuel, in their 'Conversations pour Demain' series. The title of the French publication was *Cybermonde, La Politique du Pire*. Three years later in 1999, Semiotext(e) in New York published an English translation, by Michael Cavaliere, of the whole interview between Virilio and Petit. The partial translation of the title left the book called, strangely, *Politics of the Very Worst* in English. I cannot recommend this interview highly enough to beginners in Virilio studies as well as veteran Virilio watchers. It is wide-ranging, and Petit, who has also conducted excellent interviews with Jean Baudrillard amongst others, is a good listener. He even probes Virilio on personal issues like 'love' (though he does not get very far in that regard!).

The supplementary path to enlightenment about Virilio's work is to investigate some of the many art exhibition catalogues to which Virilio has contributed over the years. He has tended to be less oblique, and much less guarded, in these publications and far clearer on what he really thinks than in some of his myriad articles, reviews and books. Very little of this facet of Virilio's work has actually been translated into English as yet. The best example of the revealing exhibition catalogue which has in fact passed into English translation is *Unknown Quantity*, a volume which is extracted in this reader. In that profusely illustrated exhibition catalogue promoted by the Fondation pour l'Art Contemporain in Paris in 2002 and published by Thames and Hudson in London in 2003, the reader gets a considerable insight into Virilio's thinking through: firstly, several long written treatises on the theory of the accident which serves as the textual part of the catalogue; secondly, a detailed interview involving Virilio on the 'accident' that was Chernobyl; and thirdly, the dozens of photographic and (still) video illustrations from the exhibition itself inspired and chosen in many cases by Virilio as organizer. Another, related way of revealing Virilio is to concentrate on some of the short books and pamphlets he has written about specific artists, architects and the like. Little of this work has appeared so far in English. A good example of this part of Virilio's career would be *Etudes d'Impact*, a publication written about the artist Peter Klasen and put out by Expressions Contemporaines in Paris in 1999.

There are dozens of critical commentaries to be found on Virilio. If I had to select one critical commentary over all the others, it would be Mike Gane's essay 'Paul Virilio's Bunker Theorising', published in the *Theory Culture and Society* special double issue on Virilio (vol. 16, nos 5–6 in 2000, edited by John Armitage and published simultaneously as *Paul Virilio: From*

Modernism to Hypermodernism and Beyond by Sage in their influential TCS book series). Gane is similarly excellent on Jean Baudrillard, a friend and colleague of Virilio in the intellectual and political milieu of Paris. On Baudrillard, see Mike Gane's *Baudrillard: Critical and Fatal Theory,* and *Baudrillard's Bestiary: Baudrillard and Culture*, both published by Routledge in London in 1991. Also recommended are Mike Gane's edited volume *Baudrillard Live: Selected Interviews*, published by Routledge in London in 1993, and his more general book on the history and social context of French theory entitled *French Social Theory* published by Sage in London in 2003.

Apart from Baudrillard, it is instructive to read French phenomenologists such as Maurice Merleau-Ponty to get an idea of where Virilio is coming from. See, for example, Merleau-Ponty's *Phenomenology of Perception*, published by Routledge and Kegan Paul in 1962. In addition, I would recommend reading at least two other lesser-known French theorists who have influenced Virilio, in order to get a broader picture of Virilio, the theorist and the human being. But they are not the sort of theorists to be found regularly in Mike Gane's book on French theory. First and most important is Jacques Ellul, both for his religious ideas and his technological theorizing of urban culture. Ellul was born in France in 1912 and his death in 1994 had a profound effect on Virilio. Indeed, Virilio explicitly acknowledges Ellul as a major influence on his life and work throughout his writing from the 1950s to today. To get an idea of Ellul's position one or more of the following English translations from the original French editions are useful: *The Technological Society*, published by Vintage Books in New York in 1964, with an introduction by functionalist sociologist of deviance Robert Merton; *The Meaning of the City*, published by W. B. Eerdmans in Grand Rapids, Michigan in 1970; *Autopsy of Revolution*, published by Knopf in New York in 1971; *The Judgement of Jonah*, published by Eerdmans in Michigan in 1971; *False Presence of the Kingdom*, published by Seabury Press in New York in 1972; *Hope in Time of Abandonment*, published by Seabury Press in New York in 1973; *The Ethics of Freedom*, published by Eerdmans in Michigan in 1976; *The Technological Bluff*, published by Eerdmans in Michigan in 1990; and *Anarchy and*

Christianity, published by Eerdmans in Michigan in 1991. The other French theorist is Pierre Teilhard de Chardin, a more tangential influence on Virilio but worth noting nonetheless. Virilio refers to him as 'that strange Jesuit'. Teilhard de Chardin's Christian dissent can be seen in one or more of the following English translations from the original French: *The Future of Man*, published by Collins in London in 1964; *Hymn of the Universe*, published by Collins in London in 1965; *Building the Earth*, published by Chapman in London in 1965; *The Appearance of Man*, published by Collins in London in 1965; *Activation of Energy*, published by Harcourt Brace in New York in 1970; *Let Me Explain*, published by Collins in London in 1970; and *Christianity and Evolution*, published by Collins in London in 1971.

Another very important, consistent background influence on Virilio is the philosopher and scientist Albert Einstein. Born in 1879, Einstein died in 1955, a time when Virilio, having recently converted to Christianity, was becoming equally interested in the role of science and technology. Any of the following Einstein extracts are useful for background reading: *Albert Einstein: Philosopher and Scientist*, edited by Paul Schilpp and published by Tudor in New York in 1951; his own *Ideas and Opinions*, published by Souvenir Press in London in 1973; and *Albert Einstein, The Human Side: New Glimpses from his Archives*, edited by Helen Dukas and Banesh Hoffman and published by Princeton University Press in Princeton, NJ in 1979.

Finally, Virilio's military influences are many but perhaps two are worth noting above any other. Firstly and most significantly, there is Sun Tsu's *Art of War*, first written over 2,000 years ago and published by Wordsworth editions in London in 1990. Secondly, less influential but still sitting there in the background in Virilio's theorizing of 'pure war', is Karl von Clausewitz's *On War*, published by Princeton University Press in Princeton, NJ in 1989. It is worth noting that, a great deal of Virilio's pervasive influence in theorizing military technology and media events can be seen in a book which never even mentions his name: Michael Ignatieff's highly readable account of 'Kosovo and beyond', entitled *Virtual War*, published by Chatto and Windus in London in 2000.

Index

EUROPEAN PERSPECTIVES

A Series in Social Thought and Cultural Criticism

LAWRENCE D. KRITZMAN, Editor

JULIA KRISTEVA	*Strangers to Ourselves*
THEODOR W. ADORNO	*Notes to Literature*, vols. 1 and 2
RICHARD WOLIN, editor	*The Heidegger Controversy*
ANTONIO GRAMSCI	*Prison Notebooks*, vols. 1 and 2
JACQUES LEGOFF	*History and Memory*
ALAIN FINKIELKRAUT	*Remembering in Vain: The Klaus Barbie Trial and Crimes Against Humanity*
JULIA KRISTEVA	*Nations Without Nationalism*
PIERRE BOURDIEU	*The Field of Cultural Production*
PIERRE VIDAL-NAQUET	*Assassins of Memory: Essays on the Denial of the Holocaust*
HUGO BALL	*Critique of the German Intelligentsia*
GILLES DELEUZE and FÉLIX GUATTARI	*What Is Philosophy?*
KARL HEINZ BOHRER	*Suddenness: On the Moment of Aesthetic Appearance*
JULIA KRISTEVA	*Time and Sense: Proust and the Experience of Literature*
ALAIN FINKIELKRAUT	*The Defeat of the Mind*
JULIA KRISTEVA	*New Maladies of the Soul*
ELISABETH BADINTER	*XY: On Masculine Identity*
KARL LÖWITH	*Martin Heidegger and European Nihilism*
GILLES DELEUZE	*Negotiations, 1972–1990*
PIERRE VIDAL-NAQUET	*The Jews: History, Memory, and the Present*
NORBERT ELIAS	*The Germans*